CITIZENSHIP
Across the
CURRICULUM

Scholarship of Teaching and Learning

Jennifer Meta Robinson
Whitney M. Schlegel
Mary Taylor Huber
Pat Hutchings
editors

Across the
CURRICULUM

Edited by
Michael B. Smith,
Rebecca S. Nowacek, and
Jeffrey L. Bernstein

Foreword by
Mary Taylor Huber and Pat Hutchings

Indiana University Press
Bloomington · Indianapolis

This book is a publication of

Indiana University Press
601 North Morton Street
Bloomington, Indiana 47404-3797 USA

www.iupress.indiana.edu

Telephone orders	800-842-6796
Fax orders	812-855-7931
Orders by e-mail	iuporder@indiana.edu

♾ The paper used in this publication meets the minimum requirements of the American National Standard for Information Sciences—Permanence of Paper for Printed Library Materials, ANSI Z39.48-1992.

Manufactured in the United States of America

Library of Congress Cataloging-in-Publication Data
Citizenship across the curriculum / edited by Michael B. Smith, Rebecca S. Nowacek, and Jeffrey L. Bernstein ; foreword by Mary Taylor Huber and Pat Hutchings.
p. cm. — (Indiana series in the scholarship of teaching and learning)
Includes bibliographical references and index.
ISBN 978-0-253-35448-8 (cloth : alk. paper)
ISBN 978-0-253-22179-7 (pbk. : alk. paper)
1. Citizenship—Study and teaching—Cross-cultural studies. 2. Curriculum planning—Cross-cultural studies. I. Smith, Michael B. II. Nowacek, Rebecca S. III. Bernstein, Jeffrey, date-
LC1091+
378'.015—dc22   2009036264

1   2   3   4   5   15   14   13   12   11   10

To seven young citizens:

Zachary Meir Bernstein
Bradley Viktor Nowacek
Solomon Eliezer Bernstein
Samuel Ian Brennan Smith
Zachary David Nowacek
Isaiah Peter Brennan Smith
Benjamin Elijah Nowacek

Your future motivates our work.

The ultimate test of a moral society is
the kind of world that it leaves
to its children.

—DIETRICH BONHOEFFER

CONTENTS

FOREWORD

Civic Learning: Intersections and Interactions

Mary Taylor Huber and Pat Hutchings

Educating citizens is one of the oldest aims of liberal learning in the Western tradition, but it has not always coexisted peaceably or on a par with other goals that higher education also serves. Now, after a longish lull, "citizenship" is back on the agenda, and a large and diverse group of educators have signed on. *Citizenship Across the Curriculum* provides a unique window into this recent resurgence of interest in preparing students for civic and political engagement and its different disciplinary styles. By foregrounding intersections with concurrent reforms in undergraduate education, particularly integrative learning and the scholarship of teaching and learning, these essays also offer entrée to the kinds of collaborative interactions that are reconfiguring the pedagogical lives of professors and students today.

Let's start with "citizenship," one of those seemingly simple terms that turn out to provoke debate and strong emotions, especially when they enter the education sphere. To be sure, there are some who think citizenship best—and exclusively—addressed as a subject for study in appropriate political science or history courses, the traditional home of civic education. But for those who see preparation for citizenship as a *goal* of undergraduate education, the possibilities for where it can be taught expand. The contributors to this book, for example, come not only from political science and history, but also from chemistry, communication, English literature, mathematics, and science education. Indeed, as this list suggests, faculty from virtually any discipline can teach with civic learning in mind. But when they do, when faculty from different disciplinary communities teach their fields wearing a civic lens, both the concept of citizenship and even the field itself (as taught and learned) are subject to change.

Most obviously, faculty bring different disciplinary understandings to bear in thinking about why it's important to prepare students for lives of civic and political engagement, and what exactly this conviction calls upon them, as teachers and scholars of their fields, to do. As a political scientist, Jeffrey Bernstein believes that his field has important expertise and knowledge to offer: "Students should know about checks and balances, the president's cabinet, and the policy-making process," he says. But at the same time he believes that he and his disciplinary colleagues "must do more." Thus, he argues for a "citizenship-oriented perspective" to political science, with a focus less on factual knowledge than on helping students "find their political voices" through developing the skills and knowledge needed to manage political information, to understand how the political system operates and how to use that information in activism, and to work with others to pursue political goals.

Going further, English professor Howard Tinberg, who teaches a course on Holocaust literature, cites Elie Wiesel's view of citizenship as extending beyond national borders to a moral and ethical identity as a world citizen. Not surprisingly, this view of citizenship shapes his thinking about his field: "As a teacher of literature, I feel that I must be especially mindful of the following: that writers, far from being the removed spectators of political and civic engagements, are so often sounding notes of alarm for citizens to hear. We must all be ready and willing to listen." Thus, he argues that Shoah educators must work hard "to offer students glimpses not only of nations and citizens that fail but also restorative models." Emphasizing the political value of thoughtful and quiet engagement, he notes, "We educators have an obligation to offer hope."

Communication scholar Carmen Werder brings yet another perspective to bear, worrying about a conception of citizenship that might seem to imply mere dutifulness and as a result cultivate passivity. She calls on work from her field to emphasize the importance of teaching not just responsibility but "response-ability," especially to "enfranchise" students to disagree respectfully and to develop a sense of themselves as capable agents of change. For Werder, citizenship is therefore an issue of identity and personal development. She emphasizes the importance of engaging students as citizens of their campus communities *right now*, as well as of preparing them for future lives of national and global citizenship.

Coming to an understanding of one's goals is only one element in redesigning a course to foster civic learning. As these essays show, changing one's priorities to include citizenship can also mean modifying a panoply of pedagogical practice:

materials, activities, assignments, assessment. And this is where things get particularly interesting, because *these* are the choices that most clearly influence how students experience the field as represented through the course. Will they see multicultural communication, environmental history, science education, chemistry, or mathematics (take your pick) as something that's really accessible, something that they can use to deepen their understanding of public issues and their skills of civic and political engagement?

The answer to these questions is far from certain. All these fields can be taught in abstract and distanced ways. But for teachers like Rona Halualani, Michael Smith, David Geelan, Matthew Fisher, and Michael Burke in this volume, the "citizenship lens" brings with it the need for more active pedagogies. As their essays attest, they have found ways to teach basic concepts through real-world problem solving and have designed activities that enable students to explore far-reaching issues in local settings. And while something (usually coverage) is always lost in such choices, these teachers' assessments and analyses of student learning convince them—and, they hope, others—that for most students, something significant in regard to civic learning is gained. As student reflections from Rebecca Nowacek's capstone seminar make clear, these gains involve some increment in students' capacities to connect academic study to complex social issues, and to work with people who bring different experience, perspectives, and expertise. Or, as a student from Carmen Werder's course Civil Discourse as Learning Interaction explains, "It's the first time I've ever thought of myself as part of something bigger."

It is, of course, this sense of connection to "something bigger," to larger issues and varied experiences, where educating for citizenship intersects with the movement to help students pursue learning in more intentionally integrative ways. And this is why the contributors argue for "citizenship *across* the curriculum." Yes, they are pleased with what their students can accomplish in a course that is designed to help students integrate learning across contexts. As we've seen, different disciplines can offer different ways for students to develop integrative knowledge and skills and values that can enrich civic life. And yes, some have seen cases (as reflected in the comment by Werder's student above) of what can best be called transformative learning, where a student's outlook on the world seemed to have taken a decisive turn. But these faculty are appropriately modest in their expectations for what most students can accomplish in a single course. Looking across those experiences and disciplines, as this volume does, it's clear that there's an additional argument to be made: opportunities for citizenship education should occur not only across the curriculum but through the developmental arc of the college years.

This is a tall order. But it is one that the concurrent development of a scholarship of teaching and learning in higher education is placing within reach. Faculty members become interested in civic learning for many reasons, including their own passions and interests in building a better world. But how to act on that commitment in the classroom, how to empower and encourage students to be more informed, empathetic, and active citizens are questions that faculty in many fields are just beginning to explore. The landscape is daunting: to cross it successfully requires integrating civic and academic learning, avoiding indoctrination, and designing activities to engage students' hands and hearts along with their heads. But a growing number of instructors have taken it upon themselves to map the way. When these innovators get systematic about where their goals and methods are taking them, asking questions about their students' learning and refining their route based on what they're finding out, they become scholars of teaching and learning. And when these explorers document the experience in ways that colleagues can critique and build upon, the landscape of civic education becomes better known. It won't be so necessary for newcomers, or even veterans, to continue to travel alone.

Citizenship Across the Curriculum exemplifies the new collaborative teaching culture that scholars of teaching and learning are beginning to form. Indeed, as editors Michael Smith, Rebecca Nowacek, and Jeffrey Bernstein explain in their introduction, the contributors to this book first met as participants in the national fellowship program of the Carnegie Academy for the Scholarship of Teaching and Learning (CASTL)—where we (as members of the CASTL leadership team) had the privilege to meet and work with them. They have shared their questions with each other over the past few years, worked together to refine their ideas, learned from each other's successes and failures, and have now found a genre to make that conversation public. The essays themselves bear telling traces of this exchange, laced as they are with cross-references to one another, but each essay is also followed by two commentaries and a response that give readers a glimpse at how pedagogical ideas can travel among very different scholars who have established a community of shared interest and trust. Matthew Fisher (chemistry) notes in his response to commentary by Carmen Werder (communication) and David Geelan (science education):

> As I've become more concerned about educating for citizenship and altered my courses to support this goal, I've become more convinced that I can't do this in isolation. I need colleagues in other disciplines in a variety of ways—as "sounding boards" for specific things I want to try, as collaborators in exploring issues that cross disciplinary boundaries, as people with expertise in things that I'm not as familiar with. . . .

Attentive readers will note that Fisher is describing for pedagogy something very close to the kind of engaged citizenship the whole set of authors hope to instill in their students. This is also, we would note in conclusion, similar to citizenship in that larger republic of letters that we have elsewhere called the "teaching commons," where "communities of educators committed to pedagogical inquiry and innovation come together to exchange ideas about teaching and learning, and use them to meet the challenges of educating students for personal, professional, and civic life . . ." (Huber and Hutchings 2005, ix–x). From this perspective, *Citizenship Across the Curriculum* is not just for faculty focused on civic learning, or on integrative learning, or on the scholarship of teaching and learning more widely cast. This book is for everyone who cares about what it could mean to be a college or university teacher responsible for educating students in a world where engagement and commitment are so urgently needed.

Work Cited

Huber, Mary Taylor, and Pat Hutchings, *The advancement of learning: Building the teaching commons* (San Francisco: Jossey-Bass, 2005).

ACKNOWLEDGMENTS

Editing a book such as this one is no easy task; it does not just happen, but instead evolves over time and through many relationships. The end of this project gives us the opportunity to reflect on how this book came about, and to express gratitude to so many for helping to make it possible.

Our first debt of gratitude is to the Carnegie Foundation for the Advancement of Teaching, for bringing us together as Carnegie Scholars during the 2005–2006 academic year. Our three residencies at the Foundation helped us develop our projects, and enabled us to make the connections among our projects that are reflected in these pages. While a great deal of work was done at the Foundation, we would be remiss were we not to mention the Rose & Crown Pub in Palo Alto, where this idea took shape (with notes written on a paper plate).

At the Carnegie Foundation, we had the pleasure and honor of working with facilitators such as Marcia Babb, David Reichard, and Whitney Schlegel, who helped improve our work. Richard Gale provided a hospitable environment, hard questions when we needed them, and encouragement, always. There was always "moresoon" and it was always good. Pat Hutchings and Mary Huber not only helped guide our work at the Foundation, but graciously responded when we asked them to write the foreword for this book. Our debt to them for their support, and for their contribution to this book, is immeasurable.

Rebecca in particular would like to thank Marcia, Richard, Mary, and Pat who, when Rebecca announced that she would like to come to the first residency with her seven-week-old baby (and her indefatigable mother to provide childcare), were immediately and unconditionally supportive. Their kindnesses great and small—a few extra moments here and there to check in on the baby, a place to store milk, affection lavished on a baby taken on an evening's social outing— made all the difference. Too often working parents feel forced to choose between time with a beloved child and a remarkable professional opportunity: the Carnegie Foundation deserves a public thanks for making it possible to enjoy both.

We also want to acknowledge and to thank the other twelve Carnegie Scholars from our cohort who do not have chapters in this book; through many conversations at the Foundation, on the phone, over e-mail, and at conferences, you have all enriched our work, and we are sincerely appreciative.

Lee Shulman was president of the Carnegie Foundation during our time as Carnegie Scholars. We will be forever grateful to him for the work he has done promoting the scholarship of teaching and learning movement, and for mentoring each of us so much along the way. Each of the members of our Carnegie cohort is proud to call Lee a friend; we, and the academy, are all far better off for what he has done to advance teaching and learning in higher education.

Wearing our editor hats, we want to thank our colleagues who have chapters (and commentaries on others' chapters) in this volume. Thank you for putting up with three first-time book editors, for (usually) meeting deadlines with good cheer, and for always believing in our joint work, and in us as editors. In addition, we want to thank David Scobey and Edward Zlotkowski for agreeing to write concluding chapters for this book. We very much appreciate what their words add to it.

Michael would like to thank two mentors at Indiana University: David Pace, whose own work in the scholarship of teaching and learning has been transformative at so many levels, and Dave Thelen, whose thinking and writing about citizenship has influenced a generation of historians. He also wishes to thank Zenon Wasyliw, Howard Erlich, and Peter Bardaglio, who, in their various administrative capacities at Ithaca College, supported a Carnegie Scholar fellowship for someone who was not even on a tenure-eligible contract at the time.

Rebecca would like to thank Honors Program Director Tony Peressini for inviting her to teach the Full-Circle Seminar; Dean Michael McKinney of Marquette's Helen Way Klingler College of Arts and Sciences for providing financial support and encouragement; and especially her department chair, Tim Machan, for proving once again that administration is indeed "the art of the possible" and providing the many kinds of support and kindness that only a department chair can.

Jeff would like to thank Karen Busch and the many participants in Eastern Michigan University's Faculty Development Seminars in the Scholarship of Teaching and Learning for providing a hospitable environment for his work. In addition, he would like to thank Sarah Ginsberg, Matt Kaplan, Debbie Meizlish,

Joe Ohren, and Raymond Rosenfeld for their friendship, and for innumerable conversations about teaching and learning.

We wish to thank Rebecca Tolen for her encouragement and sponsorship of this book at Indiana University Press. Laura Macleod, Miki Bird, Brian Herrmann, and Candace McNulty were also indispensable in bringing the book to fruition.

We are grateful to each other; our friendship has made this a joyous and productive collaboration. As we have worked on editing this book, together we have experienced births, deaths, illnesses, broken bones, and contentious pennant races pitting our beloved baseball teams against each other—and emerged stronger for it. Knowing that a friend was always there to pick up the slack when life got in the way made this project much more manageable, and a great deal of fun.

Our families have provided a loving environment from which to work, and to which we could return after working. We thank our spouses—Kristen Brennan, David Nowacek, and Lisa Bernstein—for their love and support. And, most of all, we thank our children. Although they are all too young to fully appreciate what we are trying to do here, their unconditional love keeps us going. We hope that by the time they reach college (tuition payments start within a decade for the oldest of our children), higher education will have reacted to the call we have made in this book and provided them, and their classmates, with more and better opportunities to learn the skills and dispositions of citizenship.

Michael B. Smith, Rebecca S. Nowacek, and
Jeffrey L. Bernstein

In his classic article "Teaching as Community Property: Putting an End to Pedagogical Solitude," Lee Shulman (1993) decries the loneliness of teaching in the academy. In our more traditional scholarly pursuits, Shulman notes, scholarly communities form around interesting questions and the search for answers. In Randy Bass's (1999) provocative formulation, research "problems" become invitations to talk and collaborate as we attempt to build knowledge within a field. Teaching "problems," though, rarely lend themselves to these productive discussions: nobody wants to admit having a problem with their teaching, or to accuse others of having problems with theirs. The scholarship of teaching and learning, as we see it, is largely about viewing teaching problems as ripe for conversation and careful scholarly investigation. Doing so requires that we put an end to pedagogical solitude and join as a community to solve teaching problems just as we do more traditional research problems.

One of the central problems facing the academy is how disconnected many students feel their classroom learning is from what so many of them refer to as "the real world." The problem for these students is not one of solitude so much as a sense that their education is unfolding in isolation from the world beyond the boundaries of their campuses. If students feel their learning is often disconnected, if they are not sufficiently engaged in the world with a fully developed sense of agency, faculty bear some responsibility for this. This book was written with the assumption that colleges and universities need to do more to prepare students for lives as engaged citizens and that every discipline in the curriculum can contribute to this goal.

Educating for citizenship certainly entails helping students become more civically engaged in the traditional ways: as actors in the political process, as volunteers in the community, as leaders in campus organizations. But the authors of this volume also believe that citizenship education embodies more abstract qualities: learning how to become more comfortable with ambiguity and complexity, how to disagree without being disagreeable, and, perhaps above all, how to be more empathetic. Clearly, inculcating such an expansive capacity for citizenship is beyond the reach of a single instructor or a single course. To be most effective, the themes and practice of citizenship should be conveyed throughout the college experience. Certainly activities beyond the classroom play a significant role in teaching citizenship: students learn a great deal from their volunteer work, their participation in extracurricular activities, and the experience of living with a diverse group of students in residence halls (Hamrick, Evans, and Schuh 2002). In this volume, however, we tackle the question of how we can sponsor citizenship education in the classroom, across the curriculum. Just as importantly, we present evidence of the learning that has resulted from our efforts to build the capacity for citizenship.

William Hastie, the first black judge on the federal bench, once described democracy as "a journey, not a destination" (Boyte 2005). We think of our work as scholars of learning and as proponents of citizenship education in much the same way. All education is, and should be, a work in progress. Both with the "origin story" that follows and within each chapter in this volume, we share the pedagogical journeys we have taken, along with the evidence of students acquiring the tools of citizenship. The power of building community is one dimension of citizenship visible in almost all the studies in this volume. We therefore begin our story by describing a unique experience that put an end to our pedagogical solitude, helped us to explore how we educate for citizenship across our very different disciplines and classes, and established a "teaching and learning commons" (Huber and Hutchings 2005) that we hope to keep expanding through this book.

Building a Community

The golden foothills of the California Coastal Range just west of Stanford University are habitat for mountain lions, red-tailed hawks, western bluebirds, and California live oaks. Perched among these hills is the headquarters for the Carnegie Foundation for the Advancement of Teaching, the habitat where the investigations of learning described in this volume were incubated, hatched, nurtured, and fledged. Over the course of three residencies in 2005–2006, twenty-one college and university instructors came together to refine our skills as scholars of teaching and learning (nine members of this cohort are authors of chapters 1–9 of this book). We certainly accomplished that—and finished the year as confirmed evangelists of the importance of the scholarship of teaching and learning.

We also became a community. In that habitat for thought we came together with some shared values, with a commitment to improve the practice of teaching and learning in our respective disciplines, with differences of opinion, with widely ranging life journeys. The constant dialogue, respectful but often forceful differences of opinion, and accommodation to the complexity and ambiguity that is a part of all learning became, in retrospect, one model for the capacities of citizenship the contributors to this book hope to cultivate in their own classrooms. Both the content and the spirit of this book, then, owe much to the environment the Carnegie Foundation created for us that year. It is our hope that such collaborative and multidisciplinary spaces can be created for instructors elsewhere, so that they in turn might create habitats that cultivate citizenship in their classrooms.

At the beginning of our Carnegie year none of the authors in this book recognized how congruent our investigations into learning were. One of the many virtues of the residencies we attended that year was the time allotted for unstructured conversation about our projects and for the organic evolution of discussion groups geared around topics of mutual interest. Speaking initially in pairs or in small groups, we eventually convened as a larger group committed to exploring how our investigations into student learning converged around the idea—expansively construed—of citizenship. We were intrigued by the fact that despite our very different fields we had all in one way or another been trying explicitly to cultivate a capacity for civic engagement.

Moreover, as scholars of teaching and learning we had each designed studies to determine the extent to which we had been successful in this endeavor. Not one of us had set out to frame our work as a contribution to the very robust scholarly dialogue about the need for citizenship education in the academy, but we soon recognized that we might make a significant contribution to this citizenship literature—a contribution that rests on the inquiry into and assessment of student learning taking place in our own classrooms. As David Scobey and Edward Zlotkowski observe in their concluding overviews of this project, the ways we understand and implement an institution of higher education's commitment to civic engagement (and public scholarship) have evolved considerably over the past decade. Through initiatives like Imagining America that promote public scholarship, organizations such as Campus Compact that advance service-learning, and investigations of civic education like those undertaken by the Association of American Colleges and Universities (AAC&U), the Carnegie Foundation, and the Center for Information and Research on Civic Learning and Engagement (CIRCLE), there is an emerging consensus that cultivating an enduring ethos of civic engagement is one of the most important things higher education should do.

At the same time, public frustration about the cost-to-value relationship of a college education and the shortage of meaningful assessment tools for evaluating just what a college or university graduate has gained from her passage through our classrooms has stimulated initiatives like the Commission on the Future of Higher Education convened by then-Secretary of Education Margaret Spellings in 2005. Although the work of the Spellings Commission may have been partly animated by an ideological agenda determined to send No Child Left Behind to college, the commission's conclusions (2006) about the need for better assessment of a college education should resonate with every scholar, teacher, administrator, student, and parent. The form such assessment will take in the coming years (and the degree to which it will be mandated) is still very much open to discussion. The work represented in this volume, in all its methodological variety, exemplifies an overarching approach to providing persuasive evidence of student learning in a variety of disciplinary settings across a wide range of institutions: namely, to allow instructors, in critical dialogue (i.e., a process of peer review) with colleagues, to pose questions meaningful for a particular institutional context and to gather and analyze evidence of student learning that can directly inform classroom practice.

These studies also illuminate the manifold possibilities for inculcating in our students a strong sense of themselves as civic agents who better understand political institutions and processes, and as empathetic members of a pluralistic polity who can communicate themselves more effectively. The ambitious goal of developing such capacities is an important—perhaps *the most* important —element in the charter of higher education in this country. Our collective contribution to the already ongoing scholarly conversations, then, is to argue that courses in different academic disciplines can facilitate different capacities of citizenship; and to demonstrate how this can be done, using examples drawn from across the curriculum.

Our understanding of citizenship has evolved as each of us has learned from our individual inquiries and from each other. As noted above, we find the conventional definitions of what constitutes an engaged citizen important but insufficient. If our courses produce more politically informed and engaged students (as Jeff Bernstein's do), or college graduates more inclined to perform voluntary service in their communities, that is all to the good. But we have also learned that citizenship embodies other capacities as well. Some of these are quite practical: the kind of numeracy Mike Burke examines in his chapter, for example, or the ability to maintain dialogue through disagreement, something students in Carmen Werder and Rebecca Nowacek's classes learned. Other capacities of citizenship cleave more closely to those "habits of the heart" Robert Bellah et al. (1985) explored more than twenty years ago: the greater sense of empathy central to Howard Tinberg and Rona Halualani's work in the classroom or the development of ethical consciousness through science that Matt Fisher cultivates.

These less overtly political, more apparently personal dimensions of citizenship are more than a soft-hearted view of citizenship as mere affect, as interpersonal skills writ large. Instead, our definition of education for citizenship encompasses both the political and the personal: the very reasons for individuals to be politically informed and active are inextricably linked with their sense of empathy, ethical consciousness, and capacity to engage in dialogue with others. This view of citizenship resonates with Danielle Allen's call for a "citizenship of political friendship" (2006, 140). Insisting that Aristotle's conception of political friendship is "not merely a metaphor for citizenship but its crucial component" (136), Allen argues that to conceptualize citizenship as friendship "captures the conjunction of faculties—the orientation toward others, knowledge of the world, developed practices, and psychological effects—that must be activated in democratic citizenship if it is to succeed" (137). Similarly, the authors in this volume seek to educate for citizenship by providing students with the means and motivation to cultivate both the personal and political dimensions of citizenship.

The many valences of citizenship make it difficult to create a taxonomy of outcomes that effective citizenship education can produce. In part this difficulty arises because every chapter in this volume describes learning environments that have enhanced students' disposition to citizenship in multiple ways. We see evidence of a greater sense of agency emerging—whether as political actors (Bernstein and Burke), as learners (Nowacek and Werder), or as community members (Smith). We see evidence for an emergent understanding of the universality of citizenship rather than viewing citizenship as membership in one political entity—and the attendant growth of empathy that must accompany such an understanding (Fisher, Halualani, Tinberg). We see a tolerance for ambiguity, uncertainty, and contingency in the evidence of learning presented (Bernstein, Halualani, Smith, Geelan). If, as Rebecca Nowacek argues in her chapter, we are not to allow narrow disciplinary boundaries to become the kinds of intellectual and spiritual ghettos that are antithetical to citizenship, we want to see students able to integrate knowledge across different disciplines and different perspectives. Again we see ample evidence that this dimension of citizenship is being cultivated in many of the chapters that follow (Nowacek, Fisher, Geelan, Burke, Smith).

Not only is this agency/universality/ambiguity/integration taxonomy incomplete, but it cannot do justice to the ways the chapters in this book are greater than the sum of their parts. Only when taken together does the work of each author illuminate the full spectrum of citizenship education and show how this work really can be undertaken *across* the curriculum. We hope that readers of this collection will learn not only from those authors with whom they share disciplinary affinities but also from those whose understandings of citizenship and pedagogical strategies for inculcating it are different.

We begin the volume with an investigation of citizenship education that successfully—one might even say against the odds—enhances the political efficacy of students in an introductory political science course. In chapter 1, Jeff Bernstein shows us how powerfully an active learning technique like a simulation can transform both students' understanding of the material and sense of agency in the realm of politics. By themselves these would be enviable learning outcomes, but Jeff goes further. By exposing his students to conflicting information about controversial issues, Jeff helps them understand that intelligent people can disagree on issues like school prayer and affirmative action. The class is not about finding the *right* point of view on an issue, but rather aims to help students weigh evidence in order to reach a careful, considered judgment on an issue. Students become more comfortable with the elusive nature of "correct" answers.

Finding ways to reasonably disagree—surely one of the cornerstones of a *civil society*—and to be comfortable with multiple perspectives on the workings of the world are also central elements of citizenship education. These are capacities that require the development of one's sense of empathy. Trying to understand how others experience the world and learning from difference are central to the pedagogical narratives of the next four chapters.

Rona Halualani's chapter (chapter 2) on multicultural understanding reveals that some students want a "fact sheet" to memorize, one that will simplify the complex process of cross-cultural communication. In time, however, they discover that studying complex and unpredictable groups of people, and how these groups behave in unique situations, is much harder than receiving a list of cultural groups and how they behave. By the end of her course, Rona shows not only that her students have learned new information, but that they have become more empathetic to different life experiences and embraced the uncertainty that attends studies in her discipline.

Carmen Werder's students (chapter 3) become more engaged by first developing self-awareness, both of themselves as learners and as "part of something bigger," as one of her students put it. As students become more aware of their identities as learners and of their greater social agency, they become more empathetic and engaged with their fellow students and their communities beyond the campus boundaries. "Too often in our univer(c)ities," Carmen observes, ". . . it seems as if we share the same spaces, but we remain distanced and unengaged from true relationship." As Carmen's students learn about themselves through metaphors, they begin to bridge that distance.

Howard Tinberg's study (chapter 4) of how students read the literature of the Shoah (Holocaust) is another example of building bridges of empathy that can play an important role in building a civil society immune to the prejudice that, in its worst form, can lead to genocide. He shows us how one of his students struggled to enter this literature, but was eventually able to use tragedies in her own life to help her understand and engage with the perspectives of the authors—and, ultimately, with the suffering of others. Howard quotes Elie Wiesel's exhortation not to "stay at the window" but rather to become intimately involved with the subject. That Howard himself is involved in the story as more than the course instructor (he is the child of Holocaust survivors) further enriches his story of engagement.

The multidisciplinary capstone course described in Rebecca Nowacek's chapter (chapter 5) makes understanding and integrating multiple disciplinary perspectives the central task of the course. Rebecca's students, drawn from a wide range of majors, are asked to be the experts on their disciplines—first by teaching their classmates about the knowledge and ways of knowing important to their disciplines, then by representing their disciplines in group projects. As these students apply their disciplinary knowledge to complex social problems like teen pregnancy and pollution, they also begin to integrate and reconcile multiple perspectives into a richer understanding of those problems and to recognize the limitations of their own expertise. The result is not only enhanced empathy but enhanced problem-solving capacity and the confidence to *be* a solver of problems.

Using one's disciplinary expertise for the good of the world is also the focus of Matt Fisher's (chapter 6) investigation of learning. By infusing his introductory biochemistry course—one usually taught using textbooks that remove biochemistry from "the real world"—with applied examples, such as AIDS and Alzheimer's disease, Matt teaches the technical aspects of biochemistry through these subjects; he also uses them to help students recognize that chemists have a unique perspective on societal issues that they must share with the rest of society. His students learn that science is not value neutral. Matt's vision of chemical education is that it cannot be done in isolation; rather, chemical educators must themselves engage, and help students engage, with the world outside the lab.

When students enter Mike Burke's precalculus and calculus classes, numbers and mathematics may seem as remote from the most pressing issues facing the world today as they do to Matt's burgeoning chemists. But by forcing students to use their developing math skills to address issues of public policy, Mike helps his students understand that numeracy, like literacy, is fundamental to the exercise of citizenship (chapter 7). Mike's efforts to develop his students' quantitative literacy represent integrative learning at its best: students take knowledge gained within the class, incorporate new perspectives and issues, and emerge with a better understanding of the course material. They also leave his class as better citizens, with a richer understanding of how knowledge is created around public policy matters.

Central to David Geelan's approach (chapter 8) is an understanding that a scientist is "able to participate in an *informed* way in the ongoing social conversation around the issues and problems . . . facing a society." David's project aims to educate science teachers not just in how to teach, but also in how to transmit citizenship skills to their students by helping them to see science as socially contingent. Moreover, science reveals the extent to which so many of the issues and problems we must deal with in the twenty-first century are transnational and therefore require that we be citizens of the world rather than of a nation-state. While we may be citizens of towns, cities, states, and nations, we are also citizens of the planet. Effective citizens realize that in addition to solving the problems that confront our immediate surroundings, we must also attend to more global issues.

In addressing this theme, Michael Smith's chapter (chapter 9) on a service-learning project in his environmental history course brings us full circle. Michael connects his students to the local community in which they attend college by asking them to work with a local historical society to understand the environmental history of the region. Michael's students report feeling more connected to—and feeling more like citizens of—a particular place. As the evidence of student learning he presents makes clear, this civic connection resonates with conventional notions of citizenship. But a broader set of commitments (what Michael calls "ecological citizenship") emerges as well, the concerns of which transcend political boundaries. Environmental study is situated in a place, to be sure, but the lessons are universal, not bound by the specific place.

The foregoing map of the ways the authors of this collection have defined and inculcated citizenship suggests one possible path for exploring this book. Each of the chapters, however, offers manifold ways for thinking about citizenship education, and readers will no doubt see other points of congruence among them. As David Scobey (chapter 10) and Edward Zlotkowski (chapter 11) observe in their concluding reflections, the web of connections among these chapters is testament to our claim that citizenship *can* be taught across the curriculum and that the tools of the scholarship of teaching and learning can help us understand just what learning citizenship looks like. Long at the vanguard of engaged learning in higher education, David and Edward also help put these essays in historical perspective.

Citizenship *Across* the Curriculum

One additional perspective proved essential in the conceptualization of this project. By titling this book *Citizenship Across the Curriculum* we quite intentionally invoke the name, and many of the ideals, of the writing across the curriculum

(WAC) movement. The WAC movement has demonstrated tremendous institutional vitality, having existed in the university system for nearly forty years (McLeod and Miraglia 2001, 1), and offers some valuable lessons as we advocate the inclusion of education for citizenship across the curriculum.

To sequester the responsibility for education for citizenship within a single discipline (like political science) or even a single class (like Introduction to American Government) is a grave mistake. A central premise of the WAC movement is that to become good writers, students require more than a semester or two of first-year English; a college or university committed to graduating skilled writers must offer its students extended opportunities to develop writing abilities in multiple contexts. Similarly, we believe students need multiple opportunities to develop skills and aptitudes that facilitate effective citizenship. Through engagement with education for citizenship in multiple contexts over time, students can learn to see citizenship not simply as a duty to vote but can begin to see how being an engaged and effective citizen intersects with their own interests and goals and abilities. In other words, students need practice over time and in multiple contexts.

WAC scholarship also offers a powerful way of imagining a variety of relations between education for citizenship and the disciplines. WAC scholars have long distinguished between two distinct but complementary approaches to incorporating writing across the curriculum. The "writing to learn" approach encourages instructors to think broadly about how writing assignments can scaffold students' thinking and learning: students in a literature class might keep a double-entry journal, students in a physics class might write an imaginary "Ask Dr. Physics" column answering questions about real-world applications of torque and friction and simple harmonic motion. On the other hand, the "writing in the disciplines" approach encourages instructors to identify genres and conventions that are particularly meaningful for their academic or professional community and to help students enter into that community by writing in these genres: nursing students might practice charting, psychology students might work to master the experimental lab report. The first approach views writing as a mode of learning quite broadly, one that can creatively direct students' time and attention on the subject matter we wish them to be learning; the second focuses on how particular genres and conventions scaffold specific disciplinary ways of knowing.

An analogous (if somewhat different) tension arises as we consider education for citizenship across the curriculum. There is a difference, potentially a significant one, between simply situating citizenship in a variety of courses and reconfiguring citizenship via the lens of particular disciplines. Is citizenship simply a tool of engagement, a way of helping students to find meaning and to think more carefully about our various subject matters? Or do our various subject matters help us (and our students) to recognize different dimensions of citizenship?

However we conceptualize the relationship between citizenship and the disciplines, WAC scholarship warns that to ask colleagues to add a unit on citizenship disconnected from other course goals and activities would be to invite burnout and failure. A central premise of the WAC movement is that writing can and should further the already existing goals of a course. The aim is not to teach writing but to teach *with* writing. Writing activities should be creatively designed and sequenced in ways that support the student learning that would (or should) be going on already. In some instances, incorporating writing may lead instructors to rethink and considerably revise their courses, but in all cases the goal of using writing to engage students in the intellectual work of a discipline is to help them improve their understanding of the discipline as well as their writing.

Similarly, we encourage our readers to think creatively about how to design activities and assignments that will achieve their course goals while also helping students become more aware of citizenship. Education for citizenship should not be crowding out the "real" focus of the course; it should be a way to engage students in that work, perhaps by contextualizing it in a new way. In our enthusiasm to "preach the word" (the "missionary" metaphor is a common, and problematized, trope in WAC work) of citizenship across the curriculum, we cannot close our eyes to the very real curricular constraints facing teachers. We therefore urge our readers to embrace the idea of citizenship across the curriculum with what WAC scholar Chris Anson (1993, xv) calls "intellectual caution" as well as "emotional zeal," working to forge meaningful connections between education for citizenship and other disciplinary goals.

The cross-disciplinary faculty workshop has been the key faculty development strategy of the writing across the curriculum movement; workshop participants are frequently amazed by how informed and inspired they are by the work of colleagues in very different disciplines, teaching very different students. Although it would be a mistake to ignore the real material differences in classroom structures (e.g., a lecture of 150 vs. a seminar of 15), the act of making connections across such differences is illuminating. Conversation and collaboration across disciplinary lines is a central support mechanism for the development of citizenship across the curriculum initiatives as well. To support this end, each of the chapters that detail class projects also features two commentaries from other authors, and a response from the chapter author. These suggest the generative power of such conversations—for our own collaboration in particular and as a faculty development strategy in general.

A final lesson from the writing across the curriculum movement is its ability and willingness to ride the wave of other institutional initiatives. Such institutional entrepreneurship is necessary—for despite a broad agreement that colleges and universities should graduate students with strong communication skills, there is little institutional reward for the kinds of commitments such teaching entails. To find the time and money to encourage such work, WAC directors and instructors frequently hitch their wagons to other initiatives: assessment, teaching with technology, learning communities, and many others. A similar impulse is in evidence throughout this volume: Michael Smith's work is bound up with his commitment to service-learning, Michael Burke's work offers one model of quantitative reasoning across the curriculum assignments, Rona Halualani's work on citizenship grows out of her long-standing immersion in multicultural education. A cynic might dismiss such piggybacking as mere opportunism; to us, however, this is simply a necessary step to support innovation within the academy.

Ultimately, what education for citizenship looks like is not a one-size-fits-all affair. Citizenship may mean different things within different disciplines. In all cases, we need to teach for citizenship in ways that are meaningful for students and colleagues within our disciplines—even as (and as the cases of Matt Fisher, Mike Burke, and Jeff Bernstein illustrate) we may challenge the ways some of these courses have traditionally been taught.

Bridging to the Future

As we write this introduction in the wake of the 2008 presidential election, it is clear that more Americans exercised the right most associated with citizenship, voting, than had in two generations. If their turnout is any indication, young voters—that is, people from the demographic group we are most likely to be teaching in our classrooms—seemed to be more civically engaged than at any time since the 1960s; we hope that engagement will continue and that this election is the beginning of a new trend, and not a mere blip interrupting a familiar one. Whether the learning experiences students had in college classrooms around the country have anything to do with these trends is the work of another book . . . and of college and university educators everywhere. Moreover, exercising one's right to vote represents only the first step, and arguably the most passive step, toward the kind of citizenship required to sustain civilization in the twenty-first century.

We also write during a time of enormous anxiety in the face of an economic crisis unparalleled since the Great Depression, during a time when the deadlines for achieving carbon neutrality or facing catastrophic climate instability move closer to the present with each scientific study, during a time when ideological differences and socioeconomic inequality in both the United States and abroad have made even heavier the responsibilities of citizenship. All educators, regardless of discipline or institutional affiliation, have an obligation to cultivate the problem-solving capacities that will be required of all of us as twenty-first century citizens. We hope that the models of citizenship education and the evidence of their effectiveness presented in this book will inspire a thousand new initiatives in teaching citizenship across the curriculum to blossom.

Works Cited

Allen, Danielle S. 2006. *Talking to strangers: Anxieties of citizenship since Brown v. Board of Education.* Chicago: University of Chicago Press.

Anson, Chris. 1993. Introduction. In *Writing across the curriculum: An annotated bibliography,* ed. Chris M. Anson, John E. Schwiebert, and Michael M. Williamson., xiiv–xxiv. Westport, Conn.: Greenwood.

Bass, Randy. 1999. The scholarship of teaching: What's the problem? *Inventio.* 1.1: http://www.doiiit.gmu.edu/Archives/feb98/randybass.htm.

Bellah, Robert N., Richard Madsen, William M. Sullivan, Ann Swidler, and Steven M. Tipton. 1985. *Habits of the heart: Individualism and commitment in American life.* Berkeley: University of California Press.

Boyte, Harry. 2005. Taking democracy seriously. *The Christian Science Monitor.* March 14, 2005.

Commission on the Future of Higher Education. 2006. *A test of leadership: Charting the future of U.S. higher education.* Washington: U.S. Department of Education.

Hamrick, Florence Aileen, Nancy J. Evans, and John H. Schuh. 2002. *Foundations of student affairs practice: How philosophy, theory and research strengthen education outcomes.* San Francisco: Jossey-Bass.

Huber, Mary Taylor, and Pat Hutchings. 2005. *The advancement of learning: Building the teaching commons.* San Francisco: Jossey-Bass.

McLeod, Susan H., and Eric Miraglia. 2001. Writing across the curriculum in a time of change. In *WAC for the new millennium: Strategies for continuing writing-across-the-curriculum programs,* ed. Susan H. McLeod, Eric Miraglia, Margot Soven, and Christopher Thaiss, 1–27. Urbana: National Council of Teachers of English.

Shulman, Lee S. 1993. Teaching as community property: Putting an end to pedagogical solitude. *Change* 25: 6–7.

Jeffrey L. Bernstein

The class was in the middle of the first day of its affirmative action simulation and students had gathered in different corners of the room based on their attitudes toward the issue. Johanna was the only student in the back left corner, the designated meeting place for students who "absolutely, completely opposed affirmative action." Later, as students discussed the issue with their classmates, Johanna (who is white) found herself sitting with four students, three African American and one white, who strongly favored affirmative action. The more they discussed the issue, the more confused they became. When I wandered into that group a few minutes later, I could actually see them processing their discussion in the silence that greeted my arrival. Finally, one of the students looked at me and said, "This issue was a lot easier before this discussion." Johanna, still processing, could only nod in agreement.

I teach political science at Eastern Michigan University, a regional comprehensive institution. For students who entered the university before fall 2007, the introductory American Government course is required for graduation. The course presents many challenges: beyond the fact that it has a large and essentially captive audience, students represent a true cross-section of a student body that is quite diverse in terms of its preparation for college and its motivation to do college-level work. Teaching one hundred of these students, usually in a lecture hall designed to hold far more, and keeping the focus on student learning is a daunting task.

Despite its challenges, this course has traditionally offered my department a golden opportunity to ensure students have some exposure to American government. Asked to justify why this should be a required course, political scientists respond with broad platitudes: "Our students will be citizens and need to know how government works," or "Politics is all around us and students need to be exposed to it," or "Whatever field our students go into, the political system will have an impact." These arguments rest not on the importance of disciplinary knowledge, but instead on broader citizenship issues—specifically, on our role as political scientists in training future citizens.

This is not to argue that disciplinary knowledge is unimportant. Students should know about checks and balances, the President's cabinet, and the policy-making process. Political scientists are well positioned to teach this, and do it well. But we must do more; disciplinary knowledge alone is quickly forgotten by our students. A citizenship-oriented perspective can give students tools and dispositions to be more effective participants in their government and community; these lessons will last longer than lessons about checks and balances ever will. Moreover, for academics who strive to better the world while teaching their courses, the rewards can be profound, as they have been for me.

Political Affairs Today: Three Disturbing Trends

As we move deeper into the twenty-first century, the engaged citizen has to look at the political order with concern. Whatever one's policy positions, the *process* seems broken. Campaigns push wedge issues in an attempt to divide. The ubiquitous role of money in American politics has rarely been clearer; in the presidential primaries, those who cannot raise millions of dollars more than a year before the next election are quickly deemed nonviable candidates, their voices silenced. Inability to compromise commonly stalls important legislative initiatives. It seems undeniable that the political system is failing in its role of aggregating mass opinion to inform those who make policy.[1]

Three overlapping trends illustrate the level of interest and engagement American citizens currently have in politics. First, as documented by Putnam (2000), Americans have experienced a dramatic decrease in social capital, defined as the societal value gained from interactions among people. Americans join groups—fraternal, service, political—much less frequently than they did in previous generations. Moreover, the political groups people join tend to require much less of their members; rather than chapter meetings, most groups require people to do little more than write a check (Skocpol 2003). This trend is disturbing; Putnam notes that lack of social capital makes it harder for people to engage in collective action. It also deprives people of the interpersonal ties that make life more pleasant.

A second trend is the decline in trust of the political system. Widespread disaffection toward politics is not new; Americans' political discontent helped make wags such as Will Rogers and Mark Twain famous. But the rise of discontent is accelerating (Dionne 1991; Hibbing and Theiss-Morse 2002) as politics gets nastier. Moreover, the reasons behind the acceleration are, in themselves, troubling. Dionne (1991) argues that Americans resent the false choices offered to them by polarized political parties; while most Americans are fairly moderate, the parties offer extreme choices. The result, Fiorina (2005) suggests, is perceived "culture wars," where the red state/blue state dichotomy appears to divide the country more than it actually does. As candidates employ negative campaigning and focus on wedge issues, differences rather than commonalities are emphasized (an emphasis reflected in this volume by Rona Halualani and Rebecca Nowacek).

Hibbing and Theiss-Morse (1995, 2002) argue that the problem lies in the political *processes* followed by American political institutions, particularly Congress. They suggest that the issue is less the policies Congress passes than the way the work gets done—the arguments, debates, partisanship, etc. In their judgment, people like democracy but hate its messier by-products. Since the passage of laws can never occur absent these by-products, little can be done to make Congress popular short of hiding its procedures from the populace, something that would be unacceptable in a democracy.

Finally, Americans know less about politics (Bennett 1988; Delli Carpini and Keeter 1996). Surveys show disturbingly low levels of civic knowledge; for example, more Americans can name the Three Stooges than can name the three branches of government.[2] The consequences of this trend are less clear. For some (Bennett 1988; Somin 2006), lack of knowledge indicates a disengaged populace, lacking skills or ability to actively participate in politics. For Lupia (2006), however, lack of knowledge does not necessarily imply inability to make sense of politics, or to reach informed political decisions. Citizens can use shortcuts, or cognitive heuristics, to make difficult choices, even with incomplete information. For example, it would be good if I knew my senator's voting record on the Iraq War, or on minimum wage legislation; it would be even better if I knew her opponent's positions on those issues. Ideally, I should even know how long a Senate term is, and the powers that the Senate has in the political system. But, absent this information, knowing the political parties of both candidates, or even their positions on the one issue of greatest importance to me, will help me reach a voting decision that is "good enough" (Popkin 1991; Zaller 1992).

Amplifying these disturbing trends is the fact that their effects are not distributed equally. Women show lower levels of objective political knowledge than men (Bennett and Bennett 1989; Delli Carpini and Keeter 1996). African Americans and Latinos rank lower not only in political knowledge, but also in trust toward the political system (Delli Carpini and Keeter 1996). And, most salient to this chapter, youth rank lower than other groups in traditional measures of social capital, political trust, and political knowledge (Dalton 2007; Delli Carpini and Keeter 1996; Zukin et al. 2006; Niemi and Junn 1998; Putnam 2000). Significantly, all three of these factors correlate highly with political participation.

Despite their lower levels of social capital, political trust, and political knowledge, it is incorrect to say that young people take no interest in the broader world (Dalton 2007; Zukin et al. 2006). Today's youth show high levels of engagement in various civic (as opposed to political) behaviors, such as volunteering in their community (Kirlin 2003). Noble though serving meals in a soup kitchen may be, however, these volunteers' failure to see hunger as tied to politics and political structures is cause for concern.

How can educators engage their college students politically? Colby et al. (2003) offer some encouraging vignettes of schools that have made institutional commitments to civic education; their examples function as "visions of the possible" (Hutchings 2000), showing education can have positive civic effects. Service-learning shows transformative promise, particularly if students reflect on their experiences and tie them to the academic content of their classes (e.g., Hepburn, Niemi, and Chapman 2000; Hunter and Brisbin 2000; Strain 2006). Michael Smith's chapter in this volume also shows the promise of service-learning in giving students the means for engagement.

More explicitly political, Niemi and Junn (1998) show that using active learning techniques can lead to the acquisition of more political knowledge, although they show minimal change in political attitudes. Bernstein and Meizlish (2003) demonstrate that students who participate in a large-scale simulation emerge less politically cynical and more politically efficacious than those who do not; no differences appeared in students' self-reported knowledge. Thus, it appears *possible* for attitudinal change to arise based on activities in government classes. Here, I explore whether the simulation-based approach I use has a meaningful effect on developing both the attitudes *and skills* required for effective citizenship education.

Why a Focus on Citizenship?

What role should citizenship themes play in an introductory government course? One view suggests that the focus of the course should be to learn content as dispassionate scholars. Attempts to change the world are fine, but should be reserved for the nonacademic part of a student's life (building houses for the homeless with the Office of Community Service), or in one's life outside college. An opposing approach suggests that coursework cannot be divorced from taking political positions and becoming activists. Advocates of this position would ask what the purpose of learning is if we do not directly use what we learn to address problems in our communities.

As a teacher and a citizen, I have erred on the side of the latter approach in inculcating citizenship as a goal in my classes. While not wishing to abandon my responsibility to teach course content to my students, the need to leave them with something more lasting, and to leave the world just a little bit better off, led me to forsake the approach of the dispassionate scholar and focus on student involvement and activism. Educating my students as future citizens will prove a better legacy for my work than educating my students as future political scientists.

This chapter is about the evolution of a course, but is also about the evolution of a citizen. Like most people who grow up to teach political science, I was a political junkie long before I entered the academy. My father taught high school government, and political discussions at home were common. I have many memories of intense political discussions in middle school, high school, and college. I am a politically efficacious person, perhaps more than empirical reality says I should be, and cling to the belief that individual action *can* change the system. The attempt is often its own reward, especially when we know that attempts to fight City Hall fail more often than they succeed. By the end of the course, I want my students to be able to monitor the government, discuss political issues with others, and understand the role government can play in the lives of all people.

Perspectives on Citizenship

The desire to teach a course around a citizenship theme led me to explore what citizenship means. Technically, citizenship is conferred by the state, and offers certain rights that noncitizens do not enjoy (i.e., the right to vote or hold elective office). People can be born as citizens of a nation-state or can undergo a naturalization process. The naturalization process in the United States is, in itself, telling. The requirements include swearing an oath to the new county (no country would be expected to offer citizenship to those who wish to overthrow its government), living in the country for some time, and passing a test about American history and politics.

One might expect such a test to represent a coherent statement of what society wants citizens to know; if so, the U.S. citizenship test is quite puzzling.[3] While it might be good for citizens to know what the stripes on the flag represent, or the exact year the Constitution was written, or the exact number of times the Constitution has been amended, is this knowledge *essential* to being a citizen? I do not believe this, which begs the question of what we would want people to know in order to be "educated citizens."

With this question in mind, I began to explore where I wanted my students to be at the end of the course, and how I would get them there. I came to characterize my destination as "civic competence" (Lupia 2006). I wanted to help my students build the *skills* necessary to be active and engaged participants in politics. While I hoped they would acquire the interest and sense of efficacy that would make them more likely to participate, that goal seemed difficult to attain in fourteen weeks. So, I settled on the goal of cultivating students' civic skills so they could use them when the spirit moved them; as a secondary goal, I wanted to set them along a path toward increasing interest and efficacy.

There are many citizenship skills; I focused on three. First, civically competent citizens can manage the vast array of political information they confront. The citizen who wants to understand a complex issue and reach an opinion has much information to process: not just written information but also information obtained in discussion with other people. This information is sometimes accurate and sometimes not, sometimes biased and sometimes not. The citizen who cannot effectively process this information is at a loss when attempting to understand politics. Imagine, for example, such a citizen googling "Barack Obama" to learn about his policies.

Second, a civically competent individual understands how the political system operates and how the skillful activist can use this information to his or her benefit. Frantzich's (2005) vignettes about neophyte political activists showed the need to learn some basics of the political system: for example, to whom certain concerns are best addressed, or how to motivate people to act. Political scientists understand that rules help determine outcomes. Therefore, attempts to change the results require one to understand how specific rules privilege some outcomes, and how to act accordingly to achieve the desired effect.

Finally, a civically competent citizen can work with others to pursue political goals. In a democracy, one individual cannot change the system alone; forming coalitions is vital to gaining political influence. Yet, declining levels of civic engagement and social capital threaten to erode this skill. Linked to this ability to work with others is the ability to disagree civilly, something both Rebecca Nowacek and Carmen Werder examine in their chapters. Too often in politics, "my opponent" becomes "my enemy." A perusal of recent political bestsellers, such as *Stupid White Men* (Moore 2002), *How to Talk to a Liberal (If You Must)* (Coulter 2004) and *Lies and the Lying Liars Who Tell Them* (Franken 2003) and of the loud volume on political talk shows suggests that civility in politics is a dying art. We won't all agree on political outcomes. But as a society, we must learn how to inject our politics with civility.

I also aim to affect the political dispositions of my students. My ability to do this is limited; I teach them in one course, for only four months. I compete for my students' attention with other courses, friends, families, Facebook, and jobs. Moreover, I am not writing on a blank slate; I have years of political socialization to overcome. Many students enter the course politically uninterested, disengaged, and cynical. But, if educating citizens is my goal, I must get my students to view political activity as valuable. They must come to view political participation as worth the time in their already full lives.

The Evolution of the Course

STAGE 1: GRADUATE SCHOOL-ITIS

I began to teach this course while in graduate school. Like a good graduate student, I immersed myself in the literature of the field and formed my own intellectual perspectives about what I was studying. When given the opportunity to design this course on my own, I assigned readings based upon my own understanding of the field ("Mayhew makes an important contribution to the literature on Congress. I *must* assign it to my students"). A colleague termed this "graduate school-itis." My lectures were heavy on content; after all, I had limited time to convey a wide range of material to my students; I had much to fit into a narrow window of time.

Looking back, I managed to succeed despite what I now realize were significant design flaws in the course. I have been told I am an engaging lecturer, and my offbeat humor does seem to keep the students' attention. I believe I have a strong grasp of the material and how it fits together; therefore, the presentations I would offer my students did seem to make sense (at least they told me they did!). And, I did have some experience with, and interest in, active learning techniques, so I was spicing things up with short simulations, group work, and other such activities. Still, in retrospect, my work seemed to come firmly out of the teaching paradigm rather than the learning paradigm (Barr and Tagg 1995) and seemed wedded to the notion of "covering" the material rather than "uncovering" the challenge, mystery, and relevance of what I was teaching (Wiggins and McTighe 1998).

STAGE 2: THE FIRST SIMULATION

Early in my career, I began to use a large-scale simulation in the class. In this simulation students played actual members of Congress, lobbyists for interest groups, members of the president's administration, and journalists. In its first iteration, the task was to create a federal budget; in later incarnations, the students created legislation on any topic, which would be assigned to committees that determined whether the bills would come to the House floor. The simulation took three weeks and was, in many ways, fantastic. The room had the feel of a bustling legislature; I took particular pride when two former members of Congress visited class one day and commended me on having captured the feel perfectly.

At the beginning, the design and the challenge of doing this captivated me; and, to be honest, it was a lot of fun to do! Pedagogically, I had sound reasons for using this innovation. The simulation provided meaningful integrative learning opportunities; rather than teaching course topics like Congress, the presidency, interest groups, political parties, and the media in separate weeks, the simulation combined these topics and let students see how learning one required understanding the others. I also wanted to balance a traditional book-heavy approach with a module that gave different types of learners opportunities to excel. Citizenship goals, such as giving students the opportunity to learn about critical issues and giving them the chance to practice speaking and persuading others, were present, but they were secondary. In truth, I was most attracted to the challenge of running the simulation, the desire to integrate across different topics, and the need to reach a more diverse population of learners than those I was accustomed to reaching.

Over time, I came to look skeptically at what I was really achieving. This happened in two stages. First, Deborah Meizlish and I (Meizlish and Bernstein 2003) wrote a conference paper for which we carefully read student essays designed to evaluate their learning. The question asked students to advise the Speaker of the House on how to get a controversial bill through Congress. We were disappointed to see many students tell the Speaker to prepare "campaign fliers" for favored candidates and to offer "pork chips" to sway votes in Congress. While the students' instincts were good, their failure to translate simulation activities (such as making up campaign fliers and giving out pork chips) into the actual political concepts they represented (offering campaign funding and providing particularized, pork-barrel benefits) raised a troubling concern: was I training students to play a game first and understand politics second?

This concern was furthered during a conversation with Rebecca Nowacek, a co-editor of this volume. While discussing writing assignments students did for the simulation, I told her about the role profile assignment, in which students describe who they will play in the simulation. Students playing legislators, for example, would write in the first person, composing an autobiography of the legislator and a summary of his or her policy positions. Why, I wondered aloud during this conversation, was I giving students an opportunity to write about policy issues but forcing them to do it in someone else's voice? Wasn't it my responsibility to help students find *their own* political voices? This "light bulb" moment gave rise to the simulations that I currently use.

STAGE 3: THE CURRENT SIMULATION

The design of the new simulation is relatively straightforward. On four occasions during the semester (later reduced to three), students have a week off from the regular class and instead participate in a three-day simulation. The one-hundred student class is divided into four groups, each of which has its own simulation. I have no graduate teaching assistants: therefore, two undergraduate students facilitate each simulation. These students are honors students concurrently enrolled in an honors seminar, Cultivating Civic Competence; as the "laboratory" part of their seminar, they work in the government class. These students receive extensive training in how to run the simulations. As instructor, I visit each simulation each day, offering insight and guidance. The honors students, however, are linchpins in making this arrangement work.

Each simulation deals with a controversial issue—school prayer, the war on terrorism, affirmative action, eminent domain—in some depth. Two weeks before the simulation, students are given a set of readings which typically include 8–10 pieces of 1–2 pages each, from a range of genres (newspaper articles, press releases, op-ed columns, etc.) Collectively, the articles are meant to represent the types of materials and ideological positions that might confront someone seeking to learn about the issue.

Once the students read the articles, they write a three-page paper on the issue. The paper requires them to elaborate their opinion in some depth, making explicit references to the articles they agreed with and arguing against articles with which they disagreed. It is unusual for people to have to seriously consider arguments on multiple sides of an issue; most people tend to filter out those positions with which they disagree. By forcing students to make explicit reference to sources with which they disagreed, I hoped to improve students' abilities to make persuasive arguments.

The simulation begins the class period after the students hand in their papers. Students receive a one-page sheet that details the "status quo" on the issue, laying out current policy in bulleted points. They then take out a piece of paper, summarize their position on the issue, and jot down the best arguments they can make and the arguments they anticipate hearing from the other side. They next pair off with another student to discuss their respective positions and arguments. The think-pair-share is repeated a second time, giving students the opportunity to articulate and practice expressing their opinions; in all, it takes one-half of the first day.

Following this, students write proposals to address elements of the status quo they found objectionable. For instance, the school-prayer status quo sheet indicates that teachers are not permitted to participate in prayer with their students. Participants who disagree can propose an amendment permitting teachers to pray with students. Students are encouraged to make their proposals as clear and compelling as possible; they are expected to work with others and consult widely with potential allies as they draft their proposals. Once they are satisfied with their proposal, they must get three signatures on it before submission. This process consumes the second half of the first day and the entire second day of the simulation.

During Day 2, students begin the process of selecting a Rules Committee, which, similar to the Rules Committee in the House of Representatives, is the "traffic cop" for the legislative process. In the simulation, the Rules Committee determines the order in which proposals will be debated, and for what length of time. Given that there are always more proposals (typically between 8 and 12) than there is time to debate them, Rules Committee members can exercise a great deal of power in determining which proposals can be debated and which will be defeated through not being debated. Students are often slow to realize how powerful the committee is, initially viewing it merely as a policy-neutral efficiency device.

The Rules Committee meets at the beginning of Day 3 to select the proposals that will be debated; following this, debate and discussion begin. Typically, three to four proposals can be dealt with in a particular class, each for around ten minutes. The undergraduate honors students facilitate. While conversation is typically led by a small group of students, one-half to two-thirds of the students actively participate in this discussion; although not perfect, it is far better than the level of participation I would achieve when lecturing. Debate is not of extraordinarily high quality; students rarely attain the level of sophistication needed to have an extremely erudite debate. But it is usually pretty good; by the end of the simulation, the key issues have been raised and debated.

What Might Be Gained

There are three major effects I wish the simulation to have on my students. First, students should gain the aforementioned political skills. By having to read multiple sources and write a coherent paper based upon them, I hope students learn to effectively manage political information. Coming up with a political position and understanding how to defend it is an important skill. Forcing students to work together discussing the issues, writing proposals, and lobbying one another to get their proposals passed should help them build skills in the interpersonal aspects of politics; remaining in the same simulation group all year encourages students to view each other as opponents (with whom they might need to work as allies on the next issue) and not as enemies. Finally, the Rules Committee ideally drives home the point that rules matter; good proposals can die because the Rules Committee does not bring them up for debate. After a while, students learn that success requires not just writing a good proposal, but also getting allies on the committee to shepherd the proposal successfully through this hurdle.

In addition to cultivating their political skills, I also hope students' attitudes toward their role in the political system change as well. For many students, politics seems distant, complicated, and something for *others* to do. Students do not believe they have the capacity to effect political change; often, they do not even believe they have something to contribute to discussions. If I can get students to believe that they can be effective, competent political actors, I maximize the chance that they will *use* the skills they have acquired when the spirit moves them.

Finally, I would like to see politics matter more to my students. When they line up in their mind what is important to them, influencing the political system, or even keeping up to date with public affairs, is unlikely to rank high on their list. If following politics were as entertaining as *American Idol*, as fun as a fraternity party, or as financially rewarding as a shift waiting tables, voter turnout would not be as low as it is. It is difficult to imagine politics puncturing this pantheon of importance for most students. Yet, students do care about the world around them; my hope is to get them to connect their civic caring and engagement with the political world.

Data and Methods

The scholarship of teaching and learning requires not only that we act with intentionality in the classroom, but that we subject the work we do there to the same rigorous standards of evidence and proof that we would use in more traditional research (what Boyer [1990] called the scholarship of discovery). To this end, below I present data that speak to the claims I have made about the potential efficacy of this course. At the start of each semester, I gave my students a survey to assess their political knowledge, attitudes, and behaviors. At the end of the semester, they were given the same survey. Pre-class and post-class surveys were matched based on the last four digits of student ID numbers (in accordance with my university's IRB regulations). Surveys were collected by a research assistant and held during the semester so that I did not know who consented to participate. The vast majority participate; since some students enter the class late, or "leave" early, not every student in the study has completed both surveys. The results reported here are limited to those who completed both surveys.

This chapter reports on data from the fall 2006 and winter 2007 surveys. In addition, as a control group, six other American Government courses were surveyed during fall 2006. These classes, taught by a cross-section of faculty members and lecturers in my department, used a range of active learning techniques but did not use simulations or have such a strong focus on citizenship.

This control group allows me to determine whether the gains experienced by my classes were directly tied to what I did with them, or whether these are more typical gains that can be expected from any American Government course. Students in both the treatment and control groups are drawn from the same distribution of students, allowing me to assume they are like one another before the term begins (see Bernstein [2007] for an empirical demonstration of this fact).

One significant limitation of these data is that they are limited to student self-reports of attitudes and skill levels. Elsewhere (Bernstein 2007), I present data that speak directly to more objective measures of student skills, coding student essays to demonstrate that students show improvement during the term in their ability to deal with conflicting viewpoints while making a coherent argument. Here, however, I rely on self-reports. Self-reports are the best approach for measuring changes in attitudes and dispositions of citizenship; they detail what students believed about the political system and their place in it before and after the class.

A second potential limitation of the data is that the students may be merely telling me what they think I want to hear. I do not worry very much about this, for three reasons. First, I heavily emphasized to students that I wanted their *honest* answers on the survey; I did this both at the beginning of the class and at the end. Second, I did not find out who had and had not completed the survey until the class was done and grades submitted; thus, no "credit" could have accrued to any student for giving the "correct" answer (students knew this). Finally, while I do report results here consistent with my aims and expectations, it is worth noting that various items on the survey (for example, the interest that students had in various political issues) evidenced no increase. Thus, a blanket statement that students gave socially desirable answers is inaccurate.

A third limitation is a common critique of surveys: expressing an attitude on a survey can be an empty act that need not be backed up by behavior. Anyone can claim that they have gained an increased sense of the importance of public affairs; genuine evidence of this, however, comes in the form of behaviors (such as starting to subscribe to a newspaper, watching the news and political talk shows, or attending meetings or rallies). There is no way around this problem, particularly within the timeframe of a semester-long course. Attitude change is important in its own right; moreover, if we believe that attitude change is a prerequisite for behavioral change, understanding attitude change becomes important.

Results

Table 1.1 shows a pre/post-class comparison of skill levels for students in the treatment group. The skills are divided into information skills (e.g., ability to explain views, weigh the pros and cons of issues), people skills (persuading

Table 1.1. Pre- and Post-Class Differences in Political Skill Levels

Attribute	Pre-Class Mean	Post-Class Mean	Difference	T-statistic Difference of Means
I. Information Skill Items				
I can explain my political views	3.75	4.44	0.69	4.005***
I can write well about politics	3.07	4.04	0.97	6.004***
I can weigh pros and cons of political issues	3.68	4.44	0.76	4.591***
II. People Skill Items				
I can persuade others on political issues	3.19	3.78	0.59	4.154***
I can help groups work together	3.34	3.89	0.55	3.687***
I can deal with conflict	4.26	4.55	0.29	2.036*
I can talk about social barriers like race	4.21	4.68	0.47	3.144**
I can reach compromise	4.41	4.58	0.17	1.270
III. Strategy Skill Items				
I can develop effective political strategies	2.63	3.65	1.02	5.885***

N for all items is 70 or 71.
For all items, 1=I cannot do this and 6=I can definitely do this
* denotes difference of means significant at p<.05
** denotes difference of means significant at p<.01
*** denotes difference of means significant at p<.001

others, helping groups work together) and a single item on strategy skills. The table reveals a dramatic increase across the range of items, typically over one half of a point on a six-point scale (higher scores indicate more self-perceived skill levels). With the exception of the item indicating the self-perceived ability to reach compromise, all items were statistically significant at p<.05; in most cases, the results were even more significant than that. Generally, the smallest gains were seen on items on which students entered the course with the highest skill level (reaching compromise and dealing with conflict); the biggest gains were found on the items on which students believed themselves least skilled at the beginning.

Table 1.1 shows that students consider themselves more skilled political actors after the class ends. In table 1.2, I compare my students' gains with those of their peers in the control group. In every case, skill gains claimed by members of the treatment group are larger than those of the control group—in three cases (writing well about politics, weighing pros and cons of political issues, and talking about social barriers like race), the difference is statistically significant. In numerous other cases, the difference approached statistical significance but did not

Table 1.2. Increases in Political Skill Level—Treatment and Control Groups

Attribute	Treat. Group Diff.	Cont. Group Diff.	Diff. in Diff. of Means	T-statistic— Difference in Difference of Means
I. Information Skill Items				
I can explain my political views	0.68	0.44	0.24	1.450
I can write well about politics	0.96	0.59	0.37	2.175*
I can weigh pros and cons of political issues	0.72	0.37	0.35	2.040*
II. People Skill Items				
I can persuade others on political issues	0.59	0.36	0.23	1.425
I can help groups work together	0.54	0.29	0.25	1.494
I can deal with conflict	0.25	0.00	0.25	1.620
I can talk about social barriers like race	0.47	0.04	0.43	2.796**
I can reach compromise	0.13	0.11	0.02	0.083
III. Strategy Skill Items				
I can develop effective political strategies	1.02	0.66	0.36	0.926

N for the treatment group is 70 or 71; N for the control group ranges from 270 to 273.

* denotes difference of means significant at $p < .05$

** denotes difference of means significant at $p < .01$

quite get there. It is heartening to see that government classes almost always increase self-perceived skill levels; with this said, it is also evident that my approach has a positive effect on student skill-building, relative to other approaches to the course.

Apart from skill levels, it is also important to consider students' dispositions toward politics, specifically their internal efficacy (how confident they are that they can understand what is going on politically) and external efficacy (how confident they are in their ability to make a difference in the political system). The first three items in table 1.3 deal with aspects of internal efficacy and show statistically and substantively significant positive effects. By the end of the term, students feel more confident that they understand politics, that they have something to say when political issues are discussed, and that they are well qualified to participate in the political process. The gains on each of these items range from 0.62 to 0.71 on a six-point scale.

On the external efficacy item (whether the student feels he or she can make a difference in politics), the change is modest (0.43 on the six-point scale, statistically significant at the .05 level) but still meaningful. It is not surprising that external efficacy gains lag behind those of internal efficacy; changing one's degree

Table 1.3. Pre- and Post-Class Differences in Political Dispositions

Attribute	Pre-Class Mean	Post-Class Mean	Difference	T-statistic Difference of Means
I feel I have a pretty good understanding of the political issues facing the country	3.36	4.07	0.71	4.735***
I feel I have something to say when political issues are being discussed	3.38	4.07	0.69	4.200***
I consider myself well-qualified to participate in the political process	3.12	3.74	0.62	3.435**
I believe I can make a difference in politics by becoming involved	3.79	4.22	0.43	2.420*
How often do I follow government and public affairs?	3.33	3.64	0.31	2.681**

For the first four items, 1=very strongly disagree and 6=very strongly agree
For the final item, 1=never and 6=most of the time
* denotes difference of means significant at p<.05
** denotes difference of means significant at p<.01
*** denotes difference of means significant at p<.001

of external efficacy requires changing one's view of how others will act, in addition to changing one's own attitudes. Still, this difference is a significant one. Finally, the bottom line in the table begins to explore hypotheses about political behavior. Here, we determine that students have a greater chance of saying that they are more likely to follow public affairs after the course. The difference is substantively smaller, but still important.

Table 1.4 compares student gains to those of the control group. The pattern observed in table 1.2 recurs here; both groups show significant gains, but the gains for the treatment group are larger in every case. The difference in gains between the groups is largest on the item for feeling a student has something to say when political issues are discussed: this difference in differences is 0.41 (on a six-point scale) and is significant at p<.05. The differences on understanding political issues, considering oneself well-qualified to participate, and believing one can make a difference in politics are about half this size. There is virtually no difference between the treatment and control groups in the size of the increase in how often students follow government and public affairs.

Developing political skills is certainly important. I view this as akin to the tools on a carpenter's tool belt; a skilled carpenter knows how to use each tool, but only reaches for a particular tool when the problem at hand calls for it. My students are, most typically, eighteen years old. Most work many hours a week and have active social lives and full course loads. They typically do not have some of the attributes most associated with political engagement: they rarely

Table 1.4. Increases in Political Dispositions—Treatment and Control Groups

Attribute	Treat. Group Diff.	Cont. Group Diff.	Diff. of Diff. of Means	T-statistic— Difference in Difference of Means
I feel I have a pretty good understanding of the political issues facing the country	0.69	0.46	0.23	1.437
I feel I have something to say when political issues are being discussed	0.69	0.28	0.41	2.494*
I consider myself well-qualified to participate in the political process	0.59	0.37	0.22	1.193
I believe I can make a difference in politics by becoming involved	0.41	0.20	0.21	1.146
How often do I follow government and public affairs?	0.28	0.24	0.03	0.243

* denotes difference of means significant at p<.05

own homes, or have spouses or children. Given this, there is a limit to how much one fourteen-week course can get students to change their behaviors. All I can expect is that I will put the tools in their belt, to be used when the situation warrants it.

But while behaviors may not change, perhaps the importance students attach to politics may change. At the beginning of the course, students were asked to rate the personal importance of a variety of items (see table 1.5). The ratings were 1 (not important), 2 (somewhat important), 3 (very important), and 4 (essential). As with previous items, the same questions were repeated at the end of the term to allow for comparisons. Results are presented in table 1.5.

Table 1.5 shows that the two least important items, by a wide margin, are the ones for "influencing the political structure" (an explicitly political item) and the quasi-political "becoming a community leader." "Keeping up to date with political affairs," another obviously political prompt, is the third-least important. The most important items are "raising a family," "helping others who are in difficulty," "improving my understanding of other countries and cultures" and "being very well-off financially." These are not explicitly political items. Thus, at the start of the term, politics does not matter very much to my students.

By the end of the term, much remains the same. The basic ordering of items remains, both at the top and the bottom. All items, with the exception of being well-off financially, now appear to be more important to the students. What has changed, slightly, is the extent of the increase in the importance of each item.

Table 1.5. Pre- and Post-Class Differences in Importance Attached to Aspects of Life

Attribute	Pre-Class Mean	Post-Class Mean	Difference	T-statistic Difference of Means
Influencing the political structure	2.07	2.25	0.18	2.260*
Becoming a community leader	2.19	2.47	0.28	3.048**
Keeping up to date with political affairs	2.53	2.72	0.19	2.410*
Developing a meaningful philosophy of life	2.97	3.13	0.16	1.496
Helping others who are in difficulty	3.21	3.32	0.11	1.304
Volunteering in the local community	2.58	2.72	0.14	1.598
Helping to promote racial understanding	2.79	2.93	0.14	1.396
Raising a family	3.38	3.48	0.10	1.306
Being very well off financially	3.03	2.94	(0.09)	1.229
Improving my understanding of other countries and cultures	3.10	3.10	0.00	0.000

* denotes difference of means significant at $p < .05$
**denotes difference of means significant at $p < .01$

Becoming a community leader, keeping up to date with political affairs, and influencing the political structure show the largest gains over the course of the semester. These increases are the largest of any for these ten items; the gains on these three, and only these three, are statistically significant.

A final piece of the puzzle is examining whether there are differences in the size of the gains on the political items for the treatment and control groups. This is presented in table 1.6. There are small differences in the size of the gains across the two groups: on the item for influencing the political structure, the gain is 0.20 for the treatment group compared to 0.08 for the control group. For becoming a community leader, it is 0.29 versus 0.09 (the only statistically significant difference, albeit at the modest 0.10 level), while for keeping up to date with political affairs, the differences are 0.20 and 0.12. The course appears somewhat effective in raising the importance of public affairs for students.

One single fourteen-week course provides a limited opportunity to have a life-long effect on our students. Moreover, the results presented here are modest enough to make it difficult to conclude that the life priorities of these students have been completely reordered, or that they are completely changed political beings. Still, it is possible to conclude that the students have been at least modestly transformed. At least in the short term, students emerge from my American Government class believing that they are more skilled political actors, able to reach political opinions and express them better than they previously had been.

Table 1.6. Increases in Importance Attached to Aspects of Life—Treatment and Control Groups

Attribute	Treat. Group Diff.	Cont. Group Diff.	Diff. of Diff. of Means	T-statistic— Difference in Difference of Means
Influencing the political structure	0.20	0.08	0.12	1.254
Becoming a community leader	0.29	0.09	0.20	1.809*
Keeping up to date with political affairs	0.20	0.12	0.08	0.869

* denotes difference of means significant at $p < .10$

Students seem to emerge from the course attaching somewhat higher priority to political activities in their life; they are likely to think that following politics and becoming a community leader are more important.

It is notable that the control group classes show improvement in these areas as well. The instructors of these classes all emphasize citizenship themes in their classes; in every case, their students believe themselves to be more skilled politically once the class ends than they had been at the beginning. None of these instructors, however, made citizenship the class's focus to the extent I did; moreover, none used simulations or other techniques with the explicit aim of building citizenship skills. While it may be premature to link educational outcomes so strongly with pedagogical approaches, these results at least tentatively endorse such a relationship.

As I have noted repeatedly, politics is often perceived to be remote from the lives of students in college, at least when it must compete with other obligations and desires. It may well be impossible to convince college students otherwise, although I certainly will continue to spend my time trying. I hope my students learn that engaging in political and civic pursuits can be a worthwhile use of their life, even in the face of other obligations and opportunities. When one segment of our society does not participate in collective decision-making, it is unlikely those in power will listen to them. As I frequently remind my students, there is a reason Social Security is known as the "third rail of American politics" (touch it and you die!) while welfare (the poor do not participate in politics as much as the rich) and student loans (young voters participate less than older voters) are always on the chopping block.

Ultimately, however, if I wish to encourage my students to participate in the civic and political life of their communities, I must help them build the skills necessary to do so—to weigh political positions, consider alternative scenarios, write and speak well about politics, and build strategies for political action. The critical element is skill-building, rather than the transmission of factual information or even the development of zeal to participate. Factual knowledge matters, but students must learn how to apply that knowledge; this is a key goal of my course. And, while I do aim to get students fired up and ready to participate, I suspect they will be reluctant to do so if they do not know how to do it effectively. My goal is to help students find their political voices; this project demonstrably provides them with the tools to do so.

Dialogue

A COMMENTARY FROM MATTHEW A. FISHER
Department of Chemistry, Saint Vincent College

My first reaction on reading Jeff's chapter was that here was a political science professor who had incorporated into his class a marvelous laboratory experience! At its best, the laboratory component of a science course—one of the "signature pedagogies" (to use Lee Shulman's phrase) of undergraduate science education—is an ideal learning environment to engage students in the process of scientific inquiry, which in the words of the American Association for the Advancement of Science's *The Liberal Art of Science* (1990) focuses on "active engagement with the natural world and social interaction among the members of the community."

Several powerful consequences arise from Jeff's explicit emphasis on citizenship through these simulations. First, what students learn through the active engagement with inquiry highlights different ideas and perspectives than they would encounter in a more traditional course. Second, teaching political science (and perhaps many other disciplines) in this way opens up the possibility of engaging students affectively in ways that would otherwise be very difficult. There has been much recent discussion of the importance of the affective dimension in student learning (articles in *The National Teaching and Learning Forum*, sessions at Lilly conferences, even workshops within scientific disciplines, e.g., geosciences). The simulations Jeff has developed are a wonderful addition to that broader discussion. Finally, I am optimistic that using this particular pedagogy of inquiry opens up new opportunities for integrative learning. The statement on integrative learning released jointly by the Association of American Colleges and Universities and the Carnegie Foundation for the Advancement of Teaching (Huber and Hutchings 2004) points out that integrative learning can come through "connecting skills and knowledge from multiple sources and experiences" or "applying theory to practice in various settings." Jeff's use of simulations encourages students to make those connections and engage in those applications.

I'm left wondering how my students would react if they took a political science course like this. From conversations with students over the years, I know that many see their non-science courses as largely irrelevant. But the parallels between Jeff's simulations and the process of open-ended scientific inquiry (toward which many undergraduate science courses have moved) are clear and striking. They certainly aren't what my students would expect to see in a political science course. These are exactly the sort of situations our students require if they are to develop a more mature understanding of evidence behind arguments and the importance of working together. I wonder if taking such a course would, in some way, transform their understanding of science and scientific inquiry. I envy them such an opportunity.

A COMMENTARY FROM REBECCA S. NOWACEK
Department of English, Marquette University

I've had the privilege of talking with Jeff a lot about this project, and as I read this chapter I find myself wanting to pull back the curtain and tell readers a few things they might not know otherwise. First I want to highlight an innovation that's acknowledged only briefly in Jeff's chapter: the honors students who helped to facilitate the simulation's breakout sessions. I can imagine a reader picking up the chapter and, after noting that Jeff had undergraduate assistants to help facilitate discussion, deciding that a model like this isn't applicable to his or her own situation. "I don't have teaching or research assistants," our reader might say, "so anything like this would be impossible in my large lecture course." Jeff didn't have undergraduate assistants to start with either. But he needed some, and so the honors seminar that explores scholarship of teaching and learning issues with advanced political science majors was born. It was a win/win idea: Jeff could run smaller simulations in a class of one hundred, and the students received a tremendous opportunity to explore issues of teaching and learning in their academic field.

Second, I want to acknowledge the ways in which Jeff's empirical survey research has started to inform the way I think about gathering evidence of student learning in my own classes. My institutional home is the Department of English and we don't talk much about t-tests there. And, because I teach writing, most of my classes are much, much smaller. Consequently, I never seriously considered using survey methods. But after getting to know Jeff's work, I've started using a version of his survey instrument—both to see what changes I find in my own students and to draw comparisons between my students and his (at two very different kinds of universities). And this road runs both ways: Jeff and I have talked at length about analyzing student papers for evidence of student learning, work I'm far more at home with. One of the many benefits of establishing long-term working relationships with colleagues in different fields is that it can slowly help us to broaden the repertoire of tools we use to gather and analyze evidence of student learning.

I confess I have always looked upon laboratory research in the sciences with envy. It seems a nice model of collaborative inquiry: a group of people working together on the same broad questions, using their collaboration to do work that would be impossible for any single one of them to do. From the outside, this model seems more "social" than the solitary scholar in the stacks; as an extroverted person, working in close proximity to others in the lab is appealing. I've found other aspects of teaching in the sciences equally appealing: students spend time in lecture hearing about scientific concepts, then go into the lab to make these concepts come alive. Students, I presume, own the knowledge they themselves create in the lab.

I thank Matt Fisher and Rebecca Nowacek who, in the juxtaposition of their comments, make clear this influence on my work. Rebecca notes that my student facilitators are essential to this project; I simply could not run these smaller, more intimate sessions in a one-hundred-student class without them. These students perform more than this function, however. They are also my constant sounding boards for new ideas and for debriefing what went right and what didn't quite go the way we wanted it to in class; over the years, they have been invaluable companions on the walk back to the office after class. While social scientists do not typically speak in such terms, these students are working as part of my "research lab."

Matt's comparison of my class to a laboratory in which students have an opportunity to connect what they are learning in one aspect of the class to a different situation is an apt one, I would hope. I strive to connect the regular, "lecture" portion of this class to the simulation "laboratories." The simulations give students the opportunity to apply course concepts (such as the critical concept of the importance of rules on results) to a different situation; the readings and simulation discussions immerse students in this different context. As I read the descriptions of integrative learning and scientific inquiry, it strikes me that these are goals which I actively pursue; my scholarly work addresses how successful I have been in striving toward these goals.

Taken together, these commentaries point out something important. The group inquiry process is critical for my students' learning. As Matt suggests, discussing what they are reading and thinking helps my students better understand what they are studying. And, as Rebecca suggests, collaborating with students in teaching the class, and in studying learning in the class, helps me better understand what *I* am studying. The benefits of collective inquiry in both contexts are strikingly similar; this project has convinced me further that we need to find more opportunities for collaborative learning to occur in the academy.

Notes

1. I do not argue that political officeholders must *follow* mass opinion when making policy; rather, I argue that the system must create effective mechanisms so mass opinion can *inform* policy debates, even as officeholders insert their own considered judgments into policy decisions.

2. See http://www.tcdailyplanet.net/node/6742 (accessed May 21, 2009).

3. Sample questions are available at http://www.msnbc.msn.com/id/13442226/ (accessed May 21, 2009).

Works Cited

American Association for the Advancement of Science. 1990. *The liberal art of science: Agenda for action.* Washington, D.C.: AAAS.

Barr, Robert B., and John Tagg. 1995. "From teaching to learning: A new paradigm for undergraduate education." *Change* 27(6): 12–25.

Bennett, Stephen Earl. 1988. "'Know-Nothings' revisited: The meaning of political ignorance today." *Social Science Quarterly* 69: 476–490.

Bennett, Stephen Earl, and Linda J. Bennett. 1989. "Trends in Americans' political information, 1967–1987." *American Politics Quarterly* 17: 422–435.

Bernstein, Jeffrey L. 2007. "Managing political information as a pathway to political participation." Presented at the American Political Science Association Teaching and Learning Conference, Charlotte, N.C., February.

Bernstein, Jeffrey L., and Deborah S. Meizlish. 2003. "Becoming Congress: A longitudinal study of the civic engagement implications of a classroom simulation." *Simulation and Gaming* 34: 198–219.

Boyer, Ernest L. 1990. *Scholarship reconsidered: Priorities of the professoriate.* San Francisco: Jossey-Bass.

Colby, Anne, Thomas Ehrlich, Elizabeth Beaumont, and Jason Stephens. 2003. *Educating citizens: Preparing America's undergraduates for lives of moral and civic responsibility.* San Francisco: Jossey-Bass.

Coulter, Ann. 2004. *How to talk to a liberal (if you must): The world according to Ann Coulter.* New York: Crown Forum.

Dalton, Russell J. 2007. *The good citizen: How a younger generation is reshaping American politics.* Washington: CQ Press.

Delli Carpini, Michael X., and Scott Keeter. 1996. *What Americans know about politics and why it matters.* New Haven, Conn.: Yale University Press.

Dionne, E. J. 1991. *Why Americans hate politics.* New York: Simon and Schuster.

Fiorina, Morris P. 2005. *Culture war? The myth of a polarized America.* New York: Pearson Longman.

Franken, Al. 2003. *Lies and the lying liars who tell them: A fair and balanced look at the right.* New York: Dutton Adult.

Frantzich, Stephen E. 2005. *Citizen democracy: Political activists in a cynical age,* Second Edition. Lanham, Md.: Rowman & Littlefield.

Hepburn, Mary A., Richard G. Niemi, and Chris Chapman. 2000. "Service learning in college political science: Queries and commentary." *PS: Political Science and Politics* 33: 617–622.

Hibbing, John R., and Elizabeth Theiss-Morse. 1995. *Congress as public enemy: Public attitudes toward American political institutions.* New York: Cambridge University Press.

———. 2002. *Stealth democracy: Americans' beliefs about how government should work.* New York: Cambridge University Press.

Huber, Mary, and Pat Hutchings. 2004. "Integrative learning: Mapping the terrain." Washington, D.C.: Association of American Colleges and Universities.

Hunter, Susan, and Richard A. Brisbin, Jr. 2000. "The impact of service learning on democratic and civic values." *PS: Political Science and Politics* 33: 623–626.

Hutchings, Pat. 2000. "Introduction: Approaching the scholarship of teaching and learning." In Hutchings, Pat (ed.) *Opening lines: Approaches to the scholarship of teaching and learning.* Menlo Park, Calif.: Carnegie Publications.

Kirlin, Mary. 2003. "The role of civic skills in fostering civic engagement." The Center for Information and Research on Civic Learning and Engagement: CIRCLE Working Paper 06.

Lupia, Arthur. 2006. "How elitism undermines the study of voter competence." *Critical Review* 18: 217–232.

Meizlish, Deborah S., and Jeffrey L. Bernstein. 2003. "Unpacking the 'education' in civic education." Paper presented at the International Conference on Civic Education Research, New Orleans, La.

Moore, Michael. 2002. *Stupid white men . . . and other sorry excuses for the state of the nation.* New York: Regan Books, 2002.

Niemi, Richard, and Jane Junn. 1998. *Civic education: What makes students learn?* New Haven, Conn.: Yale University Press.

Popkin, Samuel L. 1991. *The reasoning voter: Communication and persuasion in presidential campaigns.* Chicago: University of Chicago Press.

Putnam, Robert D. 2000. *Bowling alone: The collapse and revival of American community.* New York: Simon and Schuster.

Skocpol, Theda. 2003. *Diminished democracy: From membership to management in American civic life.* Norman: University of Oklahoma Press.

Somin, Ilya. 2006. "Knowledge about ignorance: New directions in the study of political information." *Critical Review* 18: 255–278.

Strain, Charles R. 2006. "Moving like a starfish: Beyond a unilinear model of student transformation in service learning classes." *Journal of College and Character* 8: 1–12.

Wiggins, Grant, and Jay McTighe. 1998. *Understanding by design.* Alexandria, Va.: Association for Supervision and Curriculum Development.

Zaller, John R. 1992. *The nature and origins of mass opinion.* New York: Cambridge University Press.

Zukin, Cliff, Scott Keeter, Molly W. Andolina, Michael X. Delli Carpini, and Krista Jenkins. 2006. *A new engagement? Political participation, civic life and the changing American citizen.* New York: Oxford University Press.

2

De-Stabilizing Culture and Citizenship

Crafting a Critical Intercultural Engagement for University Students in a Diversity Course

Rona Tamiko Halualani

One afternoon in a diversity/intercultural communication course . . .

"Dr. Halualani, excuse me, can I bother you for a moment?" Lita[1], a Filipina business major, tapped me on my shoulder as I reached for my books. The first day of my COMM 174: Intercultural Communication class (a required general education diversity course) had just concluded. I was packing up my books when Lita approached me. "Of course," I replied, "Do you have a question for me?"

Lita burst out: "I just want to let you know how excited I am about this course and how I can't wait until you tell us about all the cultures out there, what they do and think, so we know how to communicate with them. Are we going to get a huge list of all the information, you know, of all the cultures and how they behave?"

I smiled. I have been teaching this course for twelve years and this is not an uncommon question. Students come to this course year after year, expecting and wanting a comprehensive guide to "knowing" all cultural groups: their world views and communication styles. Their desire to immerse themselves into the already known and certain world of culture speaks volumes about how these students under-

stand and act toward culture. They see culture as fixed, known entities that are consumable and "out there"—detached from their own influence, imprint, and perspective.

In that moment with Lita, I debated whether to ask her why she presumed that intercultural scholars and cross-cultural psychologists possess the full range of information about complex and unpredictable cultural groups. But, as I always do every semester, I held back. "Lita," I said, "you'll be exposed to many different points of view about many different cultures. We'll see what you think about them, what you think can truly be known about a culture, and what information and questions still linger after our exploration." She smiled back with a puzzled look. We parted ways and I knew that the entire process of opening up a critical intercultural engagement for my students was about to begin.

Citizenship and Culture

Engaged citizenship can refer to many things: an active and participatory group of individuals who draw connections between themselves and their surrounding society; an experience in and through a community to help it solve a problem and address a significant issue; or a positionality that requires the formation of incisive questions and demands regard for the sociopolitical shifts within a community. In context of specific university courses, "engagement" is strongly influenced by a given discipline's subject matter and the ways in which disciplinary knowledge and authorial claims are established within that discipline.

In this essay, I focus on a Communication Studies course, highlighting how course material on "culture" and "intercultural communication" presents a distinctive challenge in crafting an engaged positionality for students. The challenge lies in dismantling the widespread view (often encouraged by intercultural scholars, anthropologists, and cross-cultural psychologists themselves) of culture as "known," "fixed," "certain," and "apprehendable." As experts in the field have unintentionally and intentionally framed culture as a product and commodity, it is no surprise that university students have similarly approached culture as fixed tablets of knowledge to be applied and consumed without hesitation.

Likewise, the notion of "citizenship" presumes that one is actively involved and immersed in one's surrounding community and civic society. However, the framings of citizenship used in the academy do not adequately unpack the problematic dilemmas associated with citizenship—especially in the context of a diverse society. Conventional conceptions of citizenship carry with them a great deal of historical and political baggage insofar as they rely on a national/ governmental body to officially recognize an individual as a legitimate, full-fledged member of a society with rights and a voice. In this country and others, many members of society are not formally recognized as citizens by virtue of their country of origin, the conditions of their arrival, and their socioeconomic positionality. "Undocumented" immigrants, for example, are never understood or recognized as citizens. Sojourners and "temporary" residents (many of whom are in political and religious exile in the U.S.) are also not viewed as citizens. Thus, "citizenship" in context of a diversity/intercultural communication course comes under scrutiny as notions of "citizenship," "culture," and "power" clash with one another.

This chapter describes the strategic pedagogical process I employ in an upper-division diversity/intercultural communication course in order to craft a critical intercultural engagement for my students. By "critical intercultural engagement," I mean a positionality through which students interrogate the conditions around which culture is formed and intervene in its seamless production by articulating what is absent and what should be. This kind of engagement does not happen in one fell swoop. It is a process that I facilitate in steps for students and one that requires them to traverse the limits of culture as they presume it to be. I *want* them to feel frustrated and stifled by the limits of "culture as a knowable entity." Then, I slowly introduce them to a positionality through which they explore unfamiliar questions about culture and citizenship: What seems to be known about culture? Can we ever truly know a culture, let alone our own? How is culture positioned? Who benefits from specific versions and interpretations of culture? Which power forces and structures help to shape and represent culture in these ways? What can we not know? What does that mean for us in a complex intercultural world? How does this position us in our own lives to create positive intercultural interactions?

The critical questioning of "culture" in the larger sense and as it is experienced in their own lives is a difficult transition point for students, but they leave this course with a radically different perspective than the one they have gained from their home societies, ethnic communities, and disciplinary majors. Simply put, we are typically not taught how to question and closely examine culture; culture is afforded a sacrosanct, untouchable status. Woven throughout this essay are narrated moments (as recounted from my own teaching journals that span twelve years) in which students' initial expectations "hit up against" the limits of culture as knowable, and the emotionally mixed enactment of a critical intercultural engagement. Critical intercultural engagement pushes the boundaries of engaged citizenship because it does not merely make explicit the connection between the political, the communal, and the personal but actively and continually questions that very connection. Who defines culture? Who defines what it means to be a citizen? By inviting students to explore these questions, the definitional, naming, and framing processes around culture and citizenship in a diverse, multicultural society are examined, unveiled, and questioned for remaking.

Inviting Curiosity

When students enter my course, they come with the "banking" mentality of education; they are quick to accept and memorize extant cultural knowledge produced by influential scholars like Geert Hofstede. Some arrive having memorized several grids or flowcharts they had inherited from other courses. This passive approach to understanding culture illuminates the challenge in reorienting college students' learning about what constitutes culture and their role in its construction. The following example illustrates my students' predisposition to receive information about culture and the need to dismantle this acceptance of culture as fixed and naturalized truth.

I distribute the handout found in Table 2.1 to my students in the second week of the semester.

Having just discussed the Dutch cross-cultural psychologist Geert Hofstede's pioneering work (2001) that summarizes and classifies the cultural patterns and world views of many national groups (e.g., the Japanese, Americans, Australians, among many others), I set down my chalk and ask, "What does Hofstede's work tell us about culture?"

Looking up at my students, I only see the tops of their heads. All thirty of them are scribbling furiously in their notebooks, writing notes in the margins of the grid handout. Jim, a top International Business student, is writing so hard that his face turns red and his mechanical pencil stub breaks at least twice. I hear the endless "click, click" of his jotting.

Table 2.1. Top Portion of the Ranking of Forty Countries on Individualism and Collectivism

Country	Ranking
Argentina	23
Australia	2
Austria	18
Belgium	8
Brazil	25
Canada	4
Chile	33
Colombia	39

Note: A high score means the country can be classified collective; a lower score is associated with cultures that promote individualism. Ranking list continues in original source.
Source: Presented in Table 4.1, Hofstede 2001

"Anyone?" I ask, surprised at their unusually high level of interest in taking notes.

"Sorry, Professor" Jim replies. "We're trying to get everything you said about what Hofstede found to be the thought and behavioral patterns of cultures."

I knew what was going on: my students had latched onto Hofstede's work as the defining knowledge source and accounting of all cultural groups. They raise no questions during this session. I have found that this unit on cultural patterns and world views inspires almost no questions from students—not because my students aren't interested or curious. They simply presume that there is no reason to be engaged, that this important intercultural scholar has already discovered the absolute truth of culture and how it operates in a universal way across situations, contexts, and groups of people. My students feel confident in Hofstede's claims, empowered by his conclusions, and prepared to apply this knowledge to their own contexts. Hofstede is the spoken authority today and throughout the first part of this course. His magnetic presence is very much here and on the minds of my students.

The Course and Its Context

For the last twelve years, I have been teaching COMM 174: Intercultural Communication, a diversity general education course at my doctoral institution (Arizona State University) and my current institution (San Jose State University). This course enrolls juniors and seniors from across the university interested in learning about different communication styles, patterns, and forms of expressions across a variety of cultures. Every year, thirty-two students flock to the course, many from International Business, Psychology, and Nursing majors.

Over the last ten years, I have noticed a growing ambivalence (and disengagement) among intercultural communication students about the relationship between intercultural communication education and the dramatic diversity trends that surround them. These students typically enter my class overwhelmed by mixed messages stressing both the importance of diversity and the necessity of colorblindness. In addition, students have come to believe that knowledge is complete, stable, and true. They believe their role is to absorb this knowledge (when it is proffered) for the purposes of practical application and skill improvement (rather than to gain a larger theory-based understanding of the interrelationship among culture, power, and history). Intercultural communication course materials have fed this perception, detailing knowledge that is largely skill-based and style-oriented, which tends to oversimplify the hidden, power-laden, and historical framings of intercultural communication. Exhausted by these contradictory messages, students have grown disinterested in engaging intercultural communication as a dynamic arena very much connected to sociopolitical, economic, and historical issues.

Intercultural communication instructors need to address this student ambivalence and work toward reengaging them with the dynamic, multilayered nature of intercultural relations. Moreover, we must also impart to our students that intercultural communication necessitates their active role as critical readers/participants who will analyze, reflect, deconstruct, and reimagine their intercultural worlds; that culture and intercultural communication are not finished products in and of themselves but ongoing societal constructions influenced and shaped by historical, economic, and political forces. I have come to these conclusions in large part from my "trial and error" experiences teaching this course.

Experiencing the Limits of Culture

One major obstacle to developing a critically engaged society is the narrow purview built into each individual's cultural perspective, world view, and identity. We are raised in cultures that by default assume that that particular culture is always right, true, and central. Through such built-in ethnocentrism (Allport 1954), cultures stand as isolated and insular framings of the world that impede intercultural sharing, dialogue, and understanding. The lack of intercultural sharing and dialogic exchanges with other views and identities makes for a fragmented society. If our ultimate goal is engaged citizenship, each one of us should ask: Which groups and individuals are actually working together? Which are not? If we are not working together across identities, perspectives, and backgrounds, then how involved, committed, and cooperative are our societal members? Below, I share a class exercise I conducted with my students through which they experience firsthand the limits of culture and then begin to ask questions about the politics of culture and its insularity.

"Okay, everyone: you have your card," I yell outside on the main campus lawn to thirty-two smiling faces. They nod and clap.

I go on. "That card I gave you tells you what culture you come from, what national culture you represent for this simulation, as well as different attributes of your culture. I am going to read some attributes and characteristics and you will step forward or backward based on what your card says about your assigned culture for the simulation. Got it?" A few giggles erupt. My students are happy to be outside on a bright, warm day in April in San Jose, California.

"Take one step forward if you come from a culture that has gender equality—men and women can both attain a college education and apply for similar professions. Those of you with cultures as indicated on your cards that do not have this, take three steps backward," I yell out, starting the simulation.

All my students pause, intensely reading their provided cards.

Twelve students step forward, a handful are extremely happy. One screams, "I get to move up!" The remaining students hop to the back of the lawn. Many are still looking at their cards. Three women who have to move backward look upset. One African American woman, Lisa, raises her hand and asks me, "Professor, do I have to do this?"

"Does it say that on your card as being an attribute of your culture?" I respond. "If so, yes, go ahead and step back."

"Do I have to though?" she asks again.

I wait a moment before responding. "Remember this card represents your assigned culture, not you," I remind Lisa.

"I know, but it feels weird." Several other students, both male and female, nod their heads in agreement.

I smile. This is an important teachable moment. "Let's talk about this. How do you feel, Lisa, right now?"

"Like if I move back, I am saying that gender equality is not a reality. That I as a woman am saying that that is okay. That this culture cannot have that. That they are stuck like this."

"Okay, tell me more. If you are a member of this culture and this is what your culture is slated to be—that it has this cultural pattern or logic, how does that make you feel?"

"It . . . it . . . makes me feel. . . . like that can't always be. . . . that I'm trapped. That it could be that way but not because it is the right way or the only way but just because I am told that it is that way," Lisa explains.

Another student, V, a Vietnamese female, jumps in. "I can see that too. You know my culture is like this, always has been. Everyday you get this but it's not because it is. . . . how do you say . . . natural . . . destined to be. . . . The government, the churches, the whole society is run by men, men who want to keep that power and rule. Women in my culture know this, we see that. It's not always what you see or think a culture is like."

Our simulation has taken a dramatic turn. We discuss how frustrating it is for many of the female students (from individualistic, egalitarian cultures as well as collectivistic, high power distance cultures) who resent the "stepping backward" to represent the patterns of their assigned culture. Male students scoff at this as well. The physical movement of their own bodies to represent the supposed attributes of a culture has a jarring effect on my students. Suddenly they are emotionally and cognitively experiencing the limits of culture as static, known, and predictive entities. After wading through six more attributes, we continue our discussion.

By the end of the hour, the students (each representing a different culture) find themselves in a zigzag pattern relative to one another. None are on the same line or same level, all are differently positioned—literally embodying the point that cultures are hierarchically positioned. Subsequent discussion and journal entries following the simulation reveal that students felt a range of emotions: satisfaction in applying cultural patterns from class material to an assigned culture; frustration in physically moving against one's own cultural attributes; anger at having to move "backward"; disbelief at seeing the hierarchy of cultures; and refusal to believe that cultures are completely one way, especially when talking about gender relations and power distance. John, a European American junior who lives on campus, states at the end, "That was hard. It brought up too many questions. I didn't like that."

I smile again. In my mind, the day was successful precisely because the students raised new questions. Furthermore, the kinds of questions they asked in their journals and the subsequent paper assignment on theories of culture and world view reflect their intellectual curiosity about a) how their culture came to be, b) who does it really reflect and include (and who does it exclude and marginalize), and c) why certain attributes of their culture move to the forefront and become fixed. In this particular class of thirty-two students, every student identified at least one question that touched on one of the above areas and stated that they felt some important attributes are not reflected in the publicized and well-circulated cultural patterns of their culture/nation. Their relation to culture—a position that once seemed so obvious, natural, and commonsensical—was beginning to change.

De-Stabilizing Constructions of Culture

Students enter the Intercultural Communication course with a specific notion of culture from larger society and media: that of the scientization and objectification of "culture." This framing of culture was created in part by academic work in anthropological and cross-cultural psychology disciplines. John B. Thompson (1990) argues that anthropological scholars, among others, treat culture as a "complex whole" whose components constitute a system that can be compared against other groups. Such a tendency represents an attempt to classify culture "in a systemic way."

Methodologically, then, culture was studied as a systematic, scientific template, with its regularities and reality verifications—meaning, the scientization of the concept of culture via description and measurement. The anthropological conception of culture was born of the spirit (and spread) of science in which analysis, classification, and comparison reigned. During this time, in the intellectual climate of the late nineteenth century, positive sciences were applied to different fields and Darwin's ideas became widely held.

Anthropology was unduly affected: in the 1930s and 1940s, Malinowski (1944) touted his scientific theory of culture, arguing for a functionalist approach to culture in which human development would be traced via cultural analysis of human needs through bodily/physical characteristics (physical anthropology) and social/cultural heritage (cultural anthropology). But, interestingly enough, the social/cultural heritage aspects were to be broken down (or diluted) into components which would then be compared and broadly related to supposedly universal human needs. Thus, anthropologists engaged in a universalizing/humanizing focus of culture—this was a descriptive conception of culture, or as Thompson explains, the conception of "the culture of a group or society as the array of beliefs, customs, ideas, and values, as well as the material artifacts, objects and instruments, which are acquired by individuals as members of the group or society" (129). This study of culture invoked scientific analysis via classification and comparisons of cultural phenomena—as well as Levi Strauss's approach to structuralist linguistics.

Thompson (1990) argues that this conception of culture is vague, methodologically weak, and based on problematic undergirding assumptions: (1) that culture is a stable, neutral reality outside of ourselves; and (2) that there are objects and behaviors of culture that are attainable and ultimately unmediated (this second assumption accounts for the importance of scientifically capturing and analyzing components of stable wholes—and by a value-free researcher with accurate instruments and classificatory schemes.) He also critiques the presupposition that culture is separate from the surrounding sociohistorical context/ structures/forms, arguing instead that culture envelops as opposed to being performed, enacted, and practiced. Here we do not see cultural members; we see humans living out their evolutionary schemes or rather, their predicament of culture, a pattern of culture that is deemed as all knowable and predictable.

It is this framework that students bring to my intercultural communication course: culture as known, predetermined, and fixed. Such a notion is embedded in the very disciplines that they study in their majors as well as the popularized representations of culture in the media (i.e., newspaper, filmic, and televisual discourses that objectify and exoticize cultural groups). It is a powerful and seductive framing of culture that lulls students into a false sense of security and accepted disengagement from culture as interwoven with societal forces.

To challenge these deep-seated ideas, the first half of my intercultural communication course focuses on understanding and applying the building blocks of culture (world views, cultural patterns, beliefs, values, and attitudes). Learning about Geert Hofstede's, Edward T. Hall's, and other scholars' frameworks of cultural patterns and communication styles is a highlight for students in that these theories reinforce and reify "truths" they have already heard and known about regarding different cultures. The familiarity of it all is comforting, reassuring, and stabilizing. Right after their midterm, however, I take my students on a much different, much rockier road. Together we experience the limits of everything they previously learned about culture by taking that information to its most logical (and sometimes uncomfortable) conclusions and interrogating that knowledge further.

For example, the "Powerwalk" simulation described on the previous pages asks students to identify (perhaps emotionally as well as physically) with an assigned culture—piecing out its cultural patterns by stepping forward and back. Students had already cognitively learned about these cultural patterns, but the simulation forces students to face the consequences of a cultural pattern on a culture, on an individual, on how they might think, act, or be if they were members of that culture. The assignment to a culture and the physical movement back and forth, combined with my continual prompt to "look who is moving with you and who is not, who is on the same level as you and who is not," helps to reveal the consequences of these cultural patterns. The Powerwalk exercise helps students raise specific questions about "if this is true" or "why and how this has come to be" and "what else could be going on."

These questions emerge when I discuss cultural patterns regarding the amount of power distance (the role of power in everyday relationships in a culture) and gender in/equality in a culture. Students at an American university who come from all over the world have visceral reactions to "branding" or merely accepting a culture as "accepting of high power distance and hierarchy." Students who come from those very cultures scoff at the notion, even when earlier in the semester they had affirmed that pattern to be true. Thus, this simulation ignites a critical question-asking process (one that I term a "critical intercultural engagement") that personalizes and interrupts the larger theoretical frameworks of cultural patterns from "realities" into socially constructed values and stances for a culture that belie individual cultural members' perspectives, needs, and desires.

My students are quick to raise questions about the complex array of lived experiences within cultural patterns and how these get obscured when reviewing a nation's cultural pattern. Ken, a student from Japan, was vocal about the cultural pattern of collectivism during the Powerwalk simulation:

> Just because you are in a collectivistic culture does not mean you are without your own views, your own will or autonomy. You just make different decisions for the group based on what that society has deemed as being right for everyone. That means there is a larger society that is making the ultimate decision, for better or for worse.

Ken raised this point about his own culture only when he and other students were forced to physically and perspectively "move" like another culture. As each student experiences discomfort, delight, excitement, and resentment at having to move forward or backward and make evaluative stances on a culture, she or he begins to move beyond the gloss and appeal of predictable cultural patterns, seeing instead how cultures are lived and brought about in societies. Ultimately, students experience the limits of culture and cultural patterns and begin to ask difficult questions: What effect does representing this culture in this way have on the culture itself? What is missing from this information? What do cultural patterns do? What can't they do?

The class session after the Powerwalk simulation, I have every student engage in the same activity but this time from the vantage point of their own culture. I yell out a cultural pattern and students must decide (based on what they know from their own experiences) if they should move forward or backward and explain why. A rich, vibrant discussion always ensues; students pose questions about the presumed patterns of their own cultures. The confusion that results is crucial as students begin to delve into uncertainty, question-formation, and instability on subject matter that two days earlier they felt they "knew" and "fully understood."

Citizenship and a Critical Form of Engagement

Through intense simulations (revisited from multiple vantage points), journaling, and performative case scenarios, I have facilitated a *critical intercultural communication engagement* for my students and invite them to experience it (albeit temporarily, but with the hopes of permanency). A critical perspective is defined as one that deeply probes the ways in which power plays out in cultures and intercultural communication encounters and contexts (Halualani in press; Martin and Nakayama 1999; Mendoza, Halualani, and Drzewiecka 2002; Moon 1996). This perspective enables us to look beyond and beneath the obvious aspects of power (or what is in front of us) as well as dig down into the hidden dimensions. As "critics," then, we are to continually reflect on our own positionalities in relation to larger structures, other cultural groups, and individuals. Such positionalities shift depending on the context—meaning we benefit over others, lose out in comparison to others, negotiate and/or identify with structures, groups, and individuals. To be keenly aware of our own placement in fields of power is key to understanding the complex role that power plays in intercultural communication.

Critical intercultural communication engagement entails not taking anything in front of us for granted (in terms of both the hidden and the obvious) and analyzing issues of power that may touch our lives and those of others. This perspective requires citizens to seriously consider and engage the following questions as we go about our daily routines:

- What dimensions, structures, and forces of power are embedded in my own intercultural encounters and relationships? To what extent are these dimensions, structures, and forces of power invisible and/or obvious?

- What kind of power dynamic deeply exists in these encounters and relationships? What is the hierarchy of power interests and how are different individuals and cultural groups positioned in relation to one another? To what extent does one individual or group have more power than the other?
- How am I positioned in the intercultural relationships and encounters in my life? In different contexts (family, work, school, and to the government, corporations, courts of law, and the media)? To what extent do I gain a power advantage and gain more over others in some contexts than in others? To what degree am I marginalized and put at a disadvantage in certain contexts relative to others?
- What can I do to change and mediate the power differences between individuals and cultural groups? How might I help others who are marginalized and oppressed in society? What are some small and large acts that I can engage in to bring about equality, reconciliation, and positive/cordial relations, and to build strong communities?
- How can I take advantage of my own position in specific contexts (economic, social, organizational) that may be used to help marginalized communities?
- How can I raise important questions about culture and power with those around me (my family, friends, classmates, coworkers, and community/cultural members)?

These questions encourage us to "deconstruct" and seriously consider the different power dimensions that occur in intercultural interactions and relations. In turn, this deconstruction process pushes students to become critical analysts of the contexts in which they live and to reimagine and work toward redesigning these contexts for social justice and transformation, which stand as important features of an engaged citizenship.

Evidence of Learning to Engage

Throughout the in-class exercises and discussions I've described, I encourage students to step outside their normal routines and comfort zones to analyze issues of culture and intercultural interaction in terms of power. As Ken's reaction to the Powerwalk exercise ("That was hard. It brought up too many questions. I didn't like that") makes clear, many students find this difficult. But there is also reason to believe that these exercises and discussions can and do facilitate student learning, learning that manifests itself as a greater sense of empathy. Consider the following excerpts from students' journals:

It came up before but I never really thought about it like I have in [this class]. How being American, what that label means, is very tailored to a certain group. You have to be a certain way, be a native English speaker, be born here, maybe look a certain way. That by American we mean White or more White values. What does that mean for me, yes, a White male? What would that mean when my grandparents came here—as a Jewish man, that did not fit into that label then. It is scary to think about that. [An international studies major in his sophomore year]

"Who defines who is what? I want to know that. I am mixed, part Indian and Chinese, my mother is from Singapore where many mixed Asians live. If we were to graph out that nation and who represents that nation like in an ad, who would be placed as the "members" of that country? Like the ad put up from England and none of the Black British citizens were in there. Am I a member in the eyes of my cultural homeland? I am not here in a lot of ways because I don't "look" American. Why does culture and what it symbolizes communicate so much, and at the same time so little? [An English major in her junior year]

I still think there is a basic profile of a culture. We are a particular way. I agree with that. In Germany, we are what Hofstede concluded. I am about to reach a point when I have spent more time in this country than I have in my country of birth. Germany, when I go back, is different, my parents always tell me that too. I agree. The role of women, how we have more different people from other lands there and what you see is the impression that Germany wants to stay a certain way—we are this with these values and beliefs. They try so hard to have that image and it can't hold up any longer. They are changing but they want to show this image, to make it seem that the image lasts forever. [An economics major in his senior year]

As demonstrated in these excerpts, students in my course are formulating important critical questions about culture and their own experiences of it; they move from disbelief, disillusionment, persistent clinging onto what they have always known, and the jarring feelings of having that knowledge questioned and challenged through the concepts and processes they experience in the course. The comment from the economics student who still maintains his belief in "a basic profile of a culture" captures these students' emergent ability to reexamine their preexisting ideas of culture within a more critical context.

Through the posed questions presented earlier, together, we may gain great insight on how others from different backgrounds are feeling and the kinds of experiences they are having in relation to structures of power. We may also learn about ourselves and the aspects of our cultural identities and experiences we take for granted. As a result we can become more attuned thinkers, analysts, cultural members, and societal participants as humans attached to larger communities. These gains represent only some of the amazing gifts that can be obtained through the active practicing of the critical intercultural communication perspective in our lives and more specifically, in terms of our interpersonal and intercultural communication encounters and relationships.

The critical intercultural communication engagement I embed in my class also pushes my students toward engaging in social justice and engaged citizenship. Through a focus on social justice and engaged citizenship, this perspective seeks to analyze issues of power and inequality, and to move one step further by taking concrete action and working toward transformation and justice in relation to culture and intercultural communication. Through concrete action we can help bring about positive change and become lifelong "change agents." These actions can be big or small and can range in different degrees and levels.

For example, an individual may embark on a large-scale effort such as organizing a program in which two cultural groups that historically have had negative relations can be brought together and put into productive dialogue sessions around issues of contention. Others may work hard to organize protests and demonstrations that create awareness of another nation's historical oppression of a specific religious, ethnic, or gender group. Others may take on a smaller, more everyday but still important act of going out of their way to engage in a conversation or become friends with someone from a different (and even marginalized) cultural (racial/ethnic/socioeconomic/class/sexual orientation/regional/national) background than their own. Likewise, individuals may engage in interactional interventions in which they stand up for a coworker, classmate, or community member being treated unfairly. We may even take specific steps to learn more about other cultural groups, especially those that face great poverty and or societal discrimination, and commit to dismantling stereotypes and sharing such knowledge with others in the form of a literary narrative, a report, a newspaper article, website, or dramatic performance/reading.

By way of a critical intercultural communication perspective, we can fully utilize insights gained from critically probing a culture, an intercultural episode, or setting, and take specific actions to empathize and help other individuals and cultural groups that are marginalized and in need. The goal is not to "save and liberate" others but to engage in a commitment of reflecting upon, listening to, caring for, and helping others and participating in a larger community with a conviction for active appreciation, meaningful dialogue, and fighting injustice.

Once students feel excited about this subject matter, I aim to make them aware of the overwhelming questions, complex dilemmas, and uncertain roles brought about by contemporary intercultural communication. My purpose is not to make students fearful of this topic but, on the contrary, to have them realize the magnitude of their role as both active and critical reflectors, evaluators, and practitioners of intercultural communication. In this way intercultural worlds can be more deeply understood and analyzed, which may help to transform and change such contexts. Thus, students get to experience and enact a type of "social justice" perspective in which they will be encouraged to take responsibility for critical analysis from a variety of perspectives and, possibly, to question existing power structures and relations and how these affect various cultural groups and their relationships. Indeed, culture is made real not by its own constitution but by the critical intercultural engagement that we employ while thinking about, analyzing, and discussing all matters related to culture.

Dialogue

A COMMENTARY FROM HOWARD TINBERG
Department of English, Bristol Community College

The critical question that emerges from Rona Tamiko Halualani's essay may be put this way: "How can we promote civic engagement among our students if they see the world as already "done" and authorized by others?" On her way to framing that question, Rona begins her essay with the following, critical assumptions:

- Students see cultural patterns as fixed and cultural groups as isolated one from another
- The truth is that cultures are produced through interaction with one another and are dynamic and considerably complex
- Students see themselves as passive receivers of variously accepted and reductive views of cultural behaviors, and nothing more
- Altering such self-perception requires a sense of dislocation and indeed puzzlement on the part of our students
- The new engagement produced by such reflection ought to form the basis of social action, for the betterment of all cultures and societies

Too often students accept the view that cultural values and behaviors are, as Rona notes, "sacrosanct" and therefore beyond analysis. In the ongoing debate about the value, indeed, the nature of multiculturalism, few question what "culture" signifies let alone the presence of many cultures. But the premise in all such considerations is that each culture is unique, bearing little relationship to another. Rona's students are prompted to believe that cultures are dialogic, in other words, they co-exist and are shaped by others in proximity. I take to heart the reaction of one of Rona's students, Ken, from Japan, who observes,

> Just because you are in a collectivistic culture does not mean you are without your own views, your own will or autonomy. You just make different decisions for the group based on what that society has deemed as being right for everyone. That means there is a larger society that is making the ultimate decision, for better or for worse.

Unlike another student who is caught in a reified view of culture as monolithic and who thus feels tentative about "stepping up" to claim that her culture does not grant gender equality, Ken can begin to accommodate a complex view of his culture, one that can accommodate seemingly exclusive values of individualism and collectivism. He still has a way to go—in working out the authority of the "larger society" in relation to that of the individual—but he is on his way.

A COMMENTARY FROM CARMEN WERDER
Department of Communication, Western Washington University

Rona Tamiko Halualani's essay resonates with me for at least two reasons. Not only are we disciplinary kin in terms of our interest in relational communication, but in this piece she also emphasizes the importance of promoting self-knowledge for teaching citizenship in a way that is near and dear to my head and heart.

With its focus on interacting ethically and empathetically in interpersonal and group communication processes, relational communication is at the heart of teaching citizenship (she says with some disciplinary hubris). And as Colby et al. (2003) insist, "understanding the relationship between the self and the community" (184) is one of the primary moral/civic competencies. If we are to teach citizenship, then, we need to prompt students to continually position themselves in relationship to others.

Rona draws on practices such as simulations in order to "de-stabilize" students' "predetermined and fixed" notions of culture. By inviting students to physically walk, if not a mile, at least a ways in someone else's shoes, she enables her students to locate themselves—both physically and intellectually—in relationship to their own static notions of particular cultural groups. With reflective journals, she invites them to analyze that walk by going meta, to "continually reflect on our own positionalities in relation to larger structures, other cultural groups, and individuals."

Using simple classroom practices such as these, she teaches learners the kinds of self-reflexive moves critical for understanding that cultural identities—our own and others'—are continually being constructed *as* we interact with each other. Because she also grounds her pedagogy in the context of power dynamics, her students learn that being engaged citizens is always an incipient act, always an act of becoming—reliant on our contexts and their power structures. Rona's piece makes me intensely proud of the way that ideas from relational communication can contribute significantly to teaching citizenship across the curriculum.

A REPLY FROM RONA TAMIKO HALUALANI

Carmen Werder and Howard Tinberg both highlight the continual construction of culture among individuals, communities, and surrounding structures of power for students in a diversity/intercultural communication course. Students enter the course with shaped perceptions of "culture" and a fixed reading on the immutability and authoritative nature of "culture." Carmen highlights how students are placed in a position to understand and view culture from their own positionality in relation to the shifting terrain of power, other group identities and experiences, and the changes that occur within one's own experience of culture.

This relative position in relation to one's own culture has been neglected in my field of intercultural communication. This could be due to the difficult nature of theorizing from a position that always shifts and moves, or what noted cultural studies scholar Stuart Hall refers to as the difference between "theory" and "theorizing." The former privileges a fixed central point that can be applied to all contexts for high explanatory power and prediction while the latter is about the process of making sense between points and experiences that are in flux. The very notion that a theorizing of culture and intercultural communication is dynamic and always fastened to the identity and life-stage points of my students (and in fact, those particular students in the classroom during a certain semester) is both exciting and frightening. How do we facilitate students' understanding of culture and intercultural communication in its full complexity while also not discouraging them from the constant flux of these concepts and their relative positionalities? We want our students to realize the multidimensional nature of intercultural relations and its connection to a sense of critical citizenship in society. But we want them to feel the full sense of responsibility that this then creates for them and the urgency of their thoughtful, intentional role as critical readers, careful analysts, active citizens, and reflexive advocates and allies. This is the responsibility I take up every day when thinking about, planning for, and walking into my COMM 174 classroom.

Note

1. All student names are pseudonyms.

Works Cited

Allport, Gordon. 1954. *The nature of prejudice.* Reading, Mass. Addison-Wesley.

Colby, Anne, Thomas Ehrlich, Elizabeth Beaumont, and Jason Stephens. 2003. *Educating citizens: Preparing America's undergraduates for lives of moral and civil responsibility.* San Francisco: Jossey-Bass and the Carnegie Foundation for the Advancement of Teaching.

Halualani, Rona T. In press. *Critical intercultural communication: An introduction.* Thousand Oaks, Calif.: Sage.

Hofstede, Geert. 2001. *Culture's consequences: Comparing values, behaviors, institutions, and organizations across nations.* Thousand Oaks, Calif.: Sage.

Malinowski, Bronislaw. 1944. *A scientific theory of culture.* Chapel Hill: University of North Carolina Press.

Martin, Judith N., and Thomas K. Nakayama. 1999. Thinking about culture dialectically. *Communication Theory* 9 (1): 1–25.

Mendoza, Susannah Lily, Rona Tamiko Halualani, and Jolanta A. Drzewiecka. 2002. Moving the discourse on identities in intercultural communication: Structure, culture, and resignifications. *Communication Quarterly* 50 (3/4): 312–327.

Moon, Dreama G. 1996. Concepts of 'culture': Implications for intercultural communication research. *Communication Quarterly* 44 (1): 70–84.

Thompson, John B. 1990. The concept of culture. In *Ideology and modern culture,* ed. John B. Thompson, 122–162. Stanford, Calif.: Stanford University Press.

3

Fostering Self-Authorship for Citizenship

Telling Metaphors in Dialogue

Carmen Werder

At the beginning of the quarter, I had no idea what to write. You really expect me to think of a metaphor to describe my communication self? Finally after everyone turned in their sheets, I scribbled down "butter" because I was real smooth. Wow. I am one pathetic loser. Was that the best metaphor I could think of for myself? I had just related myself to a dairy product. When I think of butter, I think of something that melts under pressure, something weak and soft. Those are characteristics I never want to be associated with. Though it has taken me a while to figure out what I am, I have finally found it. I am like a stream, constantly moving forward, forever changing. As I push forward, I bring with me bits of sediment (knowledge). Just as a stream eventually becomes pure, I too filter what I have gathered keeping what I feel is important and depositing what I no longer need. We are all pieces of a larger system, and I appreciate my place in it. It's the first time I've ever thought of myself as part of something bigger.

—MATT, 2006 SPRING

An Identity Problem?

This excerpt from a student's closing portfolio essay in a communication course called "Civil Discourse as Learning Interaction" startled me when I first read it and continues to echo in my mind. Could it really be true that this young man, at age twenty-two, had reached his final quarter of college and had for the "first time" thought he was "part of something bigger"? I hear a sense of real satisfaction in his words, a sense of pride that finally he felt some connection to others, but I continue to be distressed in hearing that it was the "first time" he had made that connection. I recall an article by the *Boston Globe* columnist Ellen Goodman (written in the aftermath of 9/11) in which she speculated that the reason so many young college-aged people signed up for military service was because they wanted to be *part of something bigger*—and isn't it disturbing, asked Goodman, when going to war is the most attractive option we can offer them?

I share Goodman's concern that our college-aged youth may have limited views of how they might contribute to the greater good and suspect that this narrowness results from their limited or faulty views of themselves as agents of change. My interest in students' self-perceptions has resulted from a nagging concern with what students in my communication courses seem to think of themselves. Inside the classroom, I have sensed that either they have inflated views of themselves or have spent little time assessing themselves in terms of a larger context. Or both. Outside the classroom, I have noted the growing attention paid to what the student affairs literature terms "parental over-facilitation" and the popular press calls "helicopter parenting," the tendency for parents to take obsessive control of their children's lives. Based on these informal observations, I have worried that my students assume little authority for their own education. Furthermore, I have questioned whether they can be effective rhetoricians if they do not have a clear sense of their own authority and agency. As my concern increased, though, I had to admit that I had no real evidence to support this felt sense, nor did I offer them any explicit avenue for articulating their self-perceptions.

Finding an Identity Measure

In an effort to discern whether I was reading this "identity problem" accurately and, if so, how those faulty or unarticulated views of themselves might be affecting learning, I decided to find a way to capture students' self-perceptions. With the support of a Carnegie Foundation fellowship, I investigated my students' perceptions of themselves by surveying their personal metaphors. Why use metaphor? While the traditional (Aristotelian) view of metaphor represented it as a stylistic flourish, a device used by writers and speakers merely to give verve to their rhetoric, the modern view of metaphor portrays it as a significant conceptual mechanism that can reveal our mental models. Since we also know that metaphor is pervasive in our discourse and that our language is "fundamentally metaphorical," examining the "metaphors we live by" can reveal how we think (Lakoff and Johnson 1980). By surveying students' personal metaphors, I hoped to discover not only how they would represent their identities, but also what those self-representations would disclose about their sense of agency and about their sense of relationship to others—all critical habits of mind for communication students.

As a result of this study, I have come to see personal metaphors as open windows into self-perceptions. They also offer a way for learners to reinvent themselves in relationship to others, a fundamental disposition of engaged citizenship. This chapter suggests that articulating personal metaphors and entering into dialogue about them not only assisted students in understanding communication concepts, but also helped them expand their views of themselves as citizens of the university. I aim to show how using personal metaphors, in combination with entering into dialogic relationships *during* the undergraduate experience, can foster the self-authorship needed to become engaged citizens across multiple contexts.

How Metaphors Help

While traditionally investigations of metaphor aligned only with the study of literature, increasingly it has become an object of interest to others. Because of the work of language scholars, we now view metaphor as a "way of thinking" (Richards 1936) and understand that our language is essentially metaphorical; we cannot escape using metaphors if we use language at all (Lakoff and Johnson 1980). We now know that metaphor has both a linguistic structure and a *cognitive* force (Kittay 1986) in that it is a "telling" mechanism that reveals a whole conceptual framework by highlighting some ideas and hiding others.

When we use metaphor—and we always do—we point to our beliefs and values. For this reason, metaphors have become especially important to those studying political discourse. Because we think in metaphors using what Lakoff (2004) terms "frames" that not only reflect our attitudes but also determine our actions, to ignore the metaphors we think and *live by* is to risk being co-opted by others. As Lakoff further insists (2006), a study of the metaphors used in American political rhetoric reveals that we are waging metaphor "battles" over ideas. Not merely a matter of semantics, then, our metaphors reveal our worldviews and our moral views and, thus, have significant consequence in revealing our most deeply held beliefs. By letting others frame important ideas like freedom, we surrender the concepts themselves. Furthermore, since metaphors generally operate at a subconscious level, we must make them explicit in order to understand the conceptual structures they conceal. Unless we bring personal metaphors to the surface, we may be in danger of letting others frame our very identities without even realizing it.

Moreover, because of their linguistic structure, metaphors have entailments, that is, they reveal *relationships* in the way they work semantically between lexical fields and cognitive domains. For example, in Matt's initial metaphor for himself as a communicator, "butter" and all the words in that same lexical field (e.g., *soft, spreadable, melting*) are overlaid on the cognitive domain of "communicator." In reflection, that set of entailments led Matt to see himself *in terms of the relationships* across the lexical field (hence, his observation about "melting under pressure"). In this way, metaphors can open up a whole new perspective by letting us see *relationships,* in this case about how the self relates to others. Matt's butter metaphor suggests little or no individual agency; rather, it highlights a static *lump* that is easily influenced by another force, but exerts no influence in itself. In contrast, his moving stream metaphor entails not only his agency (*"picking up knowledge and filtering out ideas"*) as he moves along, but it also reveals his perception of a relationship to the rest of the (eco)system. It is understandable that his new metaphor would make him feel much better about himself as a communicator who had both a sense of individual authority *and* a connection with others and, in his case, even with a whole (learning) system.

The Context for This Study

I collected student metaphors over one academic year (2005–2006) in three sections of a 300-level communication course that explores the nature and practice of civil discourse.[1] By studying the ways civil discourse is similar to and yet distinct from other kinds of communicative modes (such as debate), students gain concepts, attitudes, and skills to be engaged learners and skilled participants in public dialogue. The course includes a twice-a-week seminar to discuss concepts about dialogic listening, writing, and speaking, as well as two practicum experiences including participation in Western Washington University's Teaching-Learning Academy (TLA), which includes faculty, staff, and *students* working collectively to study and enhance the university's learning environment.

Evolving out of our participation in the Campus Conversations Program initiated by the Carnegie Academy for the Scholarship of Teaching and Learning (CASTL) in 1998, the TLA began in 2001 and operates as a dialogue forum on teaching and learning. It includes on average 100 active members each quarter, including about half faculty of various rank/administrators/staff/community members, and about half students at various levels. Besides the 25 civil discourse students, 12–15 first-year students from a 100-level education course and 6–8 communication practicum students participate in the TLA for course credit.

Another 5–7 graduate and undergraduate students, including a few alumni, participate each quarter voluntarily without course credit.

TLA members collectively compose an umbrella question related to teaching and learning that they deem worth pursuing for the year (and which often parallels a current campus theme or issue). The 2005–2006 study question was *What does it mean to be an educated person? And what structures at WWU support that kind of education?* Participants meet in a parlor-like setting in a house (formerly home to the university president) every other week to study the shared question, a dialogue that always begins by surveying members on related sub-questions and analyzing the results. The dialogue groups move into mini-dialogue clusters designed to give participants a chance to talk across departments and ranks; scribes record emergent ideas, and the director distributes highlights via a listserv.

TLA findings frequently lead to action items that participants pursue each quarter or that students pursue for independent study or practicum credit during succeeding quarters. The TLA provides civil discourse students opportunities to practice the dialogue concepts from the class. Because the course carries upper-level credit needed for graduation and since there are no prerequisites, the class attracts a fairly broad range of students, including some primarily motivated by upper-division credit. However, many students also report on opening surveys that they enroll because they have heard about the chance to talk with faculty and staff.

Case Study Overview

In the study year, enrollment averaged twenty-five students per section and was almost evenly divided between males (54 percent) and females (46 percent), reflecting our university's profile in terms of gender as well as students of color (13–14 percent). The three sections included about 55 percent communication majors and 45 percent students from other majors, primarily others in the social sciences. The class also enrolled about 20 percent General Studies majors, a fact worth noting as Gen Studies majors tend to have little direction because they do not have regular departmental advisors, often choose the major because they do not meet expectations for other majors, and frequently complain of feeling insignificant in the academy.[2]

Evidence under Study

Data included survey information as well as informal and formal writing samples from a pool of seventy-five students across three sections over three academic quarters: Fall 2005, Winter 2006, and Spring 2006. Students identified personal metaphors for themselves as communicators and as learners at the beginning of the course, studied their metaphors as conceptual lenses, talked about their metaphors with colleagues, interpreted the communication implications of each other's metaphors, integrated metaphors into their group electronic Snapshots (simple web pages), and at the end of the quarter identified optimal personal metaphors for themselves in final portfolio essays.

Students completed two frames on an opening survey that asked for their personal metaphors—for Self as Learner and for Self as Communicator. The prompts were framed either as "What metaphor comes to mind when you think of yourself as a communicator/learner? Why?" (Fall 2005) or "When I'm at my best as a learner/communicator, I am like a _____ because _____" (Winter and Spring 2006).[3] At the end of term, students either completed a closing survey item asking about their ideal metaphor for themselves (Fall 2005) or wrote about it as part of a final portfolio essay (Winter, Spring 2006). Since each activity involving metaphor seemed to increase students' willingness to respond, additional activities resulted in data each term.

In Fall 2005, the twenty-six student participants made visual metaphors (for "what it means to become an educated person") as part of a collaborative poster activity with faculty and staff in our Teaching-Learning Academy.[4] *In Winter 2006*, the twenty-six participants also composed individual metaphor narratives: informal written commentary in which they responded to a partner's metaphor by describing what that person's metaphor implied about them as communicators, and also responded with clarifying commentary about their own metaphors. They also created group visual metaphors to capture their collective identity as part of developing online Snapshots for their dialogue practica. *In Spring 2006*, twenty-three participants wrote the metaphor narratives, did individual "attractive new metaphor" narratives for themselves as communicators, and created visual group metaphors for their Snapshot practicum presentations. I also audiotaped interviews with two students about their experiences the previous quarter with metaphor.

Telling Results

Initially, I organized the results based on features the resulting metaphors highlighted *for me*. Because I was primarily interested in what the metaphors disclosed about the students' sense of agency, I sorted the metaphors from opening surveys by whether or not they referred to something animate or inanimate. My assumption was that animate metaphors would point to a greater sense of agency, while inanimate ones would highlight a diminished sense of authority.

Approximately two-thirds of the students selected inanimate images to represent themselves on opening surveys all three quarters. For Fall 2005, the Self as

Communicator prompt resulted in 20/26 inanimate responses; for Winter 2006, 16/26 inanimate responses, and for Spring 2006, 13/22 inanimate responses. These images included a range of objects such as a boxing glove, rain drops, car keys, a cell phone, a 7-11 store, a hole, a toilet, a boat, a basketball, a cannon, a fence, a notebook, to name a few—along with many, many sponges.

Within the category of Inanimate Metaphors, by far the most conspicuously recurring image in opening surveys was the *Self-as-Sponge* (23 percent in Fall 05, 36 percent in Winter 06, and 21 percent in Spring 06). Perhaps not surprisingly, students used the sponge metaphor most frequently for Self as Learner, though occasionally they selected it for Self as Communicator. One respondent suggested a pitiful sense of self in his choice of *Half*-of-a-Sponge for Self as Learner (saying "I'm just unable to soak it all up"). The high percentage of inanimate images, especially the recurring Self-as-Sponge metaphor, seemed compelling evidence of my students' pervasive lack of agency. These inert metaphors highlighted passivity, pointed to a diminished sense of self, and implied that these students saw themselves as mere objects primarily acted upon by others.

One student's narrative was particularly revealing in what it suggested about a locus of control: "I'm not proud of my metaphor, but it's true. I'm taking mostly GURs (general education courses), so I'm a *toilet*—all I do is fill up for each test and empty out for the next one."[5] He emphasized his regret in choosing this metaphor saying, "I'm sorry." I felt sorry, too, and when I heard his explanation, I also wondered how much he was to blame for seeing himself as a receptacle. In explaining his metaphor, this student intimates that if the pedagogy of his courses was more engaging, he might be more active. This student's rueful explanation and the conspicuous number of inanimate metaphors represent powerful indictments of educational practices that objectify learners. These results could also intimate the effects of having parents who have done so much for them that they had not assumed any responsibility for their own learning. While my study did not shed light on the etiology of the metaphors, it did suggest that the majority of my students generally saw themselves as objects, rather than as agents, when they began the course.

As discouraging as many of these personal metaphors seemed to be, when students explained them, more encouraging accounts emerged. Students would often give reasons for their metaphors that were in sharp contrast to my assumption of apathy. The most conspicuous example of this tension between a stated metaphor and its accompanying rationale was in connection with the ever present sponge metaphor. In oral and written comments, students would often explain their metaphors with language that suggested a desire for control and intentionality as demonstrated in statements such as "I *try* to be a sponge, but sometimes I get distracted" and "I *suck* in all the information I can." Another student explained that she "*works hard* to absorb and *retain* knowledge constantly so as to *never dry up.*" The seemingly passive metaphors assumed new vitality when students talked or wrote about them.

Significantly, by the end of all three quarters, after students had engaged in numerous dialogues and written exchanges about their metaphors, the Self-as-Sponge appeared much less frequently as a metaphor of choice: down from 23 percent to 7 percent by the end of Fall 2005, from 36 percent to 8 percent by the end of Winter 2006, and from 21 percent down to 5 percent by the end of Spring 2006. This decrease in the Self-as-Sponge metaphor suggests that students found it inadequate and too difficult to enliven with enough energy to suit them, so they chose other images. Even when students chose inanimate objects for their metaphors, the accompanying rationales became more animated as the quarter progressed. For example, one student exclaimed, "I am still a sponge, but now I am a living sponge! I can filter out what I choose to and open my pores to what I want to let in."[6]

In addition to the significant reduction in the number of students choosing the sponge metaphor, the majority of students (75–80 percent) chose new metaphors that either were animate, such as a *baker, a tree, a bird, a teacher, a point guard* (even naming a particular basketball player), or explained them in terms of a renewed sense of self (such as the sponge that came to life above). As one of my graduating students said in a follow-up interview, "Talking about my own metaphor helped me with my fear of not knowing who I am and where I'm going. Because making a metaphor involved choosing something I was familiar with, I felt safer about myself and my future." Comments like this one reinforce what Gillis and Johnson (2002) say about the capacity of metaphor to help students "re-imagine" themselves as professionals.

The mere act of telling about their metaphors animated their self-understanding and prompted the majority of students to reject their inert spongy metaphors by the end of the quarter in exchange for images that reflected an increased sense of agency. At the same time, the ongoing dialogue students engaged in with others from across campus, where their voices mattered in a different way from the classroom, played a role in prompting more lively metaphors that suggested more agency.

Implications for Communication Studies

While students' initial personal metaphors, with their heavy reliance on inanimate metaphors, affirmed my sense that students viewed themselves as having passive identities and little authority, their later metaphor narratives (oral, written, and electronic), as well as their closing portfolio essays, pointed to an enhanced self-understanding. Most significantly, the more they interrogated their own metaphors the more developed were their self-assessments. As a result of identifying their personal metaphors, students also expressed a need to improve their listening skills: over 50 percent each term reported dissatisfaction with their ability to practice civil listening. For example, one student noted in an early narrative: "I was pretty upset when the person responding to my opening survey metaphor (Self as a Cannon) said it implied that I was only focused on *shooting off* my mouth (and not listening). But the more I thought about it, the more I realized it was true and have made dialogic listening (a course term for attentive listening) my main goal as a communication major" (Ryan, Fall 2005).

Student commentary also pointed to an enhanced interest in analyzing audience needs. For example, one student suggests how her opening metaphor prompted her to change her focus from being concerned only with her own needs to responding more to the needs of others: "At first, I saw myself as a *star* kind of communicator because I concentrated on performing well, but now I see myself as more of an *improv actor*. I have some usual moves, but I try to work off others and not just try to steal the stage by myself" (Susan, Winter 2006). Comments such as this one suggest that it was the students' efforts to explain their chosen metaphors and any changes in those metaphors that prompted the most learning. Simply identifying the metaphors, without any reflective dialogue on them, would likely not have resulted in as much self-understanding. In other words, the self-disclosing nature of metaphor became even more powerful in the telling, so that communicating about the metaphors resulted in a more precise self-assessment of self as communicator. Students expressed a greater sense of agency when they commented on their own metaphors in dialogue with one another than when I interpreted their metaphors for them. Overall, the data provided evidence that the use of metaphors had enhanced their disciplinary knowledge, as Augsburg (2005) has suggested—in this case, about communication.

Metaphor and Self-Authorship

Marcia Baxter Magolda's concept of "self-authorship" (1999, 2001) provides a useful way to map various metaphor types that I observed emerging from my students' commentary. Self-authorship dimensions include the *cognitive* (how one makes meaning), the *interpersonal* (how one views oneself in relationship to others), and the *intrapersonal* (how one views one's sense of identity).

These self-authorship features align with three metaphor types observed in my students' commentary:

1) The *cognitive* dimension, what Baxter Magolda designates as meaning-making, corresponds to *situational metaphors*—those that highlight the contextual nature of meaning. As one student who changed his initial

metaphor from a sponge to a Swiss Army knife insisted, "I want to be able to adapt to different communication contexts, but not out of self-defense, but because different communication needs call for different tools." (Lee, Spring 2006) This reflection highlights the student's concern with contextualizing meaning.

2) The *interpersonal* dimension as outlined by Baxter Magolda, with its relational emphasis, matches up with *associational metaphors*—those that highlight interaction and the co-construction of meaning with others. For example, the student who identified himself as a "weight-lifting coach" explained that he "works to encourage others to build on their strengths" (James, Fall 2005). The emphasis is on building relationship with others.

3) Baxter Magolda's *intrapersonal* dimension, focusing on self, corresponds with *agency metaphors*—those that highlight control and intentionality and are marked by a focus on the "I." For example, one student announced that she had changed from a Self-as-Steering Wheel to Self-as-Car and Driver because she "want[s] to be in control." Here the main interest was locating the self in a position of agency.

Such a mapping of metaphors in terms of self-authorship dimensions relies on how students themselves constructed their metaphors. In the telling, they constructed an emphasis, and Baxter Magolda's taxonomy helps describe the development of self-authorship from their vantage points.

Self-Authorship for Citizenship

In addition to enhancing communication abilities, reflections on personal metaphors also show great potential for developing citizenship across the curriculum. In *Educating Citizens,* Colby et al. (2003) identify self-understanding, i.e. "understanding of the relationship between the self and the community," as one of the primary moral/civic competencies. They contend that individuals must understand themselves *in relationship* to others, that the kind of self-understanding required to be a moral citizen necessarily entails locating oneself in relationship to others. Simply to know oneself, in isolation, is not enough.

This definition of self-understanding complements the communication triangle with its complex interplay across the three points of the triangle and also lines up with self-authorship dimensions: between *logos* (message content—the cognitive), *pathos* (audience needs—the interpersonal), and *ethos* (speaker's character—the intrapersonal). In the academy, we tend to emphasize *logos* (the disciplinary content) almost exclusively, paying some attention to *pathos* (the needs of the audience). But we pay little or no attention to helping students become more self-aware of their own *ethos.*

If it is true, as Colby et al. suggest, that we understand ourselves best, or at least most fully, when we perceive ourselves in relationship to others, how do we teach that kind of *relational* self-understanding? Perhaps we can apply what we have learned about the development of language skills. Most notably, we know from Vygotsky (1962) that our development of language results from a *dialogic* relationship between our use of language internally to make sense of our worlds (the psychological use of language) and our use of language externally to make meaning with others (the social use of language). Perhaps we also construct our individual identity in a similar dialogic process between ourselves and others. My study demonstrates that it was not simply the identification of personal metaphors that assists students' self-knowledge, but even more the reflective *dialogue* about those metaphors. By entering into dialogue with others about their metaphors and about teaching and learning generally, students came to understand themselves anew—in relationship to others. But does dialogue belong in all courses?

A Dialogic Education and Citizenship

Tasos Kazepides (2007) invites us to "see education *as* dialogue" and claims "that nothing will improve our schools and society more than genuine dialogue" (5). He warns against an "instrumentalist" view of dialogue's value, however, and insists that "the purpose of dialogue is not to convince or influence the other person but to understand his or her perspective, concerns, values, emotions, assumptions, and goals" (59). If Kazepides is right that the best education, like the ideal dialogue, is not transactional—not aimed at persuasion, but rather at deeper understanding—then we need to consider very carefully how we talk with each other inside (and outside) the classroom and what we see as the purpose of that talk.

In popular parlance we tend to use "dialogue" interchangeably with "conversation" and "discussion," but I use it here to refer to a special relationship that we enter into with others that is marked by a collective effort to make meaning. This view honors the Greek roots of the word: *dia* (through) and *logos* (meaning). To enter into dialogue with others entails building up meaning through the parts. In contrast with "discussion" where the communicative goal is to break meaning into parts, dialogue works to build up meaning. While discussion seeks convergence, working toward one shared solution or perspective, dialogue seeks divergence and multiple perspectives (Ellinor and Gerard 1998). In this way, dialogue is more democratic, for the primary goal is not consensus, but rather liberation—the ability to make an informed choice, based on a better understanding of the choices available.

In discussing "Dialogue and the Self," Cissna and Anderson (1994) note that any talk of dialogue necessarily implies a notion of self as a social construction.

They reject an entirely individual conception of the self because "human beings, even human infants are *not some variety of sponge,* soaking up whatever self-definitions might spill our way" (16, emphasis added). Further, they wonder if a "conversational narcissism" has seeped into American culture. They worry that if people believe that individualism is the greatest good, then they may be "unable (or unwilling) to develop the respect for the other that characterizes a dialogic perspective" (16). This conversational self-centeredness reflects a similar concern expressed recently by psychologists from San Diego who created a Narcissistic Personality Inventory which they administered to approximately 16,500 college students in 2006 (Twenge et al. 2008). They noted with alarm that the narcissism quotient for college students sampled has risen 30 percent since its first administration in 1982. Attributing the increased self-absorption to young people hearing "you're so special" one too many times, these psychologists express concern about a nation of young people who seem to be pathologically focused on self-interests.

Are our college students at risk of relying so much on individual interests that they lack the capacity to respect others enough to enter into a dialogic relationship with them? And if we believe *this kind* of communicative ability is critical to moral reasoning and citizenship, what are we doing as educators to address what might very well be a crisis in self-understanding among our college students? Inviting our students into a dialogue about learning itself, using personal metaphors as prompts, represents one potent and relatively easy way to promote that self-knowledge.

In considering the use of metaphor and reflective dialogue, I propose a closer look at what we mean by "citizenship," a term that I have often resisted. In checking the *Oxford English Dictionary,* I see my concerns confirmed in the early definition of *citizen* as an "inhabitant of a city." To inhabit implies a minimalist role and denotes simply dwelling in a place. Too often in our univer(c)ities, our students play this kind of limited role in the broader learning culture. Surely, we want them to do more than simply inhabit the place: it seems as if we share the same spaces, but we remain distanced and unengaged from true relationship. And I feel sure that most of our students yearn for more. In fact, repeatedly students in our TLA say they want "to do something" to make WWU a better place to teach and learn, even when the benefits will not accrue until after they graduate. When we pay more attention to measures such as "seat time" than to head time (or heart time, or hand time), we risk neglecting that genuine yearning to do more.

Again relying on the *OED,* I know that a citizen has certain "duties, rights, and responsibilities." Yet it seems as if we linger on the duties, such as the duty to vote, for example, or to come to class. But what about the *response*-abilities?[7] As citizens of our families, classrooms, communities, nations, and world—to what extent do we need to respond? To speak with others about our unspoken assumptions and beliefs? To listen to others' views? To disagree and explain why? In "The Varieties of (Not) Listening," Stephen Carter (1998) counts our inability to disagree in the context of civil dialogue as one of our main failings as a people. I agree.

But I disagree with Carter when he suggests that individuals simply need to be more open to talking about differences, implying that the responsibility to enter into a genuine dialogue across differences falls only on individuals. Faculty and institutions need to open up ways for students to disagree respectfully. In other words, our learners need to be enfranchised so they can claim their rights of free speech and feel authorized to contribute to their learning communities from the minute they enter college—in every class. My study suggests that mindfulness of metaphors and an ability to engage in genuine dialogue about broader learning issues assist students in clarifying a sense of identity, developing a sense of agency, and feeling connected to others.

Engaging Citizens of the Univer(c)ities

Even though I care deeply about what my students contribute to the common good after they leave campus, I do not want to neglect what they might do for the common good of the campus community *while* they inhabit it. Opportunities for dialogue across differences, like the one that the TLA affords, promote the kind of self-understanding that leads to a desire to relate to others. TLA closing surveys from student participants for the last five years consistently show that their participation in this dialogue changes their attitudes about faculty and staff and, just as importantly, about themselves as learners. In particular, they cite an "increased sense of responsibility" as a result of this dialogue. As one student admitted, "I used to project all the blame for a bad classroom experience on the prof, but after getting to know faculty in the TLA, I can see that the majority of them really do care about their teaching. Now, I want to do more to help make it work for them (faculty)." Apparently, entering into a dialogue where students perceive they are *being heard* by others in authority because of their expertise as learners accounts for an increased sense of agency and connection to others.

These reports point to a greater recognition of how much faculty and staff care about students and their learning. The most common comment made on students' closing surveys (75 percent of the time) echoes this student's observation: "After participating in the TLA I can't believe how much faculty care about me and how much they care about their teaching." Similarly, the most common comment made by faculty/staff expresses the same sentiment—surprise at how much students care. In surveying the main problems in contemporary higher education, Fink (2003) cited a study by Courts and McInerney that revealed many students believed their college teachers did not really care much about them or about their learning. How is it that an attitude of caring does not come through in ordinary classroom exchanges? What influence might a broad-based perception of mutual caring have on the learning in our classrooms?

Engaging Dialogue as Significant Learning Experience

In proposing "a taxonomy of significant learning experiences," along with making "caring" a course goal, Fink (2003) proposes including the "Human Dimension" as a major course objective. Interestingly, this dimension includes many of the features discussed here: character-building, self-authorship, and citizenship, which he defines primarily in terms of "being responsible" in whatever community we find ourselves. If Fink is right in emphasizing the importance of designing courses that deliberately integrate these educational goals, then we would do well to consider practices that promote both foundational disciplinary knowledge and humanizing knowledge.

Citizens at Home in our Learning Places

By identifying personal metaphors and participating in reflective dialogue about learning, students more quickly understand who they are, both inside and outside the classroom. These practices do not require elaborate technology and can be done using minimal class time in multiple contexts. Several colleagues tell me that they have invited their students to talk about personal metaphors in their disciplinary contexts and have observed a deepened understanding of disciplinary identities as a result. When articulated and interpreted over time, metaphors can also serve as assessment measures—that is, as self-assessment measures to track the development of self-understanding. Reflecting on personal metaphors helps students develop the self-knowledge and sense of agency required to enter into genuine dialogue across differences with others. In order to listen to multiple perspectives that may diverge from their own, they first need a sense of their own identities.

Metaphors also have a generative dimension and can prompt envisioning an idealized self. Once my students "saw" themselves from metaphorical vantage points, they often wanted to locate themselves differently, with greater agency and stronger connection with others (as evidenced by Matt's disdain for the melting butter metaphor). Fink (2003) describes this vision as a "self-ideal" which results from new learning about what we want to become. Talking with others about our optimal selves can also encourage communal ideals, making communities want to become their better collective selves—as evidenced by the TLA's efforts to improve the larger learning environment of the university.

A citizen is someone who "feels at home in a place," and we educators can help lead an intellectual hospitality effort by inviting students to feel more at home in themselves as learners and more at home in our learning places. If we develop this kind of citizenship *in* our higher education learning communities, we can all become part of something even bigger and better.

Dialogue

A COMMENTARY FROM MATTHEW A. FISHER
Department of Chemistry, Saint Vincent College

I was struck, in reading Carmen's chapter, by the strong communal tone of her work. While I had heard of colleagues who invited students to form their own metaphors for something (even personal identity and learning), I'd never seen it used in a larger context where the metaphors are shared and individuals have the opportunity to hear how *others* respond to their metaphors. That interplay between self and community and giving students the opportunity to explore that interplay strikes me as critical if we hope to foster the skills and the disposition of citizenship in our students.

I was particularly moved by Carmen's comment about colleagues in other disciplines who "invited their students to identify personal metaphors in their disciplinary contexts and have observed a deepened understanding of disciplinary identities as a result," as the formation of disciplinary identities has become increasingly important to me in recent years. The scientific community struggles to attract and retain individuals from traditionally underrepresented groups, and I wonder if one factor is that the way we typically "form" disciplinary identity clashes with how the students see themselves. What would we learn about students majoring in science, mathematics, and engineering if we asked them for their metaphors as learners? Unfortunately, this is a pedagogical strategy that may not work well or be received well in undergraduate science courses. That's a shame, as I think the student responses could be very revealing. Several of the authors in this volume have made reference to the idea of engaging "head, hand, and heart," but I can imagine ways that would maintain a separation between the three elements. I see Carmen's use of metaphors (development and sharing) as a way to explicitly work against that separation by engaging students in an activity that is, by its very nature, holistic. We need more activities like that in higher education, because ultimately the responsibilities of citizenship—in the fullest sense that this volume and others advocate for—are themselves holistic.

In some ways, Carmen's work provides a very strong motivation to create experiences that bring together upper-level undergraduates *across* disciplinary lines and boundaries. While particular faculty in particular disciplines (such as my discipline of chemistry) may be reluctant to use such a pedagogical strategy in their courses, courses that bring together undergraduates from a range of disciplines could turn out to be a much more supportive environment for the description and sharing of metaphors. As I've worked with my colleagues on this particular book, I have grown much more appreciative of the learning possibilities that are created by truly interdisciplinary and cross-disciplinary settings.

A COMMENTARY FROM RONA TAMIKO HALUALANI
Department of Communication Studies, San Jose State University

In her chapter, Carmen Werder underscores what many educators forget: the perception of students as active learners and change agents in society. As teachers and mentors, we presume that students come into our classes already recognizing their critical role as learners and engaged citizens in the world. However, in fascinating fashion, Carmen uncovers through a series of assignments and metaphors evidence that indeed students do not initially view themselves as active and participatory learners. Students see themselves instead as "sponges," "depositories," and the end links on a chain through which knowledge is transmitted and stored (akin to the "banking" metaphors that critical pedagogy activist Paulo Freire so resisted).

Sponges? Have we not made it clear to our students that they are key pieces of the larger knowledge puzzles we discuss in class, of the complex problematics that emerge in society and in media headlines, of the mystifying conundrums that dominate our world and cannot be easily answered by the seemingly assuring formulae and theories that we circulate in the academy? Where along the way did we forget to bind together our students' sense of identity with their agency and their self-actualization of that agency? Our focus on students as learners first and citizens next, as if they arrived as empty vessels completely detached from the outside world until graduation, may have created this very problem.

Perhaps we have it backwards. Perhaps the most essential ingredient to shaping a critical citizenry in higher education is nurturing students' self-perceptions and reflections as citizens who are part and parcel of a society that needs them as decision-makers, leaders, question-posers and problem-solvers. In such an important role, the mission to learn as much as they can across several different fields of study and in connection with key skill sets becomes a necessary part of this role. The picture should be of citizens first with learning as a key dimension of that citizenship.

If this is the case, educators need to engage in conversations about what aspects of citizenship we are teaching (or not) and how we can foster a better understanding and actualization of citizenship in the classroom, across disciplines, subject areas, class levels, and diversity demographics. This move requires us to completely alter the way we see our students: they already are citizens who make an impact on our world in and out of the classroom, yesterday, today, and tomorrow.

A REPLY FROM CARMEN WERDER

I appreciate Matt's observation that the pedagogy I am studying (and admittedly promoting)—developing and talking about personal metaphors—has the potential to foster citizenship holistically. In his commentary, he speculates that "unfortunately" it is a "pedagogical strategy that may not work well or be received well in undergraduate science courses." I suppose he is accurate in that prediction, although I confess that when I talk about the use of metaphors with colleagues at my own institution as well as others, I have found it is often the scientists who get most excited about the possibilities of using metaphors. As authors of compelling figures such as black holes and big bangs, they seem comfortable with the practice.

I think first about a colleague in geology at WWU with whom I have had countless conversations about using metaphor, and, in fact, he became obsessed with deciding on his own metaphor for himself as a teacher. He thought he had it when he termed himself *Teacher as Fire Starter* because he loves to excite his students with a passion for learning geology. At least, he thought it was the perfect metaphor until he came into a class I was teaching on "learning reconsidered" where we were interrogating metaphors for their entailments (what they imply about others' roles) and one student innocently asked, "If you are a fire starter, what does that mean for your students? Are they the tinder?" The ensuing, spirited dialogue prompted my geology colleague to change his metaphor to *Teaching and Learning as a Campfire* where, as the teacher, he is simply the one who initially lights the flame, but everyone around the campfire is responsible for keeping it going. Better metaphor for learning as a partnership, yes?

My colleague's experience suggests that if faculty developed and shared their own metaphors for themselves as teachers—ones that entailed active roles for learners to play—then their students might understand better how to situate themselves as agents of influence in their own learning. Of course, such a move means that we have to think of ourselves *in relationship* to our students, not in control of them.

Rona's commentary, with its hard questions about what we may have done or not done to promote a sense of agency in our students, makes me turn reflexive, too. As Rona suggests, "[o]ur focus on students as learners first and citizens next, as if they arrived as empty vessels completely detached from the outside world until graduation, may have created this very problem." So if our students see themselves as powerless, we may have been complicit by perceiving ourselves as all-powerful rulers. It makes me consider a vision of the possible in the academy: What if our optimal shared metaphor were that we are engaged citizens—equally committed to the common good of learning?

Notes

1. I use the term *civil discourse* interchangeably with dialogue, i.e., *effective dialogue.*

2. Matt, whose personal metaphor changed from *butter* to a *stream,* was a general studies major.

3. I changed the sentence frame for the second and third terms so that students would consider their optimal selves in hopes of capturing more engaged responses.

4. Initially, I did not plan for the TLA to engage in this visual metaphor activity, but it prompted a heightened understanding of the value of metaphor, so I repeated the activity in subsequent semesters.

5. This student was a senior; his comment came midway through the course in Fall 2005.

6. This student was also a senior and struggled to come up with a new metaphor. He did not want to give up the idea of a sponge, but was dissatisfied with it being lifeless. When he found a photo of a living sponge on the Internet, he was ecstatic.

7. Lorraine Code (1995) talks about this issue as being "as much about response as about responsibility—response-ability" (13).

Works Cited

Augsburg, Tanya. 2005. Describing interdisciplinary studies: The power of metaphors. In *Becoming interdisciplinary: An introduction to interdisciplinary studies.* Dubuque, Iowa: Kendall-Hunt, 17–21.

Baxter Magolda, Marcia. 1999. *Creating contexts for learning and self-authorship: Constructive-developmental pedagogy.* Nashville: Vanderbilt University Press.

——. 2001. *Making their own way: Narratives for transforming higher education to promote self-development.* Sterling, Va.: Stylus.

Carter, Stephen. L. 1998. The varieties of (not) listening. In *Civility: Manners, morals, and the etiquette of democracy.* New York: Harper Perennial, 132–145.

Cissna, Kenneth N., and Robert Anderson. 1994. Communication and the ground of dialogue. In *The reach of dialogue: Confirmation, voice, and community,* ed. R. Anderson, K. N. Cissna, and R. C. Arnett. New Jersey: Hampton Press, 9–30.

Code, Lorraine. 1995. *Rhetorical spaces: Essays on gendered locations.* New York: Routledge.

Colby, Anne, Thomas Ehrlich, Elizabeth Beaumont, and Jason Stephens. 2003. *Educating citizens: Preparing America's undergraduates for lives of moral and civic responsibility.* San Francisco: Jossey-Bass and the Carnegie Foundation for the Advancement of Teaching.

Ellinor, Linda, and Glenna Gerard. 1998. *Rediscover the transforming power of conversation.* New York: John Wiley & Sons.

Fink, L. Dee. 2003. *Creating significant learning experiences.* San Francisco, Calif.: Jossey Bass.

Gillis, Candida, and Cheryl L. Johnson. 2002. Metaphor as renewal: Re-imagining our professional selves. *English Journal.* July, 37–43.

Goodman, Ellen. 2001. All in this together. *Boston Globe*. Sept. 23.

Kazepides, Tasos. 2007. Education as dialogue. Unpublished manuscript. Simon Fraser University.

Kittay, Eva Feder. 1987. *Metaphor: Its cognitive force and linguistic structure*. New York: Oxford University Press.

Lakoff, George. 2004. *Don't think of an elephant: Know your values and frame the debate*. White River Junction, Vt.: Chelsea Green.

——. 2006. *Whose freedom? The battle over America's most important idea*. New York: Farrar, Straus and Giroux.

Lakoff, George, and Mark Johnson. 1980. *Metaphors we live by*. Chicago: University of Chicago Press.

Richards, I. A. 1936. *The philosophy of rhetoric*. New York and London: Oxford University Press.

Twenge, Jean, Sara Konrath, Joshua Foster, Keith Campbell, and Brad Bushman. 2008. Egos inflating over time: A cross-temporal meta-analysis of the Narcissistic Personality Inventory. *Journal of Personality* 76 (August): 875–902.

Vygotsky, Lev. 1962. *Language and thought*. Cambridge, Mass.: M.I.T. Press.

> They'll probably tell you that it's only a play, that the actors
> are in disguise. So what? Jump onto the stage, mingle
> with the actors, and perform, you too.
> Don't stay at the window. . . .
>
> —ELIE WIESEL

> Prayer becomes trivial when ceasing to be an act of the soul.
>
> —ABRAHAM JOSHUA HESCHEL

Citizenship and the Shoah

What does it mean to be an engaged citizen? I can't imagine a more pertinent question in a class on the Shoah.[1] As my colleague from history, Ron Weisberger, often reminds our students in the interdisciplinary course that he and I teach on the subject, the Nazis came to power as a distinct minority (with 30 percent of the vote), able to manipulate a divided and somewhat indifferent electorate. How might history have turned out differently if German citizens had been more attuned to the dangers of the National Socialist party? How different might the outcome have been if German citizens had voted with the welfare of all of the nation's population in mind? I come to the topic of citizenship weighted down by the burden of this narrative.

I come to the subject for other reasons as well, closer to home and proximate in time. More than a decade ago, Elie Wiesel, noted author and Shoah survivor, confronted then-President Clinton at the ceremony marking the opening of the United States Memorial Holocaust Museum, with this question: How could the United States stand idly by when genocide was occurring in Bosnia and Croatia? In asking that question, and in framing questions like it in his writings, Wiesel is fashioning a view of citizenship that extends beyond national borders to a moral and ethical identity as a world citizen, with an obligation to end bigotry and oppression wherever they may occur. As David Geelan notes elsewhere in this collection, "Citizenship . . . is almost antithetical to nationalism and even patriotism." Given such a definition, each of us as a citizen of the world has an obligation to think and act outside the box of our own limited, national interests.

I come to the subject of citizenship informed with Wiesel's sense of urgency.

From the beginning, my collaborator and I have been concerned with positioning the crimes against Jews during the Third Reich against other crimes against humanity, both predating the Shoah and those that have occurred since. We have done so in large part because we see our role as educating against all such crimes. We also want to offer lessons from history as to what obligations true "citizenship" entails. Generating this kind of awareness amounts to global citizenship, to be sure, but plays itself out in the day-to-day interactions that our students have locally.

Our subject is not merely academic, nor is it merely historical: we realize that our students, having gone through the class, become "witnesses" to the terrible events of the past and, as such, bear a weighty responsibility to act when they perceive bigotry or indifference in the presence of bigotry. We see this aspect of the course as a work in progress: the need to develop models of active and moral citizenship. In terms of course readings and topics of discussion, such a focus requires that we provide students with not only the cost of deficient citizenship but also examples of righteous actions performed by heroic citizens who stood against the tide of the times. As educators, we ought not to compel our students to act morally and responsibly—after all, we want to promote in our students an independence of mind, a habit of critically reflecting on their actions—but we can certainly provide models of such actions.

Shoah educators must work hard to offer students glimpses not only of nations and citizens that fail but also restorative models that provide hope and grounds for emulation (Wolpow and Hanrahan). The six million Jewish martyrs must have their stories told. But so must we tell the stories of those countless righteous citizens who acted selflessly to save others from the Nazi killing machines. We educators have an obligation to offer hope.

As a teacher of literature, I feel that I must be especially mindful of the following: writers, far from being the removed spectators of political and civic engagement, are so often sounding notes of alarm for citizens to hear. We must all be ready and willing to listen. An active and engaged citizenry is a literate and sensitive one as well.

Testimony and the Complexity of Engagement

"The world cannot remain a vacuum," writes the noted scholar Abraham Joshua Heschel. "This is no time for neutrality" (1996, 75). Heschel is perhaps reflecting on his own precarious journey, having barely escaped the darkness engulfing Europe just as the Shoah began. But he is also expressing a deeply held tradition within Judaism that places a premium on action in the world, especially in the righting of an injustice. "And he is a witness," we learn in Leviticus, "whether he has seen or known of it; if he does not utter it, then he shall bear his iniquity" (Lev. 5.1). It is, of course, one thing to testify against a wrong and another to act to prevent or even to exact justice after the fact, but the requirement remains clear nonetheless: morally speaking, merely observing or sitting out is not an option.

But engagement in times of terror and injustice is far more complex than such a statement implies. Elie Wiesel, whose words begin this essay and who exhorts us all not to "stay at the window," notes in that same work the very human tendency to regard the inconceivable as a "game" or as theatrics, merely an illusion that calls for spectating only. The Shoah was like so much Greek tragedy, with the seemingly inevitable movement toward the fall of its victim, a fall that, so the playwrights and academics tell us, is rooted in the hero's tragic flaw. But even there the illusion betrays us, because as an audience, in the classic sense, we would feel something for the hero's suffering and for the suffering of others on stage. During the Shoah, such identification with the "characters" was too often replaced by indifference, which, Wiesel tells us, is nothing less than inhuman: "Evil is human, weakness is human; indifference is not" (1968, 307).

Wiesel's dictum is powerful. I feel its truthfulness every time I teach this course, and, as I hope to show, so do my students. But even as Shoah testimony calls upon all of us to fight off indifference in the face of injustice, it also speaks to the power of quiet and thoughtful engagement, sometimes unarticulated, sometimes even mistaken for detachment. The fact is that the Shoah swept away not only the millions of people who lost their lives in ghettos, camps, and battlefields but also intricately connected communities that had managed, through a complex engagement of their citizens and the inhabitants of shtetls (small, rural Jewish villages in eastern Europe), to maintain a culture and a language, all despite the fact of political oppression, poverty, and pogroms (state-supported violence against Jews). It was the lived experience of those shtetls that distinguished the civic life of its inhabitants. As Dr. Fischelson, a character in Isaac Singer's story "The Spinoza of Market Street" discovers, a life of engagement is no abstract or academic matter: it is messy, unpredictable and, yes, "foolish" (1983, 93). It was, in some sense, all that the shtetl dwellers had. They were neighbors, kinsmen, rabbis, students, teachers, worshippers, tradesmen, beggars: all were committed to a deeply meaningful way of life, each woven into the fabric of the community.

We read Singer's story early in the semester, in part to present examples or models of Jews not as victims but as citizens, with cultural bonds that were complex and strong. We mean as well to demonstrate to our students that they, too, are part of something larger, communities to which they can commit their energies and passions. They need not see themselves as merely pawns in the power politics of the day or as indifferent characters in a theatrical performance. The relationships to others within those communities matter deeply and have significance. Importantly, their ability to act within those small circles is no less awesome. A student reported to the class near the end of a semester that she overheard her partner questioning the courage of the victims who went to the gas chambers. Just a few weeks earlier, she confided, she would have let the remark go without debate, without reproof. But, given all that she had read and discussed regarding the Shoah—the complex causes and equally complex reactions to it— she spoke her mind, informed by discussions about the nature of resistance and the debilitating power of cultural stereotypes. This was engagement, of a personal nature, but engagement nonetheless. Other educators report similar transformations in students who have experienced a course on the Shoah or who have visited the camps themselves (Spalding, Savage, and Garcia 2007).

The Course

The description of the course, available on the course syllabus, reads as follows:

> The Holocaust, or, as it has come to be known, the *Shoah,* is one of the most horrific events in all of world history. Even more than fifty years after the fact, the world continues to struggle with the enormity of this human catastrophe. Nevertheless, a body of writing—both historical and literary—exists which enables us to confront this key moment in history.
>
> This course will serve as an introduction to that body of work. You will gain an understanding of the historical facts, including the circumstances leading up to the Shoah, key phases of the Shoah itself, and the event's critical

aftermath. And you will reflect on the role of literature—principally through accounts of that time written by survivors and the children of survivors—in the struggle to represent an event that many have described as beyond the limits of language to capture. (Tinberg and Weisberger)

The Fall 2005 semester, from which this chapter draws its evidence, was the fourth time that my colleague, Ron Weisberger, and I had taught the course, which is meant as an introduction to the subject of the Shoah, focusing on primary documents in the form of Shoah testimony, fiction, poetry, and memoirs, as well as historical memoranda from the time. In the past, students have been asked to complete a series of interrelated tasks: 1) keep a weekly reading journal (in which they chose a passage from the reading, described how the passage from the reading made them feel, and then described the significance of the passage); 2) attend a talk by a Shoah survivor; and 3) create a paper (subsequently, we've added the option of a poster or web snapshot) that responded to a research question. In addition, students were asked to keep a record of their responses to the reading by tape recording in "Think Aloud" sessions their reactions to the weekly reading assignments (Kucan and Beck 1997).

Who Were These Students?
What Did They Know about the Shoah?

As this was an honors seminar, enrollment was restricted. In all, twelve students took the class. Ten of the twelve students were women, and their ages varied widely: four students were nineteen years of age; two were twenty-four; two were thirty-seven. The remaining students were twenty-one, fifty, and fifty-two. Nine of the twelve students had read some work of literature from or about the Shoah—with eight having read Elie Wiesel's autobiographical novel, *Night*, and six having read *The Diary of Anne Frank*. Interestingly, virtually no one had read the works that were on our syllabus. Lawrence Langer, the editor of our textbook, *Art from the Ashes* (1995), consciously omitted these two works from the anthology in favor of works less well known and, in some cases, far more complex. Only one of the group of nineteen-year-olds described herself as a reader. However, nearly all of those older reported that they read regularly.

From Astonishment to Analysis:
A Range of Student Response to Shoah Readings

As an indication of the range of reading responses from my students (and the complexity of the pedagogical challenges evoked by that range), I'd like to begin by sharing with you two passages from the course readings, each then followed by a student response. The original texts appear in Lawrence Langer's anthology of Shoah literature, *Art from the Ashes*. The students' responses appeared in weekly reading journals.

Original Text:

> One of the Germans, a man named Sepp, was a vile and savage beast, who took special delight in torturing children. When he pushed women around and they begged him to stop because they had children with them, he would frequently snatch a child from the woman's arms and either tear the child in half or grab it by the legs, smash its head against a wall and throw the body away. Such incidents were by no means isolated. (Jankiel Wiernik, *One Year in Treblinka*. In Langer 1995, 30–31)

Student's Response:

> The passage is very descriptive and, yes, very shocking. Words to describe my feelings while reading this passage must be "disgusted," "hurt," "anger," and "complete awe." To think that a human being could have such inhuman actions toward another person, particularly a child, is disheartening to say the least. (Holly)

Original Text:

> Many years ago a well-known American poet, who had just returned from a visit to Auschwitz, suggested to me that he thought the camp should be razed and an amusement park built on the site. I was tempted to reply with Romeo's romantic riposte: "He jests at scars, who never felt a wound." (Langer 1995, 12)

Student's Response:

> The callous and shallow comment made by the poet saddened me and I found the author's proposal to quote from Shakespeare's tragedy was succinct and apropos. . . . The dichotomy between diarist Abraham Lewin's emotional lament, "Words are beyond us now. Our hearts are made of stone" and the insensitive suggestions of this poet straining to avoid hearing these voices is problematic. . . . (Amy)

Each student had been invited to respond to a standard set of prompts in a triple-entry notebook that served as a weekly reading journal. Each student had been asked to select a passage from the week's reading that resonated with her and then to discuss feelings produced by the passage. Finally, students, in a third column, were asked to subject the passage to some kind of critical analysis (What was characteristic about the author's style? How does this selection fit with the work as a whole? How, finally, does the passage broaden our understanding of the Shoah itself?). In their journals, students were asked to offer a view into their feelings.

Even now, I am stunned by the range represented in these two student responses. The first student selected a passage that was graphically rich and terrifying or, as she puts it, "descriptive." The second student, for her part, chose a passage whose power is no less impressive but located less in the power of imagery and more in its ironic juxtaposition of ideas and its sheer pathos. On the surface each response is different as well. The first student adopts wording from the prompt and stays pretty close to the task—in other words, offers an account of her feelings when reading the passage. The second student is no less fixed on the affective but demonstrates skillful, critical analysis, able to replicate the irony of the original passage by creating, as she puts its, a dichotomy or ironic juxtaposition of meaning. It is one thing to be made wordless and speechless by the Shoah; it is quite another thing to build an amusement park on the site of a camp. I might add one other observation: the first student, while seeming to divulge what she is feeling, in fact, produces a somewhat scripted response. She, like so many other readers of Shoah testimony before her, may have been stunned into disbelief, to paraphrase Lawrence Langer (1995, 11). The account is shockingly real but in its brutality so hard to believe. In retrospect, I am struck as much by what this student does not say as what she does. She does not say, as some might, that such an act seems impossible to believe. Perhaps she thought as much.

Kate's Case: A Story of Personal Engagement

The experience of one particular student bears a close examination. While I clearly cannot generalize from the experience of a single student, I think much can be gained by constructing a layered representation of one student's learning in this course. We are privy to the complex challenges the course poses. And we are witness to the possibility of renewal.

Twenty-four at the time of the course, Kate, a Liberal Arts student hoping to major in psychology, reported having read Shoah material before the class. Her first experience was reading *The Diary of Anne Frank* in junior high school, prior to going to Washington, D.C., and the Holocaust Memorial Museum on a school trip. In her Reading Profile, she expressed concerns about "remaining detached enough to process" what she was reading, while "at the same time allowing [herself] to have an emotional response to the material as well." In her critical research paper, Kate would later explore the idea that studying the Shoah can provide a lens through which to view one's own personal trauma—in her case, abuse that both she and a sister experienced as children. As she puts it in her paper, she was "startled" by the realization to that "to begin to understand another's suffering and trauma, it would mean reliving [her] own."

What Kate is suggesting here—and what I mean to propose as a model of engagement that emerges from studying the Shoah—is that citizenship in the larger world begins with "intimate engagement," as expressed through personal connections to the world. Judaic tradition offers a useful tool with which to understand the relationship between the personal and the larger world. When writing about the challenges of rendering prayer meaningful, Abraham Joshua Heschel looks to the concepts of *halacha* and *agada*, or adherence both to the demands of externally sanctioned behavior (*halacha*) and to those required by the individual and particular yearnings of the soul (*agada*) (1996,113). Without the latter, prayer is mere rote (and without the former, prayer becomes formless). Engagement with the world requires an inwardly seeking action, a mode of discovering who we are, but also who we are in relationship to the world.

KATE'S TROUBLES

It became clear in October that Kate was having difficulty working out who she was and how she fit in the course: She confided that she simply could not write. She would not elaborate as to the reasons but I was led to infer that the subject matter of Shoah trauma simply stopped her in her tracks, despite the fact that she had always been able to meet deadlines in previous courses.

She did agree to conduct two taped Think Aloud sessions, however, and was able to produce four weeks' worth of reading journal entries, about which I'll say more shortly. That said, her taped Think Aloud sessions were notable as much for the silences as for the explicit insights offered. As she noted in one session, "I honestly found that I'm censoring myself much more than if I were reading the book silently. . . . I'll admit that it is sometimes hard for me because it drags up the demons from my past." (Kate, "Think Aloud")

KATE'S JOURNAL ENTRIES

As I noted earlier, Kate was not able to keep up with her weekly journal. However, she did submit a handful of entries, three of which I quote below, with Kate's consent. It is interesting to note Kate's evolution as a reader, based on these— what shall I call them?—public exposures of private readings. I offer the original passages, selected by Kate, followed by her response. In each case, she is re- sponding to the prompt, "How does the passage make you feel?" My commen- tary then follows.

19 Sept. 2005. Reading the passage in which the historian Yehuda Bauer argues against the view that the Shoah is unique and thereby beyond study:

. . . if we label the Shoah as inexplicable, it becomes relevant to lamentations and liturgy, but not to historical analysis. (Bauer 2001, 20)

Kate's response:

In all honesty, it makes me question religious beliefs and wonder if there really is some sort of higher power. (Kate, "Journal")

My commentary:

Kate's response, at first glance, certainly answers the question posed ("What does the reading make you feel?"). The Shoah's occurrence at times moves Kate to a kind of spiritual doubt. But I notice as well a disconnect between Kate's affective response and Bauer's text. I don't see a serious engagement with Bauer's proposition: that if the Shoah remains unique and inexplicable, it cannot be studied. Why can't Kate engage this point?

---

11 Oct. 2005. Reading the passage from Nelly Sachs' poem, "If I Only Knew," which considers nature's response to the Shoah:

If I only knew
On what your last look rested.
Was it a stone that had drunk
So many last looks that they fell
Blindly upon its blindness? (Sachs 1995, 642)

Kate's response:

The first line of her poem . . . was heartbreaking to me. . . . I've never been all that proficient at deciphering poetry, but reading poetry that tries to explain the suffering of the Shoah really put me in a new mindset and made me think about things that I might not have otherwise thought about. And I swear to the universe, in my life, it NEVER even occurred to me that a human being would even have a need to write that line. I'll admit I felt more than a bit small minded. Trying to put myself in someone else's shoes and empathize with that feeling was startling.

My commentary:

In contrast with the previous entry, here Kate seems genuinely to grapple with the significant idea in the passage: the possibility of empathy in a world of stone.

Kate displays empathy of her own and a capacity to be "startled" by the poet's language. No less emotional a response, Kate's sentiment shows an awakening sensitivity to the poet's unpredictable juxtaposition of stones and feeling.

---

14 Nov. 2005. Reading the passage from Tadeusz Borowski's short story, "This Way for the Gas, Ladies and Gentlemen," a passage spoken by a camp inmate whose job it is to collect the belongings of those on their way to execution:

> I don't know why, but I am furious, simply furious with these people—furious because I must be here because of them. I feel no pity. I am not sorry they're going to the gas chamber. Damn them all! (Borowski 1995, 350)

Kate's Response:

> . . . It is hard to feel empathy for him. . . . It is hard to feel empathy when his situation is almost unimaginable. . . . I also remembered that when people are faced with these unimaginable situations, the ordinary rules of life don't apply anymore. . . . for this man to survive, it was perhaps . . . better for him to treat the people . . . in an angry manner. (Kate, "Journal")

My commentary:

Empathy remains a concern for Kate. Interestingly, she instinctively asserts the impossibility of feeling any identification with the insensitive comments of the character, whose survival in the camp depends on the extermination of others. But then Kate makes a move that I could not have foreseen a month or two earlier: she enters into the complex psychology of a literary creation and of survival itself. She begins to see that maybe he is not so unlike the rest of us in discovering a mechanism of self-preservation in a world gone mad. While she does not use the term "irony," Kate displays an awareness that points to the central irony of Borowski's story: the reader's entanglement in the behavior of the story's rather unsavory characters.

IMPLICATED IN THE ACT: THE RESEARCH PAPER

Kate and her classmates found themselves further entangled with the Shoah as they prepared for the research project required by the course:

The Assignment
For your research assignment, we'd like you to engage in primary and secondary research and to write up your results in the form of a critical essay. In other words, we'd like you to interview a Shoah survivor, child of a survivor, or

a contemporary eyewitness to the Shoah and to collect relevant secondary sources that will provide critical context for the information gained in the interview. Then we want you to write an essay that does not merely narrate important moments of your informant's story but tries to reflect on the significance of that story to our understanding of the Shoah and its consequences.

The Purpose

We see the purpose as complex. Here's a list of outcomes that we hope you gain from this work:

- An appreciation of the importance of viewing history through the powerful perspective of a participant or eyewitness and thus a chance to realize the consequences of historical events on human beings
- The opportunity to engage in genuine research, drawing upon both primary and secondary sources
- The chance to become critical readers of historical sources
- The production of a thoughtful, well-integrated, and well-written account of your research

While my colleague and I provided students with some contacts (including referring them to a speaker's bureau located at the Rhode Island Memorial Holocaust Museum where students heard a survivor speak), students were left on their own to locate and interview survivors or a child of survivors.

Topics ranged widely, as can be seen by this brief list of titles: "Alterations of Faith," "What did Liberation Mean?," "Survivor Guilt," "Suicide in the Camps," "The 'Greying' of Morality in the Camps," "Trauma, Memory, and Gender," and "Hope and Survival." As evidenced by their research subjects, students were led by interests cutting across matters of morality, faith, psychology, and gender. Only one essay, however, established a personal connection between writer and subject—Kate's.

Her research essay, "Viewing the Shoah through a Prism: How Our Own Pain and Suffering Alter Our View of the Shoah," charts her evolving view that personal trauma can enable a deeper understanding of Shoah literature. This is not to say that bringing her own personal trauma to a reading of the Shoah is without its costs. Drawing upon the words of Judaic and feminist scholar Laura Levitt, who struggles to view the Shoah through the prism of her own experience as a rape victim, Kate notes Levitt's observation, "I am overwhelmed by the incongruity of the connections that I am drawing between my own experience of trauma and what I have read about the Shoah" (2004, 190). Levitt's work was a crucial discovery for Kate, giving her permission, as it were, to offer a personalized reaction to the Shoah readings.

Startled early on by the fact that the course would bring back "demons" from the past, Kate fought off the urge to disengage:

As I contemplated dropping the class several times, I felt that I owed it to myself and to the survivors of the Shoah to stay in this class, for I began feeling it absolutely necessary to be witness to this suffering. Drawing from my own trauma and suffering in this lifetime, I felt like one of the most important things that anyone can do for a survivor of any kind is to be a witness to that suffering. (Kate, "Viewing")

In fact, Kate became a witness literally, since as part of her research project she needed to interview either a Shoah survivor or a child of survivors. Her engagement with the subject would become, as a result, even more intimate, for while her reaction to the reading resonated with her personally, it was quite another level of engagement to speak with a survivor or child of survivors. Could she manage to confront a living remnant of the Shoah tragedy?

Part of the requirements of this paper and the Shoah class itself was to find a survivor or a child of a survivor and interview them, listen to their story. The truth was, I was absolutely scared to death by this requirement and procrastinated when trying to find a "subject." How could I possibly interview someone in the name of academic inquiry when I could barely handle this class to begin with, when I could barely be unattached from the experience of this class at all? (Kate, "Viewing")

Kate's solution was to find someone not actually present during the Shoah, but nonetheless directly affected by its outcome: a child of survivors. That child happened to be me:

By talking with a second-generation survivor, I felt that I could better understand how the Shoah affected people who were not present during the actual war itself. The other reason, though more difficult to explain and again a little self-serving, was that for most of the semester, I was intrigued but at the same time almost afraid of Dr. Tinberg's quietness and intensity. As talked about in class, several of my classmates felt slightly uneasy because of the fact that Dr. Tinberg was a child of survivors. I decided to face the uneasiness and fear head-on because I believed that it might help calm me down. (Kate, "Viewing")

My own relationship to the subject of the Shoah, which I describe in more detail elsewhere (Tinberg 2005), produced an entanglement for me as an instructor and for Kate, and, apparently, her classmates. Kate goes on to share one exchange during the interview:

In my interview with Dr. Tinberg on November 29th, 2005 . . . , one of the things he talked about was his experience with his parents as a child. While he certainly didn't use the word resentment or guilt when explaining his relationship with his parents, some of the feelings he described could be viewed that way. I asked him if he wished his childhood could be different, and he responded, "Oh yeah. All the time when I was a kid. I wish my parents hadn't been quite so old, and quite so foreign. Maybe it's part of being a kid, 10, or 11 or 12, but given the context of the Shoah, looking back at it, it's probably not an accident that I felt these things. Sure, I wanted my parents to be more hip, I wanted them to be more popular with folks, be like my friends' parents, but they couldn't be like that." (Kate, "Viewing")

Kate goes on to describe her own resentment and that of her life partner for having to "pay for the sins of others" (Kate, "Viewing"). She begins as well to enter empathetically with the character of Art Spiegelman, a child of survivors, whose relationship with his survivor father and mother, described in Spiegelman's graphic novel, *Maus* (1986), is rife with guilt and loathing.

When Kate asked to interview me for her research project as a "child of survivors," I was, as I say, "implicated in the act" of the Shoah. I became part of the text; I was being read.

But I had been entangled with the subject from the start, having informed students at the beginning about my parents' status as survivors who had not been placed in a camp but rather had spent the war fleeing Nazis (who had eliminated virtually all the family on both sides) and Russians (who wanted my father for military service). I came clean, as it were, in the hopes of demonstrating my personal commitment to this course: this was in part a family matter.

What I hadn't anticipated was that my family connection to the Shoah would further complicate Kate's and the other students' response to the material by engendering silence as a response to the reading. Kate had mentioned that students felt uncomfortable in class talking about their feelings in large part because of my own connection to the Shoah. I should hardly have been surprised, given how students reacted to the testimony of an actual survivor early in the course. After listening to a survivor speak eloquently about his experience, the class sat in silence, asking no questions, offering no heart-felt expressions of consolation or empathy. Understanding how my students read the Shoah required some reflection on the meaning of silence as an expression of intimate engagement with the troubling subject.

Citizenship Redefined

When Heschel, from whose wisdom I have drawn much in this essay, considers what it would take for people of disparate religions to work together, he notes that on one level, the "encounter proceeds in terms of personal witness and example, sharing insights, confessing inadequacy" (1996, 297). Engagement with the traumatic subject of the Shoah and with the post-Auschwitz world rests, at least in part, on an inwardness and a reciprocal recognition of each other's inadequacies. Stripped to its essentials, citizenship today, like its progenitor in the camps, knows not distinctions of nation, nor culture, nor language, but rather rests in the soulful understanding of oneself and of oneself in relation to others. Just as Rona Halualani's students (whose experiences wrestling with identity appear in this volume) need to rethink the concepts of culture as "fixed, known entities that are consumable and 'out there,'—detached from their own influence, imprint, and perspective"—so we all need to reconsider our notion of citizenship as unchangeable and unaffected by the plight of those outside our personal and national boundaries. Citizenship, ever evolving to reflect a changing, interdependent world, reaches far below skin level and looks to build a soulful relationship with others. Auschwitz teaches us that much, at least.

Dialogue

A COMMENTARY FROM JEFFREY L. BERNSTEIN
Department of Political Science, Eastern Michigan University

The notion of intimate engagement is a key theme in Howard Tinberg's chapter on teaching the Shoah. Howard finds that teaching citizenship through the Shoah course paradoxically requires an intimate, but also a dispassionate, engagement. Kate, the student whose work he discusses most, demonstrates this. The literature of the Shoah touches the most intimate parts of Kate's life. At the beginning of the course, she expressed concern about "remaining detached enough to process" while also "allowing [herself] to have an emotional response to the material as well." As the course proceeds (compare her journal entries of September 19 with that of October 11), she comes to display greater empathy with what she is reading, ultimately connecting it with her own trauma of abuse as a child. The experience is intense, but her growth as a student, and as a person, appears quite significant. She has engaged with the unspeakable and emerged stronger from the experience.

For Howard, intimacy with this subject matter has been a life-long process, growing up as the child of survivors. Howard begins this essay by examining Elie Wiesel's view of citizenship as including "an obligation to end bigotry and oppression wherever they may occur." That creates in Howard a "sense of urgency." By the end of the chapter Howard is interviewed by Kate and becomes, in his words, "implicated in the act" of the Shoah. Howard's personal connection to the Shoah proves intimidating to some students; it is, in many ways, the six-ton elephant in the room. Clearly, their instructor is engaged, and urgently so, with the course material.

Howard's focus on intimacy may seem diametrically opposed to another ideal of scholarship: scholarly objectivity. The true scholar, so this mantra goes, avoids getting too close to what he or she is studying for fear of biased conclusions; a certain scholarly distance in the pursuit of neutrality may be required. But here, of necessity, that distance must be sacrificed. Howard's approach to citizenship is a normative one, informed by Wiesel's injunction to prevent tragedies like the Shoah from happening again. Howard is not neutral in teaching this class and trying to forge learning experiences for his students.

Howard's chapter makes me think about how we interject ourselves into our teaching and scholarship. All authors in this book join Howard in writing out of a sense of urgency. We see democratic citizenship as impoverished for a variety of reasons and see our own work in the classroom as enriching our students as citizens. We *must* get close to what we are teaching and, as scholars of teaching and learning, to what we are studying.

In balancing neutrality and intimacy, we must allow our students to reach their own conclusions about some things: it would not be Mike Burke's place to tell students what to believe about nuclear power (chapter 7), nor Matt Fisher's place to propagate a particular viewpoint on how to reduce the spread of AIDS (chapter 6), nor should I tell students what to believe about school prayer. That said, citizenship education requires us to show students our normative perspectives (or biases). We can hold back some of ourselves: it may not be my students' business for whom I will vote (and, as a personal preference, I will not tell them). But they *will* know that I voted, and that I think they should do so as well. My urgency to make students better citizens requires me to share myself with them, as it requires Howard to share himself with his students.

A COMMENTARY FROM MICHAEL B. SMITH
Department of History and Environmental Studies Program, Ithaca College

Shortly after September 11, 2001, Elie Wiesel reflected on the persistence of fanaticism in the world, despite the many horrors fanaticism had produced in the twentieth century. Fanatics, he argued, thrive because the atrocities they commit are, to a compassionate, rational mind, unbelievable—a reaction one of Howard's students seems to have had to an example of Shoah literature. Fanatics also thrive because we too easily forget. "To remember means to recognize a time other than the present," he wrote. "To remember means to acknowledge the possibility of a dialogue. In recalling an event, I provoke its rebirth in me. In evoking a face, I place myself in relationship to it. In remembering a landscape, I oppose it to the walls that imprison me. The memory of an ancient joy or defeat is proof that nothing is definitive, nor is it irrevocable. To live through a catastrophe is bad; to forget it is worse." (2002)

As a historian I have seen how forgetting or ignoring the past compromises the development of a robust civic culture. But I am even more stirred by Howard's chapter as a human being who, having lived an enormously privileged life, struggles to understand the atrocity of the Shoah and the other mass murders in human history. The Shoah must be learned as something more than an abstraction to those of us who have lived out our lives two generations after the Germans carried out their genocide.

The evidence of student learning Howard provides shows that the literature can function as an antidote to forgetting *and* as an invitation to dialogue. Both processes begin developing the kind of "moral citizenship" he rightly argues is perhaps our only defense against bigotry and the behaviors bigotry begets.

As the case study of Kate illuminates, some students come to terms with the trauma of the Shoah at the same time they come to terms with personal trauma. I found this insight very valuable as a teacher who recognizes that many of my students pass through my courses with undisclosed trauma, and that trauma inevitably shapes how they learn. Courses such as the one Howard and his colleague have designed provide students with tools for developing a capacity for empathy and self-knowledge that can heal on both a personal and cultural level. When we learn that pain and suffering are part of so many people's lived experience, trauma can be transformed into a commitment to help heal the wounds of the world. I cannot think of a more important element of citizenship or a more important task for higher education.

A REPLY FROM HOWARD TINBERG

Thanks to Michael Smith and Jeffrey Bernstein for their thoughtful responses to my essay. Michael's comments validate the view that citizenship has a moral component, while Jeff attests to the high-wire act undertaken by those who teach subjects that entangle us as human beings. The two responses work well together, because classroom engagement with "moral citizenship" poses peculiar challenges for students and faculty alike. When citizenship ceases to be defined by personal and national boundaries but instead calls for a deep search into one's soul even while heeding the cares of others, we are on difficult and uncertain terrain. Jeff's commentary points to this dilemma most vividly: faculty must delicately model a kind of personal entanglement with their teaching subject without simply exposing their personal biases or life stories. From the students' perspective, such modeling translates into internalizing a connection to the subject without compromising their personal integrity. Kate manages to navigate these treacherous waters, albeit at the cost of considerable pain and stress. Her interest in the Shoah was not a merely academic matter.

As to my own personal entanglement with the subject, no end point or closure has been reached (Kate, while perhaps not reaching "closure," has made significant progress to the extent that she has enrolled in a second course on the Shoah). I am hardly unique in that respect, in that Shoah educators report regularly on the wear and tear of teaching a subject so rich with trauma. But, of course, I have a personal stake in all this. While I would prefer not to reveal my own family history, I feel that I am bound to take this subject personally. While I would prefer to model a normative response, as Jeff rightly recommends, I find that the Shoah, by its very nature, challenges the normative process itself. Would that it were not so.

Note

1. Throughout this essay, I use the term "Shoah" (in Hebrew, "catastrophe") rather than "Holocaust" (from the Greek, signifying "burnt offering"). Epigraphs: Wiesel, p. 307; Heschel, p. 113.

Works Cited

Amy. "Journal." Unpublished ms.

Bauer, Yehuda. 2001. Is the Shoah explicable? In *The Shoah: Readings and interpretations,* ed. Joseph R. Mitchell and Helen Buss Mitchell, 18–31. New York: McGraw-Hill/Dushkin.

Borowski, Tadeusz. 1995. This way for the gas, ladies and gentlemen. In Langer, 342–356.

Heschel, Abraham Joshua. 1996. *Moral grandeur and spiritual audacity.* Ed. Susannah Heschel. New York: Farrar, Straus and Giroux.

Holly. Journal. Unpublished ms.

Kate. Journal. Unpublished ms.

——. Think Aloud. Unpublished ms.

——. Viewing the Shoah through a prism: How our own pain and suffering alter our view of the Shoah. Unpublished ms.

Kucan, Linda, and Isabel L. Beck. 1997. Thinking aloud and reading comprehension research: Inquiry, instruction and social interaction. *Review of Educational Research* 67: 271–299.

Langer, Lawrence, ed. 1995. *Art from the ashes: A Holocaust anthology.* New York: Oxford University Press.

Levitt, Laura. 2004. "Intimate engagements: A Shoah lesson." *NASHIM: A Journal of Jewish Women's Studies and Gender Issues* 7: 190–205.

Sachs, Nelly. 1995. "If I only knew." In Langer, 642.

Singer, Isaac Bashevis. 1983. "The Spinoza of Market Street." *The Collected Stories,* 79–93. New York: Farrar, Strauss, and Giroux.

Spalding, Elizabeth, Todd A. Savage, and Jesus Garcia. 2007. The march of remembrance and hope: Teaching and learning about diversity and social justice through the Shoah. *Teachers College Record* 109: 1423–1456.

Spiegelman, Art. 1986. *Maus*. New York: Pantheon.

Tinberg, Howard. 2005. Taking (and teaching) the Shoah personally. *College English* 68: 72–89.

Tinberg, Howard, and Ronald Weisberger. English 64 Syllabus. Unpublished ms.

Wiesel, Elie. 1968. The town beyond the wall. In *Out of the whirlwind: A reader of Holocaust literature*, ed. Albert H. Friedlander. New York: UAHC Press. 288–308.

——. 2002. "How we can understand their hatred." *Parade Magazine*. 7 April 2002. 4–5.

Wolpow, Ray, and Brian Hanrahan. "From sympathy to action: The restorative and transformative potential of Shoah education." Unpublished ms.

If, before this semester had started, I had known exactly what was going to happen in this class, I don't think there would have been any way I would have signed up for it. . . . To be frank, I had never been a fan of democracy or the democratic process, finding it mostly to be a waste of time. I had always looked upon our own government as sort of a vague, formless entity, of which I was no part. Fast forward a semester, and now I don't think there's any way I wouldn't have signed up for it. Now . . . I appreciate more how [democracy] works and what people have to do to make it work. I guess you could say that I learned the true meaning of democracy.

—SENIOR ENGINEERING MAJOR

[T]his was most definitely an enlightening experience, and I think one that has inculcated in me a sense of community with the rest of you just by its nature. I've never suggested to meet people from class randomly on the weekend for beers, and I've never given someone a high five as I was walking out of class just for the hell of it like I did with [a classmate] the other day. So aside from the successes and flaws, it

was a lot of fun, and I feel like I have connected with my classmates more than just about every other class I've taken here.

—SENIOR HISTORY MAJOR

I'm sure that some people will pontificate [on] the deep meanings and goals of the class. Not me. I think that the class . . . [was] an excellent way for me to put my four years of school to use. Nothing more. It did an excellent job doing what it was supposed to do, no question, but it wasn't some deep experience for me. It was a class, a good class, but still a class.

—SENIOR SOCIOLOGY MAJOR

The Full-Circle Seminar—a multidisciplinary senior capstone offered through the Honors Program at Marquette University—is, as the last student reflection rightly points out, just a class. But it is a class unlike any other I have taught or taken. It is a class that is meant, according to the Honors Program's director, to be multidisciplinary and integrative and to give students an opportunity to reflect on how their educations help them to make sense of the world. It is a class that enrolls students from Marquette's Colleges of Arts and Sciences, Business Administration, Communication, Education, Engineering, Health Sciences, and Nursing. And it is a class, as the first two quotes suggest, that can provide students with a powerful opportunity to enter into a practice of democratic citizenship that draws not simply on a sense of obligation (to vote, to pay taxes, to be of service) but on a feeling of opportunity to contribute real insight into real problems meaningful within a larger community.

I teach at a Jesuit university, and most of our students, whatever their religious identity, actively embrace the Jesuit goal of becoming "men and women for others," volunteering their time to social justice work in impressive numbers. And yet, like the student in the first epigraph, many of them remain wary of the obligations of democratic citizenship; for too many of our students, the prospect of democratic citizenship appears vague, formless, and a waste of time. Perhaps this should not be surprising: we live in an age of virulent partisan politics and relentless twenty-four-hour news cycles. Matriculation at a Catholic university whose mission places a heavy emphasis on service (over 80 percent of Marquette's undergraduates, for instance, participate in community service) does not exempt students from the crippling effects of living in a society dominated by the shrill talk radio of Limbaugh and Franken or the experience of "bowling alone"—phenomena Jeff Bernstein elaborates in chapter 1 of this volume. What I describe in this chapter is a model of citizenship—that of citizenship as vocation —which I believe both suggests what education for citizenship might entail and provides a language to help students bridge a commitment to service to an emerging identity as an effective citizen.

Context of This Study

The Full-Circle Seminar enrolls approximately eighteen students. During the spring 2006 and 2007 semesters that are the focus of this chapter, my sections enrolled almost exclusively second-semester seniors, from majors including accounting, advertising, anthropology, biological sciences, biomedical engineering, computer science, creative writing, economics, education, English, French, genetic counseling, history, industrial engineering, international affairs, journalism, mathematics, mechanical engineering, philosophy, physician assistant studies, political science, psychology, real estate, sociology, Spanish, speech pathology and audiology, theatre, and women's studies.

A central challenge of teaching the Full-Circle seminar was the problem of designing a course that would be multidisciplinary and integrative and still teachable by a single person. The obvious temptations were to either restrict the course to my own strengths and interests or invite a parade of colleagues to give guest lectures. Instead, I made students responsible for being experts in their own disciplines and professions. Taking the idea of democracy and democratic citizenship as our focus, we worked individually to reflect on our own disciplinary expertise and collaboratively to create dialogue across disciplines. Four assignments defined the core of the course:

- *Intellectual autobiography.* The task was to write a narrative of how the author came to choose his or her major and to explore the degree to which it is congruent (or not) with the way he or she makes sense of the world.
- *Disciplinary snapshot.* The task was to introduce the student's discipline or profession to a college-educated audience that knows nothing about the discipline or profession. Students were required to interview two experts in their field and asked to identify, among other things, key concepts, important practitioners, seminal texts, and the professional organizations of their discipline or profession.
- *Individual disciplinary research into a complex social problem.* In spring 2006, the task was to pose a question about the future of democracy in Iran that would be interesting to people in their discipline, and then to try to answer that question. In spring 2007, students used their disciplinary or professional expertise to analyze a complex social problem in Milwaukee (what we called a "knotty local problem": e.g., the problem of pollution in the Milwaukee River and Lake Michigan or the problem of Milwaukee's teen pregnancy rate).

- *Cross-disciplinary dialogue about that complex social problem.* The task was to work in groups of three to five students in order to put the disciplinary research and findings of each individual into dialogue—and then go public with that knowledge.

Citizenship as Vocation

I did not begin teaching the Full-Circle Seminar using the religious concept of vocation to conceptualize education for citizenship. I was too deeply preoccupied with the challenge of designing a capstone course that would do justice to the studies of all my students and help them to articulate their knowledge and abilities. I wanted to design a course that would give students the opportunity to identify the worldviews and ways of knowing they had cultivated during their university studies and to better understand, through dialogue with others, the strengths and the limitations of those ways of knowing. By helping them to engage in collaborative, multidisciplinary inquiries into complex social problems, I hoped to help students to develop skills and attitudes that would serve them well as citizens in nonacademic contexts in the future. It was only over time that I came to see that my understanding of citizenship was shaped in some fundamental ways by the concept of vocation that is central to the mission of the university where I teach.

The word vocation comes from the Latin *vocare* (to call) and means calling. But calling to what? Understandings of vocation have shifted over time, but the common thread is an orientation beyond oneself, toward God and toward others as a way of serving God. The Old and New Testaments include many stories of individuals being called to serve God in a variety of ways: Moses was called to deliver the Israelites out of Egypt (Exodus 3:1–15, 4:10–17), Isaiah was called to be a prophet (Isaiah 6:1–8), Simon Peter and Andrew were called to discipleship (Matthew 4:18–22), Saul was called to Christian faith on the road to Damascus (Acts 9:1–20). The medieval conception of vocation was limited primarily to the sense of a calling to join a religious order, whereas the Reformation introduced the distinction between general and specific callings (to Christian faith and to a particular job, respectively).[1]

A handful of Marquette students understand their vocation to be a religious calling to ministry; they feel called to a "Vocation" with a capital V. But most students do not. In 2002, Marquette University received a multimillion-dollar grant from the Lilly Endowment to foster curricular and extracurricular conversations about religious discernment and vocation. To encourage all our students to engage in a process of discerning their own vocation, and as a way of helping them to become men and women for others, Marquette's Lilly-funded Manresa Program introduced into campus conversations about vocation a complementary definition inspired by Frederick Buechner.

Buechner's definition of vocation focuses on the intersection of Vocation as religious calling and vocation as employment. Vocation, he writes, is "the work a person is called to by God." It is, he continues, "the place where your deep gladness and the world's deep hunger meet" (Buechner 2006, 111–112). Such an understanding of vocation resonates both with ancient conceptions of vocation and with the more modern writings of Parker Palmer, who conceptualizes vocation as a type of spiritual self-actualization, insisting that vocation "does not come from a voice 'out there' calling me to become something I am not. It comes from a voice 'in here' calling me to be the person I was born to be, to fulfill the original selfhood given me at birth by God" (Palmer 2000, 10).

As I talked with my coauthors in this volume about my experiences and goals teaching the Full-Circle Seminar, I came to realize that Buechner's understanding of vocation also offers a rich definition of citizenship. The concept of vocation helps to describe an approach to citizenship that *may* be different in its tangible results (more active, involved, committed citizens) and *certainly* is different in the way an individual experiences citizenship. To be clear, my understanding of citizenship as vocation takes a term from a religious lexicon and uses it in ways that are decidedly secular. By using a term with religious resonance, I hope to tap into a sense of citizenship as something we are called to do. This experience of citizenship is not something we are simply born (or even naturalized) into—but requires a process of reflection on our talents, passions, and expertise, and how we may best use them to serve the needs of a larger community. But we need not believe in the God of Christianity or any god at all in order to feel called or to discern how we may serve our communities.

It is education for citizenship that can help individuals discern how they are called—perhaps not by God or even by a sense of duty, but by their "deep gladness"—to contribute and participate as citizens to ameliorating the world's "great hunger." Citizenship is experienced as a vocation, as something we are called to do, when our talents meet the world's needs. It's more than membership, it's more than voting; citizenship as vocation requires active participation in dialogue based on caring for something larger than ourselves and on what we find we can contribute to that larger entity.

What does this conception of citizenship mean pedagogically? If we want to prepare students to experience citizenship as vocation, if we want them to enter the world ready to figure out where their talents meet the world's needs, then we need to prepare them in at least two dimensions. First, students need a richer sense of what their talents and expertise are. We need to help them consolidate and articulate that knowledge. Second, because the world's needs are often terribly complex problems that can't be solved by a single type of expertise (no matter how fully consolidated or articulated) students also need practice in communication across those disciplinary and professional differences.

Owning Disciplinary and Professional Knowledge

One important implication of the citizenship-as-vocation trope is the idea that we need to help students recognize that they do in fact have talents and a kind of expertise that are not possessed by everyone. For some students, especially those in pre-professional studies, this seems obvious: the engineers, the science and health professions students, the business majors readily recognized that they had worked hard to develop habits of head, hand, and heart that they did not have when they began at Marquette and that their classmates did not possess. But other students in my capstone courses seemed skeptical and at times even resistant to the idea that their studies had helped them develop a worldview and abilities not universally shared. They recognized that not everyone shared their views and they would concede that they had gained some knowledge—but they didn't see themselves as having been immersed in or apprenticed to distinguishable ways of knowing.

The reasons for this are manifold. No doubt it is partly due to structures of education that position students as consumers rather than producers of knowledge. That's not something I can undo in a single semester. But it is also the case that students are rarely if ever asked to articulate to others what they've learned through their studies. The first two major assignments of the semester—the intellectual autobiography and the disciplinary snapshot—are designed to do just that. Drawing on students' snapshots as well as their reflective writings and comments to me in and outside class, I believe that these two assignments work together to help students articulate and consolidate their knowledge—sometimes for the first time in their college careers.

There was some resistance. In the process of writing their intellectual autobiographies and disciplinary snapshots, some students actively resisted being pigeon-holed by their majors. I tried to explain that I had no desire to force them into a "little box" (the complaint of one student). I was not trying to define each student's essence according to his or her major. I recognize that choosing a major is extremely arbitrary for some students. Instead, I stressed the usefulness of articulating what is characteristic of the disciplines they've been studying for several years (even if they want to distance themselves personally from those disciplines) and thinking about their studies in relation to the disciplines and professions of their classmates.

The intellectual autobiography and the disciplinary snapshot were, without a doubt, challenging assignments. The disciplinary snapshot in particular demanded a great deal of legwork: tracking down interviewees, culling old notebooks and other texts for "key concepts" and "seminal texts," discovering (sometimes for the first time) their field's professional associations. And it required even more intellectual work: What misperceptions would they need to counteract? How could they explain things like double-entry bookkeeping to people who'd never taken an accounting class? In this sense, challenges from other students—in conversation or writing—were another useful resource for helping students develop a richer sense of their own discipline. In their final course reflections, three students wrote of their importance:

> There was a discussion we had in class one day where I was defending the need for reliability among measures used by studies. I felt my discipline was challenged and it was probably the first time I've felt like this in quite some time.
> —SENIOR PSYCHOLOGY MAJOR

> I remember when I was working on [the second draft of my snapshot] at my apartment; I was looking for clearer terms to describe some of the subject matter and key concepts—I had *four* textbooks out in various parts of the room, all opened to one topic or another. It was exciting for me to put the pieces together in my mind to better prepare myself to describe it to someone else.
> —SENIOR ACCOUNTING MAJOR

> Reading [another student's] snapshot [on the same discipline] opened my eyes. The one thing that I really learned was that my understanding and coursework in economics has been limited to primarily neoclassical economics. There are other lesser-known schools that I have learned little about.
> —SENIOR ECONOMICS MAJOR

The value of developing such meta-awareness of disciplinary backgrounds and ways of knowing was underlined by the experiences of one student working with two classmates on the knotty local problem of school choice within Milwaukee public schools. Early in the collaborative process, an English major told me she felt that the value of her disciplinary knowledge was questioned, even slighted. One of her groupmates was a political science major, well versed in questions of public policy. The other was a speech pathologist, with experience working in the local schools. What could someone who sits reading novels bring to their collaborative inquiry? Whether their skepticism was real or only imagined, the English major felt the need to articulate for her groupmates—and for herself—what her studies of literature had prepared her to contribute to the understanding of this knotty local problem.

In response, she embraced the disciplinary snapshot assignment and interviewed several of her English professors. Ultimately she delivered a superb presentation to the class about literary analysis and why it matters. In it, she addressed several myths (literary analysis has no real world application and is stuffy and elitist) and argued, to quote her handout, that literary analysis can "inform our understanding and ability to tackle knotty local problems" because it provides individuals with "the tools for critically encountering their world, enabling them to understand complex ideas, break these ideas down, and present articulate arguments." Ultimately she determined that what she could contribute to her group was her capacity to identify and tease out the significance of patterns in discourse. She conducted a careful reading of local newspaper coverage of school choice, identifying a number of disturbing trends. My sense is that this student never again felt that the value of her disciplinary training and contributions was in question.

Other affirmations of these reflective assignments—particularly the disciplinary snapshot—were common. At the end of the spring 2006 semester, each student filled in a Final Reflection Worksheet. In answer to the question "Can you identify any particular moments or interactions that influenced your current understanding of your discipline or profession?" 9 of the 18 students identified the interviews they conducted with practitioners in their disciplines. One student, who majored in real estate, described the experience of discovering how professionals in her field could use their knowledge and talents to advocate for social justice:

> During my first interview . . . I was surprised at how many issues [my professor] seemed passionate about in developing the real estate system in developing countries. He teaches commercial real estate and finance and up to that point I had thought of the business side as being separate from the culture (for lack of a better word).

Similarly, during the spring 2007 semester, a student stopped me before class shortly before the snapshot was due to tell me how much she was enjoying the process of writing it—particularly conducting interviews with practitioners in her field. In her final reflection she wrote:

> Presenting on my field really made me think about all of the various aspects of genetic counseling—both the positive and the more negative components alike—and how to explain it to an audience who probably hasn't heard of this profession before. . . . I do believe that the skills we learn from our majors (whether it's analytical reasoning, research methodology, writing skills [and not just from an English or journalism major], or how to work productively in a group) . . . add a different perspective to the class as a whole.

A second student reiterated the value of the disciplinary snapshot, explaining that it really made me think about my own discipline. I really didn't realize how much my discipline affected the way I thought of things and how I looked at the world and how I related to other issues and stuff. And so going through and having to instruct the rest of the class how my discipline worked kind of made me realize to myself how my discipline worked.

A third student offered the following observation in her end-of-semester reflection:

Reflection inspired by one of our very first assignments, the Intellectual Autobiography, has ultimately helped me better understand my own abilities as a thinker and as a democratic practitioner. I've taken the time to consider how my disciplinary lenses shape my views and direct my focus. The Disciplinary Snapshot assignment forced me to challenge any established understanding of my field and the way in which I utilize the tools and skills my major . . . seeks to cultivate. I've developed not only a better understanding of but an increased appreciation for what I supposedly "do." However, the multidisciplinary aspect of this course should not go unacknowledged. There was something about developing a better sense of my own discipline in relation to others that made this course particularly fruitful.

These reflections echo my course goals beautifully. Perhaps too beautifully. These students are, after all, honors students, good at knowing what teachers want and giving it to them. This is one of the problems of relying on student self-reports as evidence of learning. Nevertheless, these quotes feel trustworthy, in part because they were written when no grades were on the line but largely because they come from students who did excellent work on their snapshots and who seemed, from my conversations with them (and in one case with a faculty member the student interviewed) to have been extremely (perhaps unusually) engaged with this assignment. I am not prepared to claim that *all* students developed a greater awareness of their disciplinary and professional ways of knowing. But the evidence suggests that some certainly did.

Dialogue Across Difference

A second important implication of the citizenship-as-vocation trope is the idea that social problems are complex and require the cooperative insights of individuals with many different kinds of expertise. Although a number of students resisted the disciplinary snapshot assignment, all seemed to embrace the idea of cross-disciplinary collaboration as a way to better understand complex social problems. And yet, ironically, if the primary success of the semester was a sequence of two assignments that helped students articulate and consolidate their disciplinary or professional knowledge, the continued challenge of both semesters was the cross-disciplinary dialogues. These seniors struggled to engage in extended dialogue across difference.

They struggled for a variety of reasons. For many, their disciplinary knowledge was only recently articulated and so was still relatively fragile. Furthermore, the lure of pseudocommunity—the desire to favor interpersonal goodwill over epistemological conflict—is understandably strong (Grossman et al. 2000). But perhaps most importantly, the legacies of schooling that students brought to the Full-Circle Seminar worked against extended dialogue and reflection on differences. To illustrate, I offer an overview of the projects from the spring 2006 semester and a more extended account from the spring 2007 semester.

The last few weeks of the spring 2006 class were devoted to developing cross-disciplinary dialogues on the future of democracy in Iran. The assignment was to "somehow make public through our [course] website a dialogue among your disciplinary perspectives." The dialogue could be written, audio, or video; could be more or less formal; and did not have to offer a "seamless interdisciplinary synthesis." What it did have to do was "highlight both conflicts in insights and common ground among the disciplines." Because I knew that I was asking something relatively unusual of the students, I tried to leave the assignment very open. In response, one group videotaped a roundtable discussion styled after Sunday morning political talk shows; a second group videotaped a simulation of a briefing/debate in the president's situation room; a third group scripted and audiotaped a performance piece titled *The Democracy Dialogues* (modeled loosely on Eve Ensler's *Vagina Monologues*); and a fourth group created a group blog.

However, these projects—although thoughtful and well-informed by the disciplinary research projects the students had completed individually—more often resembled what I would call (drawing loosely on the language of early childhood education) parallel rather than cooperative play (Parten 1932). The analogy between the academic work of graduating seniors and preschool children has obvious limits, but I use it to stress my students' tendency to "play nicely" with each other but with relatively little extended interaction and a decided avoidance of conflict. Characteristics of "parallel play" as I define it include a dominance of consecutive monologues (in some cases constituting more than three-quarters of the putative dialogue); the frequent use of set-up questions (e.g., "Wait a minute, I thought Iran was a democracy right now. Don't they have a system of checks and balances and free elections?") rather than challenging or even genuine questions; and a preponderance of "conversational turns" that offer only the verbal equivalent of a nodding head (e.g., "Man, that is so cool. I only thought the internet was cool for downloading music."). The blog, which I consider the only example of sustained "cooperative play," on the other hand, included more elaborated connections and more extended disagreements.

I have recognized in retrospect the full importance of the fact that I was trying to get my students to engage in a kind of assignment that is not common in school. (Or, I suspect, in society.) I left the format of the collaboration open (and groups did in fact choose more creative options than the traditional group paper)—but I left untouched the expectations that students brought to the *process* of such collaborative work. Through their years in school, students learn that it is best to get group work done quickly and with minimal conflict. To become personally invested or to insist on disagreeing would slow down the collaborative process and risk negative interpersonal consequences. I told students that they needed to engage in dialogue and reflect on points of conflict, but provided little guidance in how to do so. My explicitly stated expectations thus did little to overcome the legacies of schooling evident in their reflections on the cross-disciplinary dialogues:

"I think we spent more time talking about how to present than the content of the presentation. There could have been more dialogue."

"It seemed like the group was more interested in getting it done than doing something creative."

These quotes reveal the degree to which the groups were focused on crafting a polished final project while minimizing time and conflict. Although I didn't want to encourage them to argue merely for sport, my analysis of their texts reveals multiple instances of "false consensus"—where potential disagreement was scuttled, presumably to maintain harmony and efficiency.

Students, in other words, need practice and coaching in the art of principled and civil disagreement, a point illustrated by an example from the spring 2007 semester. Here I return to the group of three women working on the problem of school choice in Milwaukee. All three women were smart and articulate. All three had elected to work on this issue because it was something they cared deeply about. But theirs was not always an easy collaborative experience: one group member was a passionate advocate of school choice, another was vehemently opposed. For a long time they tried unsuccessfully to convince one another and instead grew increasingly frustrated.

Eventually, I urged them to take what seemed like an insurmountable barrier and turn it into a strength. Instead of trying to reconcile or brush over their differences—which is what students are accustomed to doing on school projects —I encouraged them to move that conflict front and center and use it as a source of strength and insight. What if, I asked them, they tried to explain to other people (and themselves) not only what they had learned about school choice but also *why* they disagreed? What if, in other words, they sought to model productive and civil disagreement? As they tried to better understand the sources of their disagreement, the group members began to highlight the ways in which their personal, disciplinary, and professional experiences illuminated different aspects of the problems school choice was meant to address. At the end of the semester, they took this knowledge to an Introduction to Education class, delivering a presentation that offered competing views of school choice to future teachers and sought to contextualize those differing views not in terms of differing political affiliations (a commonly invoked explanation) but in terms of their disciplinary backgrounds, in terms of the units of analysis and types of evidence each found compelling.

In short, the group was finally able to move forward productively only after they had embraced their differences of opinion and found ways to contextualize and understand those differences. As one member of the group observed in her final reflection:

> Repeatedly Dr. Nowacek encouraged both my individual affinity group and our class as a whole to "capitalize on our disagreement." Though my initial reaction to these urgings was one of hesitation and, at times, confusion, I have come to believe that perhaps this is what the democratic process is all about. It's about making your own voice heard and then stepping back and urging others up to the microphone. For me, the dialogue that we have engaged in as a class has unquestionably been most valuable. I have not only learned a great deal about how my disciplinary lenses influence the way I attack problems and enter debate, but I've also acquired a better understanding of myself as a communicator—I've been forced to closely examine both my strengths and weaknesses.

Their cross-disciplinary dialogue did not take a form these women had initially imagined. They were understandably drawn toward a vision of a text that would provide a seamless, unassailable argument bolstering their already held view of school choice; instead, they modeled their disagreement. But I now believe that this is exactly the kind of work that most of my students need to do. Education for citizenship must, I believe, include opportunities to help students embrace their differences and capitalize on their conflicting insights and opinions. And, I would argue, a richer understanding of their disciplinary and professional ways of knowing helped them to transform what might have remained a bitter political disagreement into a still heated but civil engagement.

What Citizenship as Vocation Looks Like

Throughout this chapter I have argued that disciplinary meta-knowledge and extended dialogue across difference are key to education for citizenship. To conclude, I'd like to return to the idea of citizenship as vocation, offering one example of such engagement, what such a "calling" might look like in action. The spring 2007 group that focused on the knotty local problem of water pollution provides one compelling example.

Thanks to the efforts and knowledge of the staff in Marquette's Office of Service Learning, this group—comprised of three students majoring in biological sciences, computer science, and mechanical engineering—connected early in the semester with a contact at a local nonprofit, Friends of Milwaukee's Rivers. Their conversations with this local activist were vital in a number of ways, including her suggestion that the group focus its research on Milwaukee's handling of sewage processing and overflow, in particular on Milwaukee's Deep Tunnel system.

The Deep Tunnel system and the Milwaukee Metropolitan Sewage District have received a great deal of negative press over the past decade—and for understandable reasons. In April 2007 the Friends of Milwaukee's Rivers website reported that the "MMSD dumped an estimated 399 million gallons of sewage into the rivers and lake this week after continuous rainfall overwhelmed the deep tunnel system" (Milwaukee River Keeper 2007). Such overflows are reported several times each spring and summer. In the 2006 Great Lakes Sewage Report Card compiled by Sierra Legal (2006), Milwaukee received a C+ overall and a D on raw sewage discharges. Residents of Milwaukee and across the Great Lakes area are rightly horrified by the thought—and reality—of millions of gallons of untreated or minimally treated wastewater being dumped into their rivers and lakes.

The members of the pollution group sought to better understand the problem of sewage overflow through multiple avenues. Not surprisingly, they did a lot of online research and reading. They also contacted the MMSD, and two members of the group toured the local water treatment facility to better understand the treatment process. The biological sciences major used his knowledge to explain to the class the actual science behind sewage treatment. The mechanical engineering major drew on his training to analyze and explain to the class the problem of water overflow through the tunnel system. And the third member of the group drew on personal connections to meet with one of the original architects of the Deep Tunnel project.

In addition to the in-class presentations, which were significantly informed by their disciplinary and professional knowledge, the group members worked to translate their expertise and go public in two ways. First, and somewhat more conventionally, they wrote an essay for submission to *River Currents*, a quarterly newsletter of the Friends of Milwaukee's Rivers. As one member of the group put it in his final reflection, "It seems sort of selfish to me to take all of this research and thought about our community and then use it for a classroom exercise only." Less conventionally, the pollution group organized a canoe trip down the Milwaukee River for their classmates. This field trip happened entirely on their initiative and entirely through their efforts. We arrived at Milwaukee's Urban Ecology Center and saw how their rain barrels and rain gardens (ways of avoiding overflows by keeping rainwater out of the Deep Tunnel system) worked. We portaged canoes down to the Milwaukee River. We negotiated, with many laughs and varying levels of success, the river's rapids. And we saw one of the enormous pipes that dump millions of gallons of minimally treated wastewater into the river. Seeing that cavernous pipe while paddling down the river brought home to me and (I know from conversations) to others the reality of the Deep Tunnel problem. And for a number of class members, it was the first time they had visited the Urban Ecology Center or been on the Milwaukee River. They saw the city, quite literally, from a perspective they had never seen before—perhaps planting the seeds of the kind of ecological citizenship that Michael Smith describes in chapter 9 of this volume.

In their end-of-the-semester reflections, members of the pollution group identified ways in which their own thinking had developed and sometimes changed through their work on the knotty local problem (KLP) of pollution in Milwaukee's waterways:

> The KLP was something for me that seemed like a chore until I started talking to the people who work with it everyday. It became something that I was interested in, I could put a face on the problem and become emotionally attached, rather than the normal "pollution is bad" line.

> I actually did a lot of research into the KLP looking at theoretical solutions. But then I also had a talk with engineering professors and engineers that worked at Jones Island and they were like "these are all really nice ideas but here's reasons we can't do it: monetary wise, decentralization, bureaucratic and such" and so it came to the point of okay, how do you take biological theory and put it into application? And this has really opened my eyes a lot to how things actually work.

> I loved the KLP. I got the impression that most people were genuinely interested in what they were studying (I know I did) and found themselves feeling better that they took the time to investigate the problem and try to think of ways to get through the problem. I, for one, have been studying (and thus been concerned about) the environment for most of my life, and I'm

really glad that I had the opportunity to work with some local organizations to help better it. If nothing else, I learned about the problem, and what I can help do to attack it. That's something in a class that a Jesuit university could use a lot more of.

These reflections suggest the powerful and somewhat unpredictable synergy that results when citizenship is experienced as a vocation, as something we are called to do when we see how our passions and talents and expertise meet the world's needs.

To some degree, this is work that students must do for themselves: we cannot discern their passions and talents for them, we cannot compel them to participate in larger communal efforts against their will. And yet the evidence of student learning from these two courses suggests that there are things we, as instructors, *can* do. We can design assignments that help students to articulate and consolidate their disciplinary and professional ways of knowing. We can create opportunities for students to engage in sustained dialogue across difference; we can coach them to embrace conflict not as a chance to one-up someone else but to learn more and work collaboratively. We can encourage the development of these types of self-knowledge and abilities in senior capstones—but also, I believe, in general education courses and sophomore seminars and advanced undergraduate study throughout the curriculum. Students are so rarely asked to consolidate and articulate for others their disciplinary knowledge, so rarely asked to collaborate in any extended way across differences (disciplinary or otherwise), that even relatively modest additions or revisions to current curricula may have a significant cumulative effect.

Finally, whether or not individual instructors and students find the religious connotations of the citizenship-as-vocation trope appropriate for their personal beliefs and institutional contexts, I am hopeful that the core idea, the understanding of citizenship as something we are called to do by connecting our passions and talents with the world's needs, can be a powerful way of helping our students and ourselves move toward a more engaged experience of citizenship.

Dialogue

A COMMENTARY FROM MICHAEL B. SMITH
Department of History and Environmental Studies Program, Ithaca College

Over the past one hundred years higher education, like the rest of American society, has followed the path of specialization. Without question such specialization has accelerated knowledge creation during the past century (though hyper-specialization has rendered some of that knowledge so esoteric as to be useful only to a very few). As specialists we divide ourselves into "disciplines," a telling lexical choice. In many ways we have so disciplined ourselves that finding a common language for identifying and solving problems poses a real challenge. Our ways of knowing the world are "disciplined," we shy away from constructive dialogue about different ways of knowing the world (and using that knowledge to solve problems), and outcome trumps process. This is clearly not the way to develop a robust civic culture.

After four or five years of disciplinary training and many more than that of formal education, the students in Rebecca Nowacek's capstone seminar exemplify each of these phenomena. What emerges from the evidence of student learning is a clear sense that she has facilitated a learning experience through which students "undiscipline" their thinking. But undisciplining is not unmooring. The students quoted in Rebecca's chapter have come to new disciplinary awareness, often feeling validated in their choice of discipline—such validation contributing, one hopes, to feelings of vocation. At the same time they recognize the power of multiple perspectives.

Perhaps more importantly, they also engage in constructive dialogue and embrace the *process* of cross-disciplinary dialogue and problem-solving as much as the end goal of solving problems. Rebecca's case study of a group at loggerheads about their project on school choice illuminates how conditioned our students (and perhaps most of us) are to achieving false consensus in order to avoid conflict. We *all* "need practice and coaching in the art of principled and civil disagreement." Without this capacity differences fester and the cost of conflict rises. In a world in which we are all increasingly pulled toward people and media whose worldviews primarily resonate with our own, civil disagreement becomes one of the more important mechanisms for civic engagement.

Rebecca writes that "citizenship is not something we are simply born (or even naturalized) into—but requires a process of reflection on our talents, passions, and expertise, and how we may best use them to serve the needs of a larger community." In helping her students become more discerning both about the value of their disciplinary training and about problem-solving through relationships, she has helped cultivate a sense of citizenship as vocation. In so doing her work has advanced the vision of a democracy laid out by Walt Whitman in "Democratic Vistas" (1871) more than 140 years ago: "Did you, too, O friend, suppose democracy was only for elections, for politics, and for a party name? I say democracy is only of use there that it may pass on and come to its flower and fruit in manners, in the highest forms of interaction between [people], and their beliefs—in religion, literature, colleges and schools—democracy in all public and private life. . . ."

A COMMENTARY FROM MICHAEL C. BURKE
Department of Mathematics, College of San Mateo

Elsewhere in this volume, Carmen Werder writes about the importance and richness of metaphor. Rebecca Nowacek employs two lovely ones in her chapter. The first, citizenship as vocation, is central to her story; the second, parallel play, is a small gem that illuminates her discussion about the difficulties our students often have in engaging in true dialogue, particularly when they encounter substantive disagreement.

I must admit to an initial sense of discomfort when I first saw Rebecca's chapter. In fact, the title alone gave me pause: "Understanding Citizenship as Vocation. . . ." The use of a term so laden with religious history and meaning seemed problematic to me. While organizing a course around the concept of vocation is certainly appropriate in Rebecca's world (she teaches at a Jesuit university, after all), I feared that her ideas would be of little use to those of us who teach at public colleges and universities. But I find Rebecca's description of the concept, the idea that we should search for the intersection of our talents and the world's needs, and that we should do so out of a felt need to contribute to something larger than ourselves, quite powerful, and not, of necessity, religious. Rebecca makes it clear that although she is employing a religious term, and hopes to draw upon the power of the term's religious origins, she is, in the end, using this religious concept in a wholly secular way. I find that I am persuaded; I agree with Rebecca that the term "vocation" offers a compelling and engaging way to think about citizenship. And so, despite my initial misgivings, I think that Rebecca has made a convert of me.

I am intrigued by Rebecca's observation that her students have great difficulty engaging in a reasoned dialogue with those with whom they disagree. Her students, and mine, and often our citizens, frequently refuse to engage, often out of a sense of politeness; it is this reluctance to fully engage our fellow citizens in discussion by talking past each other, in a polite fashion, that Rebecca characterizes as "parallel play." No doubt the "parallel play" that we observe is partially a consequence of the current strident and vituperative political culture in our country; our students see no models of quiet, thoughtful, respectful discussion between those who disagree, no models where people who disagree come to understand each other's point of view, and create out of their disagreement new solutions to our problems, solutions that would never have occurred to them individually. I think that Rebecca has identified an important issue for us, as faculty, here. Our democracy demands genuine engagement, leading to a search for answers. How do we begin to teach our students the skills of civil, respectful disagreement? Rebecca suggests that we should provide our students with "practice and coaching in the art of principled disagreement," and offers the compelling example of her students who worked on the issue of school choice.

Finally, Rebecca's idea of asking her students to examine the disciplinary lenses they have adopted over the course of their college careers offers them a natural opportunity to reflect on the ways in which they think. I hope that, in most cases, they find that their disciplinary knowledge is a source of genuine power for examining questions they encounter in the world. When thinking about important issues, disciplinary lenses offer both sharp focus and powerful tools. At the same time, however, disciplinary lenses can act as blinders, limiting vision. By requiring her students to analyze their disciplinary perspectives in a classroom setting, Rebecca offers her students the opportunity to compare their perspectives with the differing perspectives of fellow students. The evidence supplied by Rebecca suggests that at least some of her students come to understand and embrace the particular disciplinary expertise they can bring to bear on a problem, while also seeing the limitations of their discipline and appreciating the varying perspectives offered by their classmates. This exercise strikes me as an eminently worthwhile activity, a fitting conclusion to a college career.

A REPLY FROM REBECCA S. NOWACEK

In their commentaries on my chapter, Michael and Mike make explicit a concern bubbling under the surface of my essay: my desire to temper the tendency toward disciplinary and professional chauvinism. As I wrote of "terribly complex problems that can't be solved by a single type of expertise" I was, in truth, thinking that some of these problems are caused by actions and policies that are so blinkered by one type of disciplinary or professional expertise that other dimensions of the problem remain invisible—often with devastating results.

But, and I think Mike and Michael recognized this too, I don't wish to erase disciplinary knowledge and training. Such a wish would be not just foolish but impossible. Instead, my hope is that by articulating their professional knowledge and contrasting their disciplinary ways of knowing with those of their friends and classmates, students will cultivate a more flexible and ultimately more powerful expertise—one that recognizes its limitations as well as its strengths.

Finally, I confess a certain pleasure that both Michael and Mike latched onto my claim that students "need practice and coaching in the art of principled and civil disagreement." I saw this in my own class, it is a theme that emerges in Jeff Bernstein and Carmen Werder's chapters, and it is, apparently, a chord that resonates with my respondents as well. The inquiry I conducted in the Full-Circle Seminar helped me to recognize and articulate such practice and coaching as a goal for my subsequent classes. Indeed it led me to teach a new course (called the Jury Project) and I'm currently in the midst of a new inquiry into how students engage in collective deliberation on complex social and legal problems: how, in other words, do students sustain respectful and productive dialogue across a difference of opinions? My point in mentioning this new project is to provide one example of how the scholarship of teaching and learning can profoundly influence (and, I believe, improve) an instructor's teaching. The scholarly inquiry I conducted in the Full-Circle Seminar—and the conversations I have enjoyed with colleagues in other disciplines and institutions—helped me to articulate new questions and imagine new pedagogies, questions that have led me down new paths to education for citizenship.

Note

1. I have drawn heavily in this paragraph from William C. Placher's (2005) excellent collection *Callings: Twenty Centuries of Christian Wisdom on Vocation.*

Works Cited

Beuchner, Frederick. 2006. Vocation. In *Leading lives that matter: What we should do and who we should be,* ed. Mark R. Schwehn and Dorothy C. Bass, 111–112. Grand Rapids, Mich.: William B. Eerdmans.

Grossman, Pamela, Sam Wineburg, and Stephen Woolworth. 2000. *What makes teacher community different from a gathering of teachers?* University of Washington: Center for the Study of Teaching and Policy. http://depts.washington.edu/ctpmail/PDFs/Community-GWW-01-2001.pdf (accessed May 24, 2009).

Milwaukee River Keeper. 2007. MMSD dumps sewage in rivers, lakes. April 6, 2007. http://www.mkeriverkeeper.org/newsroom/archives/2007-04.htm (accessed May 24, 2009).

Palmer, Parker J. 2000. *Let your life speak: Listening for the voice of vocation.* San Francisco: Jossey-Bass.

Parten, M. B. 1932. Social participation among preschool children. *Journal of Abnormal and Social Psychology* 27: 243–269.

Placher, William C. 2005. *Callings: Twenty centuries of Christian wisdom on vocation.* Grand Rapids, Mich.: William B. Eerdmans.

Sierra Legal. 2006. *The Great Lakes sewage report card.* http://www.ecojustice.ca/publications/reports/the-great-lakes-sewage-report-card/?searchterm=sewage%20report%20card (accessed May 24, 2009).

Whitman, Walt. 1871. Democratic vistas. http://bartleby.com/229/20022.html (accessed May 24, 2009).

6

Educating for Scientific Knowledge, Awakening to a Citizen's Responsibility

Matthew A. Fisher

> Silence has long been confused with neutrality, and has been presented as a necessary condition for humanitarian action . . . We are not sure that words can always save lives, but we know that silence can certainly kill.
>
> —JAMES ORBINSKI, THE PRESIDENT OF *MÉDECINS SANS FRONTIÈRES/* DOCTORS WITHOUT BORDERS (MSF) ON ACCEPTING NOBEL PEACE PRIZE FOR MSF IN 1999

In late May and early June 2007, there was a flurry of news stories about an airplane passenger who flew on two trans-Atlantic flights while infected with an extremely drug-resistant form of tuberculosis. It was ironic that one American infected with tuberculosis generated this much public attention: the global scourge of tuberculosis had until recently been overlooked, much like the number of annual deaths from another infectious disease, malaria. While there had been a few recent stories about funding for research to develop new drugs for tuberculosis and insecticide-treated bed nets for controlling malaria, the staggering number of deaths from these two diseases (1 million and 2 million deaths each year, respectively) had been a reality in much of the world for far longer.

But complex societal issues with a significant scientific component aren't limited to health issues in developing countries. A recent article in *The Lancet* (Ferri et al. 2005) estimated that 24.3 million people globally have dementia, with 4.6 million new cases every year (one new case every seven seconds). The authors predict that the number of individuals affected by dementia will double every twenty years. The predicted economic toll of this condition is staggering; the Alzheimer's Association (2008) reports that Alzheimer's disease cost Medicare $91 billion in 2005 and American businesses $61 billion in 2002 (Alzheimer's Association 2008). Another example can be found in the media attention directed to recent reports from the Intergovernmental Panel on Climate Change (IPCC). The Fourth Assessment reports (2007), drawing on research stretching back almost two decades and as recent as 2006, conclude that it is more than 90 percent likely that human activity is having an impact on global climate and that the extent of possible global warming could be larger than the 2001 Third Assessment estimates. The topic of global warming even made it onto the cover of the April 9, 2007, issue of *Time*.

Science, particularly my discipline of chemistry, has an important role to play in how society tries to address each of these issues. As an educator who works with students majoring in biology and chemistry, how can I help my students better understand the connection between the knowledge within a scientific discipline and these issues? How can I encourage, support, and even challenge my students to think about these connections and about their responsibilities as scientists and citizens?

Science and Society

It isn't hard to find eloquent statements about the relationship between science and society. The American Association for the Advancement of Science (AAAS) includes the following definition of science literacy in *Science for All Americans:*

> Science literacy—which encompasses mathematics and technology as well as the natural and social sciences—has many facets. These include being familiar with the natural world and respecting its unity; being aware of some of the important ways in which mathematics, technology, and the sciences depend upon one another; understanding some of the key concepts and principles of science; having a capacity for scientific ways of thinking; knowing that science, mathematics, and technology are human enterprises, and knowing

what that implies about their strengths and limitations; and being able *to use scientific knowledge and ways of thinking for personal and social purposes.* (Rutherford and Ahlgren 1990, xvii–xviii, emphasis mine)

The first chapter of the same volume, under the heading "Science is a Complex Social Activity," states that "As a social activity, science inevitably reflects social values and viewpoints" and offers some specific illustrations of this point. AAAS is not alone in its explicit recognition of the connection between science and social issues. The World Congress on Science, held in 1999 in Budapest, argued that

the practice of scientific research and the use of knowledge from that research should always aim at the welfare of humankind, including the reduction of poverty, be respectful of the dignity and rights of human beings, and of the global environment, and take fully into account our responsibility toward present and future generations. (UNESCO 2000)

Editorials regularly appear in the journal *Science* (published by AAAS) identifying specific challenges and strategies for how science can be used to address important social issues. My own disciplinary organization, the American Chemical Society (ACS), included as a primary objective in its 2004–2006 strategic plan to "lead the diverse chemically-related professions for the benefit of society" (American Chemical Society 2004). The most recent strategic plan puts forth a vision of "improving people's lives through the transforming power of chemistry" and an organizational mission that "advances the broader chemistry enterprise and its practitioners for the benefit of Earth and its people" (American Chemical Society 2007). The foregoing statements encourage scientists to use their disciplinary expertise as a unique and important way to fulfill their responsibilities as citizens.

At the same time many scientists are reluctant to grapple as a community with the full implications of these statements. Joseph Rotblat (2000) described this reluctance well in his comments to the World Congress of Science:

The detachment of scientists from general human affairs led them to build an ivory tower in which they sheltered, pretending that their work had nothing to do with human welfare. . . . The aim of scientific research—they asserted— was to understand the laws of nature . . . Arising from this exclusivity, scientists evolved certain precepts about science to justify the separation from reality. These precepts included: "science for its own sake"; "scientific inquiry can know no limits"; "science is rational and objective"; "science is neutral"; "science has nothing to do with politics"; "scientists are just technical workers"; "science cannot be blamed for its misapplication". . . .

William Sullivan (2004), author of *Work and Integrity: The Crisis and Promise of Professionalism in America,* identifies a similar problem when he writes, "The idea of the professional as neutral problem solver, above the fray, which was launched with great expectations a century ago, is now obsolete. A new ideal of a more engaged, civic professionalism must take its place."

Undergraduate science education suffers from the same tension between training students narrowly and helping them see the connections between science and social issues. In its guidelines for the approval of undergraduate chemistry programs, the ACS Committee on Professional Training states that "within chemistry courses themselves, advantage should be taken at all levels of course sophistication to point out the connections between science and society" (American Chemical Society 2003). Yet many chemistry faculty resist using class time to make these connections. A quick examination of chemistry textbooks reveals the absence of connections between chemistry and significant social issues. Revealingly, Janet Donald's (2002) work on how members of various disciplines think leads her to describe chemistry in the following terms:

- a discipline—"a body of knowledge with a reasonably logical taxonomy, a specialized vocabulary, an accepted body of theory, a systematic research strategy, and techniques for replication and validation"
- hard/paradigmatic—"logically structured, uses models or theoretical frameworks, has an acknowledged methodology"
- pure—"uses specific models or theories"

So chemistry in its own view, as demonstrated in textbooks and as described by Donald, would have ample reason to resist the inclusion of social issues in courses for majors. Such resistance may be rooted in a concern that time taken to point out the social applications of chemistry is time taken away from learning essential content. It may be rooted in the attitude that Rotblat describes as "science has nothing to do with politics." Regardless of the reason, the resistance is there.

Most undergraduate science educators seem to assume that majors who have a basic understanding of the scientific concepts will automatically make connections between those concepts and global challenges such as HIV/AIDS, access to pharmaceutical drugs, or malnutrition. They will naturally and appropriately speak up regarding social issues that have a scientific component. Yet we see very little evidence that students make these connections when they are not an intentional part of the curriculum. Many biochemistry majors, for example, seem unaware that, as Philip Ball (2004) recently wrote, "the principal causes of death in the world are ones that are easily treatable or avoidable. And the wealthiest countries suffer largely from mortalities brought on by tobacco, alcohol, poor diet and lack of exercise."

In a similar vein, an editorial in the journal *Nature* commented that "scientists, at least, should argue for a strengthening of research priorities that reflect the needs not of well-protected interest groups in their own nations, but of humanity itself" ("A Divided World," 2005). Societal issues such as the ones mentioned earlier have scientific, moral, and civic components and cross the traditional boundaries between disciplines. What they demand of students is the ability to integrate learning across disciplinary contexts including and beyond biochemistry. As the Association of American Colleges and Universities (AAC&U) report *Greater Expectations* (2002) points out, these integrative connections are significant in providing students with "challenging encounters with important issues" and helping them "cultivate social responsibility." These encounters and the skills and dispositions that develop as a result are an integral part of preparing students to assume the responsibilities of citizenship.

Yet the activities that support this integrative learning are not commonly found in the curriculum for undergraduate science majors. While increasing emphasis is placed on the importance of undergraduate research as a capstone experience (Project Kaleidoscope 1991), these experiences stimulate integrative learning *within* the discipline, not integrative learning *across* disciplines such as the natural sciences, social sciences, and humanities. So we must explore other ways of developing socially conscious integrative learning that are rooted in specific courses within the major. Otherwise few students are likely to develop the skills and dispositions for making the connections between science and society that will serve them well as citizens.

The challenge is that the social issues I have been referring to are really ill-structured problems where real uncertainty exists in how to solve them. In addition, solutions to these problems must, by necessity, be rooted in more than just science; they must also draw from perspectives of other academic disciplines and ethical values. Jacob Bronowski wrote in *The Ascent of Man* (1973):

> There is no judgment of a field or line of research that can be confined to its scientific potential. Every judgment in life contains a silent estimate of human and social values too, and the representatives of science will not be able to shirk that. There is no guarantee that scientists will make a better job of fitting science to humanity than has been done before, but it is time that they faced their moral obligations and tried.

The moral and civic learning that Bronowski's words require of undergraduate science majors needs to be brought into the courses in their major. As Colby et al. (2003) have written, "It is equally important to weave moral and civic learning into the disciplines and into the majors. . . . Disciplines and majors are the primary focus of undergraduate education. Students define themselves to a great extent through their majors . . . moral and civic learning can be integrated into every discipline in a way that will strengthen rather than distort disciplinary learning" (185).

A Personal Journey toward "Breaking the Silence"

My own journey toward a teaching philosophy and practice that would break the silence regarding societal issues within science courses for majors has unfolded over more than fifteen years. The seeds of this journey were planted in 1990–1991, when I worked with Cathy Middlecamp at the University of Wisconsin–Madison's Chemistry Learning Center. One of Cathy's ongoing concerns has been to give voice to those individuals who are often not heard in a chemistry classroom. While much of that work has centered on students from traditionally underrepresented groups, such as women, African Americans, and Latinos, it also stresses giving voice to those who are concerned about how scientific knowledge is used in our society.

The next major turning point came nearly ten years later, during discussions among natural science faculty at Saint Vincent College regarding the natural sciences' goal in our core curriculum. By this time I had been teaching two different courses designed for *non-science* majors. Those courses sought to teach chemistry in the context of some broader issue: global warming, air and water quality, nutrition, drug development. Teaching such courses had shown me the power of contextualizing scientific concepts, particularly for non-science majors. As we talked about possible ways to revise the language of the natural sciences' core curriculum goal, several of us advocated the inclusion of the phrase "one should understand the impact science has had on daily life and the human condition." The same group also felt that an understanding of science was demonstrated in part when a student could "evaluate the impact science has had on the human condition." During our discussions, a colleague from another department made the point that the core curriculum goals apply to *all* students. So if we as a group felt strongly that some understanding of the impact of science on the human condition was important for students to develop, that meant that *all* students, majors and non-majors, needed to develop that understanding.

Shortly after the discussion at Saint Vincent began, I became involved with the NSF-funded Science Education for New Civic Engagements and Responsibilities (SENCER) project. SENCER advocated using a large, complex, "capacious" issue to teach "through" to the underlying science.[1] SENCER model courses used issues such as HIV/AIDS, tuberculosis, energy, and environmental questions as the context for "drilling down" to the underlying scientific concepts. Participating in the 2002 SENCER Summer Institute as an "advance representative" for the College gave me a much clearer sense of how individual faculty were actually implementing this approach. In the fall 2003 semester I taught an honors course on Science and Global Sustainability, a new course that I had developed using the SENCER approach.

Teaching that course had a profound impact on me for two reasons. First, the focus of the course required that I become more familiar with HIV/AIDS, malaria, tuberculosis, and other global public health issues. As I became more aware of these issues, I realized how much they were missing from the undergraduate biochemistry curriculum, how much biochemistry courses and textbooks were silent on the social dimension of these topics. Second, I was able to observe first-hand how motivated these students were to "go out and change the world." To be honest, that was a level of civic enthusiasm and engagement that I had *never* observed in any of my biochemistry courses.

After teaching Science and Global Sustainability, I spent more and more time thinking about why the connection between scientific concepts and public issues wasn't part of undergraduate biochemistry. The more I thought about it, the harder it was for me to justify or rationalize the silence that I increasingly recognized in undergraduate biochemistry, a silence that I found morally unacceptable. In the spring 2005 semester I made some small efforts to connect two different biochemistry courses to global issues, and several students commented on how they appreciated my raising them since these issues were never discussed in science classes.

Thinking about the relationship between science, societal issues, and how science courses are structured has increased my concern with how my students will understand and seek to fulfill their moral and civic responsibilities as professionals and American citizens. Drawing on my experiences and a definition of citizenship found in the *Merriam-Webster Collegiate Dictionary*, I now define citizenship as the manner (skills, disposition) in which an individual responds to membership in a community and the mutual relationships that come with such membership. The practice of science is a community activity and scientists are members of that community. By that I am not referring to the communal process of critical reflection that is at the heart of good peer review and an integral part of doing science. What I have in mind is that science as we know it and as it has developed exists because of the commitment and investment of community/societal resources. I use this analogy with my students: just imagine what would happen if I went to my local bank and asked them to lend me $500,000 to support my scientific research. I can't pay that back as if it were a loan. The National Science Foundation and the National Institutes of Health in the United States (and similar organizations in other countries) exist because of a cultural commitment to the public good that results from funding them with tax money.

Like other professions, science has been given enormous freedom by society to define how it operates, how new members are trained, and what the profession as a whole works on. The peer review system for grants involves almost exclusively scientists and not the general public. Scientific societies define what constitutes appropriate science education. I find myself coming back to William Sullivan's (2004) argument that professions as a whole—medicine, law, teaching, engineering, *science*—need to recover a sense of civic engagement and responsibility. Sullivan describes professional education as essentially involving three apprenticeships—cognitive apprenticeship, apprenticeship of practice, and moral apprenticeship. Undergraduate science education has grappled with varying degrees of success with the first two apprenticeships but has been almost totally silent on the third, particularly as it relates to the relation between science and society in general.

To define citizenship as the manner in which an individual responds to membership in a community is to point toward the responsibility scientists have to others in the various communities to which we belong. Those responsibilities—which include *civic* engagement and responsibility—come with the rights and privileges that our society has given the scientific community, including the relative autonomy of the scientific profession. In his foreword to *Work and Integrity,* Lee Shulman sums up the major thrust of the book as "autonomy and responsibility" (Sullivan 2004). For me, this balance is the heart of citizenship in the context of educating future members of a profession.

Bringing the Civic and Moral Dimension to Biochemistry

How all of this actually plays out in the context of an undergraduate biochemistry course is the subject of the rest of this chapter. A typical upper-level undergraduate biochemistry course is very content intensive; my fall course covers protein structure and function, enzyme function, and roughly a half dozen distinct metabolic pathways related to how the human body metabolizes carbohydrates, fats, and proteins. The spring course examines some different aspects of protein structure, glycoproteins, membrane structure and dynamics, transport, signal transduction, nucleic acid structure, and several processes central to nucleic acid biochemistry. I redesigned these courses in three ways (additional information about this redesign can be found in Fisher, n.d.):

1. Wherever possible, illustrative examples used in class would be drawn from public health topics rather than the examples found in textbooks that had been used for many years.

2. At various points in the course, I would ask students to read and respond to articles that focused on the broader societal context of these public health issues.

3. Students would work in small groups to develop a final "capstone project" on a public health topic of their own choosing.

My goal was to provide opportunities for students to connect biochemistry knowledge with other perspectives on a public health topic, allowing them to see the importance of multiple perspectives in addressing such complex issues. Using public health topics in my course, many of which are global, provided an opportunity for students to wrestle with moral and ethical issues as both biochemists and global citizens. In that regard my approach was similar to what Howard Tinberg (chapter 4) sought to achieve in his course on the literature of the Shoah.

An example of the first principle can be found in the area of enzyme mechanisms. For years, biochemistry textbooks have used the enzyme chymotrypsin as the paradigmatic example to illustrate the chemical strategies used by enzymes to catalyze cellular reactions. This enzyme, found in the stomach, is one of the best characterized enzymes known. Using it as the primary illustrative example does not open up any opportunities to connect enzyme mechanisms to societal issues. However, many of the same catalytic strategies can be illustrated equally well with HIV protease, an enzyme critically important in the life cycle of the HIV virus and the current target of the class of antiretroviral drugs known as protease inhibitors (an important component of HAART, highly active antiretroviral therapy). By using HIV protease to illustrate the chemical strategies used by enzymes, my students encounter the same biochemical concepts in a context where it seems completely appropriate to incorporate readings from other sources. Through the incorporation of readings such as selections from *28: Stories of AIDS in Africa* (Nolen 2007), my students now encounter the basic biochemical concepts, the biochemical aspects of HIV/AIDS (a topic already of interest to them), and other dimensions of the AIDS epidemic all at the same time.

Table 6.1 lists the public health topics that I have incorporated into both semesters of biochemistry. For each topic I use the same general pattern. First, introductory readings provide the broader context for the topic; these readings have ranged from transcripts of conference talks to perspective pieces from *Science* or *Nature* to more narrative essays published in the *New Yorker*. The readings are connected to an assignment that involves reflective writing by students. These topics also provide examples of basic concepts wherever possible, e.g., using the amyloid β protein important in Alzheimer's to examine protein folding. This approach is similar to Mike Burke's assignments (see chapter 7) that ask students to do a mathematical analysis of data that comes from a real world

Table 6.1. Cases and Themes Used in Both Semesters of Biochemistry

Public Health Issue	Semester	Basic Concepts Covered
Alzheimer's disease	Fall	protein structure, stability, and folding illustrated by amyloid ß protein
HIV/AIDS	Fall	enzyme kinetics and mechanism illustrated by HIV protease
Malaria and other parasitic diseases	Fall	central metabolic pathways—glycolysis, citric acid cycle, ATP synthesis
Diabetes and malnutrition	Fall	gluconeogenesis, glycogen metabolism, fat metabolism, and integration of metabolic pathways by looking at the biochemical basis and consequences of diabetes, obesity, and malnutrition
Avian influenza	Spring	protein structure, stability, function, and glycoproteins by examining the functions of hemagglutinin and neuraminidase from influenza virus, designing a flu vaccine, and new antivirals
Multidrug resistant tuberculosis	Spring	transport across membranes illustrated by the molecular mechanisms for multidrug resistance in TB
Alcoholism	Spring	signal transduction by various pathways illustrated by the biochemical effects of chronic alcohol abuse
Cancer and the environment	Spring	signal transduction, DNA replication, and transcription (both mechanism and regulation) illustrated through the biochemical consequences of damaging DNA or incorrectly turning on/off proteins (such as estrogen receptor) that are involved in signal transduction or regulate transcription

question; we are both "contextualizing data and ideas." Finally, the take-home question for the exam concluding each section of the course is almost always related to the contextualizing topic and wherever possible focuses on the broader issue and relevant perspectives as well as the basic biochemistry.

Several of the reflective writing assignments employ guidelines rooted in the Reflective Judgment model of King and Kitchener (1994), which focuses on John Dewey's notion that ill-structured problems with no single right solution require a combination of both logic and evaluation of possible solutions in terms of the coherence of the arguments and an individual's beliefs.[2] While heavily indebted to William Perry's seminal work on stages of intellectual development, King and Kitchener's (1994) model focuses on the complex reasoning and reflective judgment that individuals must engage in as they seek solutions to complex and controversial problems.

Consequently it is a model that I find particularly useful in educating for citizenship. Because this model has been extensively studied, there are many resources to assist faculty in designing assignments that challenge students to develop their ability for reflective thinking. These resources include a body of research that identifies the stage of intellectual development typical of most undergraduates and provides a set of guidelines that help faculty understand what individuals at each stage are capable of, and what tasks are thus appropriate; it also offers developmental assignments to promote reflective thinking and help individuals at a given stage progress to the next stage. I use the suggested developmental assignments for stages 3 and 4 to help design the initial writings and the take-home exam questions.

To connect our examination of these issues to both personal and institutional values, I use an activity each semester that focuses on the values of community, care, hospitality, and stewardship—values that are central to the Benedictine tradition and its approach to education. As a Catholic Benedictine college, Saint Vincent shares with other Benedictine colleges a commitment to certain institutional values that arise from this tradition: community, care, hospitality, and stewardship thus serve as an institutionally appropriate perspective and critical lens for approaching public health topics and the question of "moral apprenticeship" in a profession.[3] Since these values are incorporated in other courses across the Saint Vincent curriculum, using them in my biochemistry courses provides another opportunity for students to make connections across courses and disciplines.

As a small-scale capstone activity for the course, students are asked to work in small groups (3–4 students) on a public health project. The project is intended to present an overview of the biochemistry central to this topic as well as other perspectives outside of biochemistry (including salient characteristics) that the group has identified as important to understanding the public health issue chosen. Students submit the final version of their projects electronically using the KEEP (Knowledge Exchange Exhibition Presentation) Toolkit developed by the Carnegie Foundation's Knowledge Media Lab (Iiyoshi and Richardson 2008).

The assignment is designed so that each group must complete several tasks. First, each group must identify and present an overview of some aspect of biochemistry central to their topic. Since it is impossible to overview *all* the biochemistry relevant to a topic, students need to focus on one or two aspects of particular importance. Second, the group must identify one or two other perspectives on the public health issue from outside of biochemistry, as well as characteristics from those perspectives that are of notable significance in understanding the issue. Students are expected (and directed) to use one or more of the core values—community, care, hospitality, stewardship—as a "critical lens" through which they approach these outside perspectives. Third, the final presentation must incorporate the personal perspectives/thoughts of each group member. In the spring 2007 semester, I added one additional component; each group was asked to present what they saw as important next steps to be taken in addressing this issue. Students have selected a diverse range of topics: dengue fever, gonorrhea, tuberculosis, alcohol consumption as a cause of thiamin deficiency, juvenile diabetes, malaria, shigella, methicillin-resistant *S. aureus*, human papilloma virus, Ebola, and rabies.

Student Work and Student Response

As I describe in more detail elsewhere (Fisher, n.d.), making public health issues central to my biochemistry class has not significantly reduced student learning of basic biochemical concepts. The final exam in each semester is cumulative, and the exam questions since 2000 have largely remained the same. From fall 2000 to spring 2005, the average was 80 ± 14 in the fall course and 81 ± 11 in the spring course. Since the public health emphasis was introduced in the fall 2005 semester, the final exam averages have been 81 ± 8 in the fall course and 79 ± 10 in the spring course. The basic concepts listed in table 6.1 of this chapter are commonly found in a year-long biochemistry course; the only concept I eliminated when incorporating the public health emphasis was photosynthesis.

Clearly, a content-intensive science course like biochemistry can be modified to incorporate explicit connections to real world issues without sacrificing understanding of important disciplinary knowledge. In some ways, the revised course is more challenging for students. For almost ten years prior to the Fall 2005 semester, the course had included as part of each exam take-home questions that were focused on more complex problem-solving and analysis skills.[4] As I have developed take-home questions connected to public health issues, I find these new questions are more challenging than their predecessors. For example, the question used for the section of the fall course focused on enzymes asked students to 1) suggest a chemical mechanism for SARS protease using enzyme mechanisms studied in class as a starting point, 2) provide biochemical explanations for the observed effects of mutations on SARS protease activity, 3) identify whether the monomer or dimer form of the enzyme is most active, 4) apply the biochemistry of dimer formation to identify possible targets for drug development, and 5) identify what other factors (beyond biochemistry) would be important to consider in responding to a SARS outbreak. What I want to examine more closely here is evidence that challenges faculty assumptions regarding how students connect disciplinary learning to broader issues.

One of my original goals was to gather evidence of what perspectives outside of biochemistry students could identify and describe as important in a particular public health issue. These abilities are clearly important in the context of citizenship, particularly with regard to the broad discussions that often surround complex societal issues. Several times I have anonymously surveyed students, asking in which disciplines they have taken at least one course and which course(s) they saw as particularly relevant to the public health perspective used in the biochemistry course. While the majority (70 percent or higher) of students have taken one or more courses in social science, philosophy, history, and theology, the only course that is consistently mentioned as relevant to public health is ethics, with sociology mentioned much less frequently. In the fall 2007 survey results, two students (out of sixteen who responded) were very critical of what they saw as the very abstract perspective of many general education courses. The majority of my students don't see much connection between public health issues and other academic disciplines; that is consistent with what I have observed in a number of the public health projects that students complete.

Providing students with more opportunities to make connections improved the quality of their work. As I grew more comfortable incorporating public health issues into my course and designing assignments that asked students to identify non-science perspectives on these issues, critique the use of evidence, and evaluate a position from the perspective of a core value, students became more effective at identifying other important perspectives. This was clearly evident in several of the more recent public health projects as well as in answers to two different take-home exam questions focused on either SARS or bird flu. With the take-home exam questions, the students' answers were richer and more developed when they were asked to evaluate a reading through the perspective of one or more core values than when they were asked to critique the author's use of evidence.

The public health projects are a particularly rich source of evidence regarding the strengths and weaknesses of how my students made these integrative connections. The quality of the student work on the first generation of public health projects was quite varied and sometimes disappointing. In the gallery of selected examples that can be found in the KEEP Toolkit, the projects on thiamin deficiency, dengue fever, and micronutrient malnutrition were completed by students in the fall 2005 semester.[5] Examination of these projects reveals that students incorporated a very limited number of perspectives, often provided minimal biochemical information on their topic, and did not create a very rich representation of their understanding of the topic they chose.

In the spring 2006 semester for the first time I explicitly asked students to look at their chosen topic through one or more of the core Benedictine values as a critical lens. The projects that semester focused on diabetes, Ebola, rabies, breast cancer, and vitamin A deficiency. They were much more developed than what I saw in the fall 2005 semester, with multiple disciplinary perspectives incorporated into the final work. One common characteristic of these projects was a richer use of the language and ideas of biochemistry, such as protein kinases and the molecules they phosphorylate, transport proteins, or proteins that bind DNA sites. While some of the student comments relating their issue to the core values can be viewed as somewhat naïve, many of the comments indicate that students are beginning to grapple with the complexity of these issues and what they as citizens might advocate for.

The projects on shigella, river blindness, and alcoholism are the richest and most complex examples of student work. In these projects students are focusing on particular enzymes and metabolic pathways, transmembrane proteins, biochemical mechanisms of antibiotic resistance, or the biochemical effects of ethanol on specific signal transduction pathways. These artifacts of student learning demonstrate a process of incipient integration. First, students use the language and concepts of biochemistry to understand and describe relationships, at a *molecular* level, between structure and function or specificity and regulation central to their public health topic. At the same time that students are reflecting in great depth on the science involved, they are incorporating other important disciplinary perspectives on how society might address these issues in a way consistent with the values of community, care, stewardship, or hospitality.

At the outset of this inquiry into student learning, I hoped to observe a change in what students identified as important over the course of a semester. But relatively early in my work it became clear that this question would be impossible to answer. In large part this was because, for many students, the biochemistry course was the first time that they had thought carefully or even at all about many of these issues. At the same time that they were describing some important aspect of the biochemistry of their topic (and often doing that well) they were responding with surprise to other aspects of their topic:

> Malaria is a disease that I always took for granted. Not living in a 3rd-world country, I never really thought about this disease. As a result of doing this project, I now see how serious the issue is. I also now see that is a serious global problem that demands the attention and resources for the international community.

> Doing the research behind this project has really opened my eyes to the seriousness of diabetes. I was not aware that there were so many complications and annual deaths attributed to diabetes. After dedicating a significant part of this semester to hormone binding and signal transduction, it was interesting to see some of these components applied through looking at insulin. It is humbling to think of how problems with one, single hormone can cause so many hardships.

My thoughts on Alzheimer's disease are sadly minimal, because of my ignorance to the disease. I think my great-grandmother may have been victim of the disease, but my interactions with her in my lifetime can be counted on one hand. All I know entering this educational session into the disease is that victims suffer from severe memory loss . . . My view of Alzheimer's disease (AD) has changed upon reading about Bill and Bea and also looking around the www.alzheimers.org website. I now realize how important it is for victims of the disease to have support and help from their family and friends.

I have never had any family members with Alzheimer's, so I cannot connect with this article on a personal level. However, the information within it is applicable for MANY individuals and their families. I may have to confront this disease myself someday, and I have to keep this in mind while reading . . . My personal understanding of this disease has certainly changed after reading the literature, as I have become much more knowledgeable of the salient facts about the disease and its treatments. I now have a better understanding of what individuals with Alzheimer's disease have to go through on an everyday basis as well as the mental strain placed on people close to them.

While students have repeatedly indicated over the past three years the tremendous interest they have in topics such as bird flu, HIV/AIDS, or Alzheimer's, the responses above suggest that they have had very few encounters with these topics. Consequently, students are not very skillful at connecting the disciplinary knowledge they have with these issues, let alone connecting the ideas and insights of other disciplines. From the perspective of educating for citizenship, this is a somewhat troubling conclusion in that it suggests our students will find it very challenging to bring their disciplinary expertise to bear in broader conversations about these important issues (a problem that Rebecca Nowacek also wrestles with in chapter 5 of this volume); it also suggests possible solutions.

Implications for Undergraduate Science Education

Many professors—in both the sciences and other disciplines—would almost certainly agree with Derek Bok (2005) when he writes that "requirements are adopted in the belief that hearing professors discuss great books and reading masterpieces of literature will develop caring, ethically discerning students or that taking a variety of courses—any courses—in several different fields of knowledge will be enough to produce educated, intellectually curious adults."

The second part of Bok's statement should be particularly applicable to students at Saint Vincent College, as the College requires students to complete 59–

60 credits in what the institution refers to as the Core Curriculum. The *College Bulletin* states, "The Core Curriculum presents all students with a broadly based education that provides a general body of knowledge in the humanities and fine arts, social sciences, natural sciences, and mathematics, an interdisciplinary view of that knowledge base, and the skills to increase that general body of knowledge throughout their lives." Yet the evidence I have gathered over three years in teaching upper-level biochemistry to science majors doesn't support these claims.

I see several implications of this work for how undergraduate science courses aimed at majors are taught and the relationship of those courses to broader general education requirements. Science teachers cannot assume that students will naturally and easily make connections on their own between scientific concepts covered in a particular course such as biochemistry, how those concepts are used in solving real-world problems, and values such as community and care (encompassing connections to other disciplines as well). Opportunities to make those connections need to be incorporated into courses for majors; many of my students who take the revised biochemistry courses have commented that my assignments are the first opportunity they have to explore such connections in a science class. While some students can make deep and rich connections with clear implications for citizenship, those students are in the minority. Based on the student work that I have gathered and examined, many of my students still have room to improve in this regard.

In the "three apprenticeships" model of professional education described by Sullivan (2004), moral apprenticeship (the obligation that the profession as a whole has to society) is an important part of becoming a member of a profession. The dimension of moral apprenticeship must be incorporated in some explicit manner into the undergraduate science major's curriculum. As regards my own discipline of biochemistry, the American Society for Biochemistry and Molecular Biology states in their curricular guidelines (Voet et al. 2003) that students in these disciplines should develop, by the end of their undergraduate education, an awareness of "major issues at the forefront of the discipline" and "ethical issues in the molecular life sciences." Yet, biochemistry teachers cannot assume that students will develop on their own an understanding of public health issues and the role that our discipline and related areas will play in these issues. The work described in this chapter supports the principle that the moral dimension—integrated through connections to public health issues which involve reflective judgment—can be developed at the same time that students develop an appropriate understanding of basic biochemical concepts.

It should be clear that what I have tried to accomplish with my undergraduate biochemistry course does not stand on its own. In content-intensive courses like biochemistry, simply providing opportunities for students to make these connections is a challenge for instructors. Whatever knowledge of other disciplines students bring to this work has to come from other courses or their own reading. Prior experience with reflective writing in other courses can provide a foundation for these assignments in biochemistry such that students will find them more rewarding and effective. Creating opportunities for students to be engaged in the "moral apprenticeship" dimension of learning science requires that instructors and students draw from other learning experiences. When such opportunities are created, disciplinary learning and moral/civic learning related to the responsibilities of citizenship can be experienced even in content-intensive courses for science majors.

Dialogue

A COMMENTARY FROM DAVID GEELAN
School of Education, University of Queensland

Three things struck me very strongly in reading this chapter. The first is the notion of a "moral apprenticeship" for professionals. This linked with reading Hugh Sockett's excellent *The Moral Base for Teacher Professionalism* (1993) some years ago, and my own efforts to instill and elicit a moral perspective on science education in the science teachers I work with. In many ways we have rejected the notion of value-free science and technology intellectually, but much of our practice still occurs as though we believed values have no place in science.

The second is the excellent counterexample provided by Matt's work (and also by the work presented in Mike Burke's chapter) to the oft-heard lament by science and mathematics educators that that curriculum is too stuffed with content to allow these kinds of more integrated, socially connected learning activities to occur. Clearly, with will and courage and skill, it is possible both to teach a large amount of science content to a deep level of understanding and also to engage students with ideas of service and citizenship. The example essay question Matt Fisher describes—which I have read in its entirety—puts meat on the bones of this belief, showing the depth of knowledge required and the authentic, rather than token, links to the issues. In fact, there's a very strong argument to be made that engaging with the science content in the context of an authentic social or public-health issue leads to a deeper and richer level of engagement with and understanding of the science.

The third thing that struck me in reading this chapter is the global perspective these activities provided. Issues such as malaria are unlikely to directly influence the lives of many of these students if they remain in the United States, but the various issues and contexts explored "raise their eyes" by giving them a vision of the whole world, and of the struggles and challenges facing people in other cultures. The statistics used create an understanding of the scope and scale of global issues that may not appear in other courses taken by the students, particularly science courses. This course links the submicroscopic world of the molecule and biochemistry with the macroscopic world of human life on a global scale. It also provides an antidote to too-narrow notions of "relevance," where scientific knowledge is linked only to contexts from the students' existing experiential worlds. Matt's work creates, not incidentally, a vision of global citizenship and global service.

A COMMENTARY FROM CARMEN WERDER
Department of Communication, Western Washington University

I heartily applaud Matt Fisher's reminder to his science educator colleagues that "we cannot assume that students will naturally and easily make connections on their own between scientific concepts covered in a particular course such as biochemistry, how those concepts are used in solving real-world problems, and values such as community and care. . . ."

One of his examples of a "real-world problem" strikes a special chord with me right now as I work to understand the biological consequences and causes of my mother's Alzheimer's. Would that I had had an instructor like Matt who would have helped me see a connection between all those terms I memorized in my undergraduate biology course and the dramatic realities of my mother's disease. He is right in reminding science faculty not to assume that their students will make *any* connection between course concepts and their lived experiences. I would go further and say that none of us should make that faulty assumption—regardless of discipline.

Grounded in William Sullivan's tri-part professional education model, Matt makes a strong case for the importance of engaging students in a *moral apprenticeship*. At the same time, he suggests how to provide the two other kinds of apprenticeships: *cognitive* and *practice*. While maintaining a clear expectation that his biochemistry students have a firm conceptual grasp of basic scientific principles, he also invites them to apply course concepts to public health topics. Acknowledging that too often, across higher education, we continue to emphasize the cognitive domain exclusively, Matt concentrates on the need for a moral dimension. Although it is not the main focus of his rationale, he also implies the crucial need for application, for practice.

Students often try to remind us of this need for genuine opportunities for practice, too. As a 2008 K. Patricia Cross Future Leaders Award Winner, Andrew Farke (a biology graduate student), said in anticipation of his career as a science educator:

If I accomplish nothing else, I want to convey my own enthusiasm for the breathtaking expanse of life's history and intricacy—whether in the dissection lab, in front of an audience, or in mentoring promising students. And most importantly, I want the individuals I reach to use their knowledge. This is why I am dedicated to academia (Miller 2008, 59).

If we listen to our students and to scholars of teaching and learning like Matt Fisher, we will understand better how teaching the knowledge of our disciplines, engaging the moral consciousness of our students, and providing them with opportunities for practice has become not a luxury, but our own intellectual, pedagogical, and societal responsibility.

A REPLY FROM MATTHEW A. FISHER

As I've become more concerned about educating for citizenship and altered my courses to support this goal, I've become more convinced that I can't do this in isolation. I need colleagues in other disciplines in a variety of ways—as "sounding boards" for specific things I want to try, as collaborators in exploring issues that cross disciplinary boundaries, as people with expertise in things that I'm not as familiar with (e.g. designing reflective writing assignments). So it is extremely heartening that both Carmen and David have responded so positively to my use of William Sullivan's "three apprenticeships" of professional education.

Now, after writing my chapter and reading the thoughtful responses from Carmen and David, I see what I have tried to accomplish with my biochemistry courses as an example of what Mary Catherine Bateson (1994) describes as spiral learning. She writes "Lessons too complex to grasp in a single occurrence spiral past again and again, small examples gradually revealing greater and greater implications . . . Spiral learning moves through complexity with partial understanding, allowing for later returns." Helping my students engage with public health topics as a context for both learning biochemistry and learning about their responsibilities as citizens strikes me as one way to set up an opportunity for spiral learning. That opportunity, of course, will only happen if students return to these issues again and again.

While it is possible that this would naturally happen in my students' lives after finishing my course, I am much more intrigued by the possibility of this return happening through repeated encounters with these issues in the context of other academic courses. Those repeat encounters could happen in a number of different ways, from faculty explicitly structuring a course to include public health issues to the inclusion of more open-ended assignments that students complete as part of a class. Regardless of the details, such courses and assignments will only flourish and have their full impact in an environment where teachers from numerous disciplines feel that they share common values and are working toward a common goal. Carmen and David's heartfelt support for the work I've done is a wonderful (and gratifying) example of what that "common space" could look like.

David commented on how he was struck by the global perspective provided by the activities I have incorporated into my biochemistry courses. That's actually something that I am concerned about. The last time I checked our institutional statistics, over 40 percent of Saint Vincent students came from the county where the college is located. If the counties to the east and south are included (which would include the Pittsburgh area), then 86 percent of Saint Vincent students come from areas less than one hour away from the college. So I'm not certain how much my students really get out of the global dimension of these issues solely from what we do in class. Fortunately, the College has identified increased student participation in study abroad as an important goal in the current strategic plan. My hope is that as more students participate in study abroad experiences, the campus culture will become more global. Who knows? That change in campus culture might provide opportunities for repeated encounters with the global dimensions of public health in different contexts . . . and thereby lead my students deeper into their own spiral learning as scientists and citizens.

Notes

1. More information on the SENCER project can be found at www.sencer.net.

2. A particularly good overview of the Reflective Judgment model is King and Kitchener's "Reflective Judgment: Theory and Research on the Development of Epistemic Assumptions Through Adulthood" (2004). There is also a website, http://www.umich.edu/refjudg/index.html (accessed May 25, 2009), which provides an overview of the model and relevant references. The developmental assignments to promote reflective thinking that I mentioned can be found in King and Kitchener's *Developing Reflective Judgment* (1994).

3. The Association of Benedictine Colleges and Universities website (www.abcu.info) has a number of essays that explore the institutional values and perspective that Catholic Benedictine colleges share. "Catholic, Benedictine Values in an Educational Environment" is a wonderful essay by three Benedictines at Saint John's University/College of Saint Benedict in Minnesota that can be found at http://www.osb.org/acad/benva11.html (accessed May 25, 2009).

4. While space limitations precluded the inclusion of one of the take-home questions as an example, interested individuals are welcome to contact me for additional information about these.

5. Faculty interested in examining a selection of public health projects completed between fall 2005 and spring 2008 are welcome to contact me.

Works Cited

Alzheimer's Association. 2008. *Alzheimer's disease facts and figures.* http://www.alz.org/alzheimers_disease_facts_figures.asp (accessed May 25, 2009).

American Chemical Society. 2003. *Undergraduate professional education in chemistry: Guidelines and evaluation procedures.*

———. 2004. *Strategic plan.*

———. 2007. *Strategic plan.*

Association of American Colleges and Universities. 2002. *Greater expectations: A new vision for learning as a nation goes to college.* Washington, DC.

Ball, Philip. 2004. "Word of honor," http://www.bioedonline.org/news/news.cfm?art= 1309 (accessed May 25, 2009).

Bateson, Mary Catherine. 1994. *Peripheral visions: Learning along the way.* New York: Harper Perennial.

Bok, Derek. 2005. *Our underachieving colleges: A candid look at how much students learn and why they should be learning more.* Princeton, N.J.: Princeton University Press.

Bronowski, Jacob. 1973. *The ascent of man.* Boston: Little, Brown.

Colby, Anne, Thomas Ehrlich, Elizabeth Beaumont, and Jason Stephens. 2003. *Educating citizens: Preparing America's undergraduates for lives of moral and civic responsibility.* San Francisco: Jossey-Bass.

"A Divided World." 2005. *Nature* 433: 1.

Donald, Janet G. 2002. *Learning to think: Disciplinary perspectives.* San Francisco: Jossey-Bass.

Ferri, Cleusa P., Martin Prince, Carol Brayne, Henry Brodaty, Laura Fratiglioni, Mary Ganguli, Kathleen Hall, Kazuo Hasegawa, Hugh Hendrie, Yueqin Huang, Anthony Jorm, Colin Mathers, Paulo R. Menezes, Elizabeth Rimmer, and Marcia Scazufca. 2005. "Global prevalence of dementia: A Delphi consensus study," *Lancet* 366: 2112.

Fisher, Matthew A. n.d. "Public health and biochemistry: Connecting content, issues and valves for majors." Unpublished manuscript.

Iiyoshi, Toru, and Cheryl R. Richardson. 2008. Promoting technology-enabled knowledge building and sharing for sustainable open educational innovations. In *Opening up education: The collective advancement of education through open technology, open content, and open knowledge,* ed. Toru Iiyoshi and M. S. Vijay Kumar, 337–355. Cambridge, Mass: M.I.T. Press.

Intergovernmental Panel on Climate Change. 2007. *Climate change 2007: Synthesis report. Contribution of working groups I, II and III to the fourth assessment report of the intergovernmental panel on climate change,* ed. Core Writing Team, Rajendra K. Pachauri, and Andy Reisinger. Geneva: IPCC.

King, Patricia M., and Karen S. Kitchener. 1994. *Developing reflective judgment: Understanding and promoting intellectual growth and critical thinking in adolescents and adults.* San Francisco: Jossey-Bass.

———. 2004. "Reflective judgment: Theory and research on the development of epistemic assumptions through adulthood." *Educational Psychologist* 39: 5.

Miller, Margaret. 2008. "Listening to students: Creating the future." *Change,* September/October, 58–62.

Nolen, Stephanie. 2007. *28: Stories of AIDS in Africa.* New York: Walker & Co.

Project Kaleidoscope. 1991. *What works: Building natural science communities.* Washington, D.C.: Project Kaleidoscope.

Rotblat, Joseph. 2000. Science and human values. In *World conference on science: Science for the twenty-first century; A new commitment,* ed. Ana Maria Cetto, Susan Schneegans, and Howard Moore, 45–49. London: Banson.

Rutherford, F. James, and Andrew Ahlgren. 1990. *Science for all Americans.* New York: Oxford University Press.

Sockett, Hugh. 1993. *The moral base for teacher professionalism.* New York: Teacher's College Press.

Sullivan, William M. 2004. *Work and integrity: The crisis and promise of professionalism in America,* 2nd ed. San Francisco: Jossey-Bass.

UNESCO. 2000. *World conference on science: Science for the twenty-first century; a New Commitment.* Ed. Ana Maria Cetto, Susan Schneegans, and Howard Moore. London: Banson.

Voet, Judith G., Ellis Bell, Rodney Boyer, John Boyle, Marion O'Leary, and James K. Zimmerman. 2003. Recommended curriculum for a program in biochemistry and molecular biology. *Biochemistry and Molecular Biology education* 31:161–162.

Michael C. Burke

Today's students, tomorrow's citizens, will have to make decisions, as citizens, about a collection of important issues that face us in the world today—issues such as global warming, energy policy, world population, as well as many social issues. Although the issues themselves are not inherently political, successful resolution of them will require political decisions. When our students think about political questions such as these, if indeed they think about them at all, how do they arrive at their conclusions? Most rely on the opinions of others— friends or parents. Some obtain information from radio or television, or search on the internet. They may even consult an expert or two. But what happens when these sources do not agree? How do our students process conflicting information to arrive at their own conclusions? It is our job to teach our students the skills they need to make sense of the world, and many of us work very hard at that. We focus, often, on skills of analysis, of argumentation and persuasion, and on what we have come to call critical thinking. What is often omitted in this effort, however, is an element that I think is central: the importance of looking at the data, and the skills needed to make sense of the data.

Lincoln at Cooper Union

In February of 1860 Abraham Lincoln of Illinois traveled to New York to deliver an address at Cooper Union (Lincoln 1860). The address, delivered before a sophisticated New York audience, was Lincoln's opportunity to convince those in the Eastern political establishment that he was worthy of the Republican nomination for the presidency. While in New York for the speech, Lincoln also visited the photography studio of Matthew Brady, who produced a dignified portrait that later appeared in newspapers across the country. The speech and the photograph were phenomenally successful, so much so that Lincoln later commented that "Brady and the Cooper Institute speech made me President" (Corry 2003, 93).

The issue Lincoln chose to address at Cooper Union was slavery, or, more precisely, the extension of slavery to the territories of the United States. In Lincoln's words, the question was "Does the proper division of local from federal authority, or anything in the Constitution, *forbid our Federal Government* to control as to slavery *in our Federal Territories*?" Senator Stephen A. Douglas, Lincoln's great rival, also from Illinois and the man who would be chosen as the Democratic presidential nominee later in the year 1860, took the position that Congress did not have the power to regulate slavery in the territories; Douglas argued that the question of slavery in the territories must be left to the residents of the territories themselves. Furthermore, Douglas had asserted in a speech at Columbus, Ohio, that "Our fathers, when they framed the Government under which we live, understood this question just as well, and even better, than we do now." In his Cooper Union address, Lincoln accepted this last statement by Douglas as a starting point, and then used the statement to attack Douglas's position. Lincoln did this by asking how our fathers (whom Lincoln took to be the thirty-nine signers of the Declaration of Independence) had acted on the question of the authority of the federal government to regulate slavery in the territories.

The manner in which Lincoln examined how the thirty-nine signers had acted is quite extraordinary by today's standards. Lincoln detailed, one by one, the instances, both before and after the Constitutional Convention, when members of the thirty-nine voted on the issue of slavery in the territories. He named those who voted both for federal regulation of slavery in the territories and those who voted against. Lincoln devoted considerable time to this analysis (thirty-two minutes of a sixty-seven-minute speech, in Sam Waterston's C-SPAN reading ("Abraham Lincoln's Cooper Union . . ." 2005), and his case-by-case discussion made a very powerful argument. He concluded, after this careful analysis, that twenty-one of the thirty-nine (a clear majority) had voted to prohibit slavery in the territories, and therefore, implicitly, supported the position that Congress had the power to regulate slavery in the territories. Lincoln thus demolished Douglas's position. He also noted that two of the thirty-nine voted against federal prohibition of slavery in the territories, and that sixteen had no recorded position on the issue. We can characterize Lincoln's method as an appeal to the data. Lincoln used the simplest of mathematical techniques to analyze the data: enumeration.

As a modern reader and viewer of a historical reenactment of the Cooper Union speech, I had two immediate reactions. The first was that Lincoln was, indeed, a masterful speechwriter. The second was that the level of political discourse today is greatly impoverished compared to that of 1860. Today's political discourse suffers from a number of faults: a focus on emotional issues of lesser importance, a tendency to attack the character of political opponents rather than to analyze the issues at hand, and an almost total disregard for the evidence pertaining to important questions. Lincoln's speech, by contrast, addressed the single most important issue of the day, used solid reasoning to build a powerful case, and built that case upon a comprehensive examination of the evidence.

The successful resolution of many of the issues that we confront today—issues such as global warming, energy policy, world population, and even many social issues—must begin with a careful examination of the world as it is. When we look carefully at the world, we produce data and evidence. The central question for us is "What do the data tell us about the world?" Much of the data is quantitative, and so an analysis of such data will necessarily involve mathematics. The good news is that the mathematics required to make sense of the data is often relatively unsophisticated. Although not as simple as the method of enumeration employed by Lincoln in his Cooper Union address, the level of mathematics required is well within the reach of any high school student who has successfully completed second-year algebra. Thus, the mathematical hurdles are far from insurmountable. I have found that other nonmathematical issues with regard to the treatment and interpretation of data are much more difficult, more profound. And so I worked to design assignments that helped students cultivate both these capacities.

Data-Based Writing Assignments in a Mathematics Class

The use of data and evidence to inform our opinions about important issues of the day has been the focus of my work as a Carnegie Scholar. Over the course of a year, I constructed six data-based writing assignments for students in my precalculus and calculus classes. The six topics addressed were global warming (based on data about carbon dioxide levels), a historical look at the population of Ireland, radiocarbon dating, global warming again (based on data about the size of the Arctic ice cap), the disposal of nuclear waste, and world population. In each assignment, the students were presented with data; they were asked to construct a mathematical model for the data (linear or exponential), and then to use a spreadsheet to implement the model by producing a table and graph. They were asked to interpret the data by making projections and/or by deciding whether or not the data were consistent with a particular theory about the underlying issue. And, finally, they were asked to embed their mathematical work into a written paper using what they had learned from their study of the data to inform their thoughts about the underlying issue. My students found these assignments extraordinarily difficult, as indicated by these post-assignment reflections:

> I thought that the paper was challenging because I have never done a paper like this before. It was hard to put what I did into words instead of just showing work. The most challenging thing about integrating mathematical thinking into the paper was explaining how the calculations made sense to the data. It was also difficult to be as un-biased as possible in writing the paper.

> The math was simple. However integrating formulas and mathematical data into a paper without sounding choppy is challenging. I also have a difficult time gathering my thoughts into a sensible order. We were asked to include a lot in a single essay.

> The idea of examining the statements in light of the data was a new idea to me. It was very challenging because when I was writing, I got off topic and forgot what I was supposed to be writing about.

> It was hard to put the paper together because it wasn't like an English essay.

As I read these reflections, I was struck by the sense that my students viewed these assignments as something entirely new and foreign. They had evidently never been asked to do this kind of writing, and thinking, before.

Intellectual Contexts

I came to this work through an interest in integrative learning (Huber and Hutchings 2004). Initially, I had three main goals. I wanted my students, for motivational purposes, to see some genuine applications of the mathematics they were studying, applications beyond the field of mathematics. I wanted to teach through interdisciplinary problems, so that my students would begin to see that knowledge is not constrained by artificial disciplinary boundaries. And I had the conviction that asking my students to write about mathematics would help them to clarify their mathematical thoughts.

In addition to my original motivation, however, I now see my work in the context of quantitative literacy. Lynn Arthur Steen has captured my intent. He writes that quantitative literacy (QL) is about challenging college-level settings in which quantitative analysis is intertwined with political, scientific, historical or artistic contexts. Here QL adds a crucial dimension of rigor and thoughtfulness to many of the issues commonly addressed in undergraduate education. . . . QL is not a discipline but a literacy, not a set of skills but a habit of mind. (Steen 2004, 22)

The papers I assign require my students to use mathematics in the ways that Steen suggests. Students' thinking is grounded by both the presence of data and the requirement to work with those data mathematically. As noted above, students find the kind of thinking required by these assignments to be quite foreign and difficult. Integrative writing assignments of this sort expose weaknesses in my students' thinking in ways that are not ordinarily apparent and, ultimately, lead to deeper, more thoughtful work.

Implementation

I teach at the College of San Mateo, a suburban community college on the San Francisco Peninsula. We have a healthy transfer program; the most popular transfer destinations for our students are the University of California (Berkeley and Davis campuses), and the California State University System (particularly San Francisco and San Jose State Universities). The two courses I worked with, precalculus in the fall semester and calculus in the spring, are standard, transferable courses populated by students who successfully make the transition to four-year colleges. Each course has a well-defined, tightly organized curriculum that has been articulated with our transfer institutions. I used standard textbooks for the courses: Cohen (2006) for precalculus and Stewart (2000) for calculus. It was quite a challenge to introduce data-based writing assignments into such content-heavy courses with strictly mandated curricula—a challenge that arose from time constraints rather than the mathematical aspects of the assignments. Linear and exponential functions are topics of study in precalculus, and so discussion and application of this mathematics fit very naturally into that course. And we assume (mostly correctly) that our calculus students have already mastered linear and exponential functions. Consequently, the mathematical requirements of the assignments demanded relatively little class time in the calculus course.

I assigned three of these assignments in each of the two courses. For each assignment, I would spend a good part of a class hour introducing the topic. The next day, I provided some time in class for students to get started on the mathematical aspects of the assignment. And a couple of days before each paper was due, we would have a "draft workshop" day during which students traded papers to read and critique.

But beyond these activities, which I had planned, we spent substantial additional class time on the data-based assignments: the assignments raised important nonmathematical issues, and discussion of these issues consumed a significant amount of time in both courses. My students simply found the questions raised by these assignments to be very compelling. Repeatedly, I would find that in response to students' questions, I had spent a substantial portion of a class hour (frequently half or more of the hour, occasionally the entire hour) talking with my students about various issues related to the data-based assignments. I provided background information about the assignments, ranging from scientific discussions about the nature of the issue, to historical context, to political considerations, to moral issues provoked by the assignments.

In addition, we addressed questions such as these: Where did the data come from? Are the data reliable? What can we conclude from our study of the data? Does the graph we have constructed clearly illustrate trends in the data? How certain are we about projections for the future based upon our work with the data? What are the implications of our projections? It is fair to say that extended discussion of issues such as these threatened, at times, to hijack the course. Yet I have never before taught courses in which the level of student interest was so high. And the data-based assignments served well to motivate the study of mathematics. I was never asked the question, "Why do we have to learn this?"

Despite the challenges of an overstuffed curriculum (an obstacle also described by Matt Fisher and David Geelan in this volume), I did successfully introduce the data-based assignments into the two courses, and I managed to devote considerable class time to them. I was able to find some wiggle room in the precalculus course, making judicious choices about the mathematical material we would cover. The calculus course was more difficult. There was no wiggle room there; virtually every topic was essential for the development of calculus. But I simply made it work. Perhaps I talked faster. More likely, I suspect that I shifted more of the responsibility for learning calculus onto the backs of my students (not a bad idea, that) by working through fewer examples and spending less time answering routine homework questions.

Did this curricular shift compromise student learning of mathematics? The brief answer is no. For comparison purposes, in each course I gave final exams that I had used previously. The precalculus students scored slightly lower on the exam than their counterparts from previous semesters, although the difference was within normal semester-to-semester variation between classes; the calculus scores were essentially the same as the scores from earlier semesters (actually ϵ higher). I have concluded that it is indeed possible to augment the standard mathematics curriculum with written assignments of this type without compromising mathematics instruction and student learning. And the students enjoy the benefit of using mathematics to explore a compelling collection of important contemporary issues.

The Nuclear Waste Assignment

For the remainder of this chapter, I take a close look at the assignment about nuclear waste in order to provide a more complete picture of the nature of these data-based assignments and the student learning they facilitated. Nuclear waste is a byproduct of the nuclear power industry. In the 1970s we reached an informal national consensus on the issue of nuclear power. We decided that nuclear power was too dangerous, and indeed, no new nuclear power plants have been constructed in this country since the 1970s. The issue has been largely dormant for thirty years. Now, we are revisiting the question of nuclear power, and properly so. The world has changed since the 1970s; the true costs of our traditional power sources, oil and coal, are more apparent today, and in the case of oil, the exhaustion of the world's reserves is in sight.

When my generation (the Baby Boomers) considers nuclear power, we bring a lifetime of experience to the question. We are aware of the horrors of Hiroshima and Nagasaki. We remember what it was like to live in the nuclear shadow of the Cold War. We traced the path of the radioactive cloud that resulted from the Soviet Union's explosion of the one-hundred-megaton bomb as it passed across the United States, as it passed over our homes. We know about the cancers caused by our own nuclear testing at the Nevada Test Site. We have heard the promise of nuclear power as a source of electricity, "too cheap to meter" in the words of Lewis Strauss, chairman of the Atomic Energy Commission in 1954. We have watched as the nuclear industry struggled to build additional plants and was ultimately stopped by citizen action fueled by a quarter of a century of fear of the possible consequences of a nuclear accident. And finally, the accidents at Three Mile Island and Chernobyl cemented the wisdom of our collective decision in the popular mind. But today's students, our students, know little of this story. The nuclear waste assignment offers an opportunity to talk about this recent history with our students.

Today's supporters of the nuclear industry assert that new, improved reactor designs are safer than the reactors built in the 1960s and 1970s. They remind us that nobody has been killed by a nuclear accident in this country, a record that compares very favorably with coal. They point to the dangers of global warming, largely a consequence of the use of oil and coal. They argue that our dependence on foreign oil has lead to an unstable and dangerous situation in the Middle East. These are all reasonable points. And, in light of this, proponents of nuclear energy argue strongly for a renewed commitment to nuclear power and for the construction of many new nuclear power plants.

I write here neither as an opponent of nuclear power, nor as a proponent. I write as a citizen and an educator who sees that the question is to be revisited, and who is concerned that our future decisions about nuclear energy, which will

Table 7.1. Radioactivity Levels Over Time

Time (in years) (t)	Radioactivity Level P (t)
0	1.0000
50,000	0.2466
100,000	0.0608
150,000	0.0150
200,000	0.0037
250,000	0.0009

be made by tomorrow's citizens, must be made wisely, with care and thought. This is exactly the sort of issue that should be examined in the classroom, and I would argue that it should be examined in the mathematics classroom, because we (mathematicians) can bring an essential dimension to the discussion that is largely missing from debate on the issue.

Most discussions of nuclear power today generally follow the discourse pattern above: one side lists the dangers of nuclear power, and the other cites advantages. If the issue of nuclear waste is raised at all, it is usually addressed in a superficial way with unsupported assertions. Yet a careful analysis of the problem of nuclear waste disposal belongs at the center of the discussion. The data-based writing exercise I designed requires just such a careful analysis. The core of the exercise is based on a statement by Hans Bethe, a Nobel laureate and the head of the Theoretical Division of the lab at Los Alamos during the Manhattan Project. In a 1976 *Scientific American* article in which Bethe argues for the necessity of nuclear power, he states that the half-life of plutonium 239 is 25,000 years, and that the nuclear waste material will not be safe until the level of radioactivity is cut by a factor of 1,000 (Bethe 1976). Beginning with this information, I ask my students to construct an exponential decay model for the level of radioactivity of plutonium 239 and then to use a spreadsheet to implement the model by producing a table and a graph. They are to address the question of how long it will take until the radioactive material is safe, and then to use their answer to inform their conclusions about the wisdom of a renewed commitment to nuclear power.

Students derive the mathematical model $P(t) = P_0 e^{-.000028t}$, where t represents time in years, P_0 represents the initial level of radioactivity, and $P(t)$ represents the level of radioactivity after a period of t years. They then construct tables and graphs similar to those given in table 7.1 and in figure 7.1. (Bear in mind that if the initial level of radioactivity is 1.000, then the level of radioactivity will be reduced by a factor of 1,000 when the level falls below .001.) In this assignment the graph

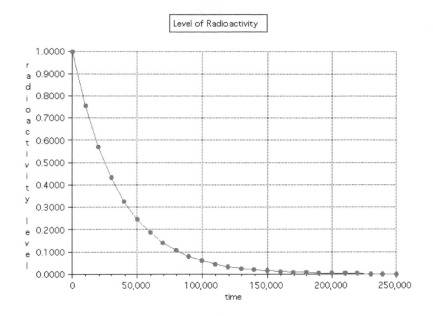

FIGURE 7.1. RADIOACTIVITY LEVELS OVER TIME

is not finely tuned enough to answer the question of how long it will take until the radioactive material is safe. But the table clearly shows that it will take about 250,000 years for the level of radioactivity to fall below .001. My students can also reach this conclusion by solving the equation $P_0 e^{-.000028t} = .001 P_0$ for t.

Student Reflections on the Assignment

Many of my students come to an assignment like this one with preconceptions, as the quotes below demonstrate. I challenge them to set aside their preconceptions, to analyze the data, and to see what the data tell them. My students succeed to some degree, as evidenced by the following reflections:

> I would say I am pro–nuclear power, but my paper reaches a conclusion that differs from my personal beliefs. . . . My conclusions were nearly direct results of my mathematical data. It's hard to fight cold hard facts, and the facts show this waste is just as dangerous, if not more dangerous, than the CO_2 emissions currently left by oil and coal burning.

I actually started with the preconceived idea that we should go to nuclear energy, but through my research and what I discovered from my mathematical model, I had changed my mind. . . . The mathematical model really put into perspective how long the waste would have to be stored. After you find out that it's going to take a quarter of a million years until it is safe, you really start to second guess the whole idea all together.

As a person interested in science, I felt as if I did have a preconceived idea about a conclusion. Specifically, that nuclear power is a safe, effective means of power generation. Still, I approached the issue with an open mind and tried to be objective with all the data given. Although I reached the conclusion that nuclear power is safe, I was able to appreciate the concerns of those who oppose it.

The extreme time durations needed to render plutonium waste "safe" really surprised me. The mathematical model, and graph, really brought out the impact of how long it really takes.

What I have found fascinating as I read these reflections and watch my students struggle with these assignments is the difficulty they have in interpreting their mathematical work. I have also gained an appreciation for the subtlety of the issues they confront. The questions surrounding the interpretation of their work become central to the course. First, students begin to recognize the importance of using data to inform their conclusions about important issues. Next, they learn to ask where the data they are working with came from. And they begin to think carefully about the implications of, and the limitations of, their mathematical models. Finally, they begin to learn that they do have the ability to use quantitative reasoning to draw their own conclusions, that they are not compelled to remain in a state of ignorance, and that they do not have to rely on experts. These are powerful learning outcomes—for both mathematics and citizenship.

The Power of the Assignment

The power of this assignment derives from the requirement that the students themselves actually work mathematically with Bethe's information. Of course, I could have simply told them that the nuclear waste must be kept safely out of the biosphere for 250,000 years and asked them to take this into account when they wrote their papers; but this approach would have had relatively little impact on their thinking. In a similar vein, Lincoln could have begun his speech by simply stating that twenty-one of the thirty-nine fathers had acted in support of the proposition that Congress had the power to regulate slavery in the territories, and then proceeded with the remainder of his speech. Such an approach would have been relatively ineffective; Lincoln's speech gains its power from the careful enumeration of the data. In the same way, for my students it is the act of grappling with the information, of constructing a table and graph, which forces them to *really* look at the issue, to focus on the implications of their work. They understand the implications of their work because they have struggled with it, and they believe their conclusions (as they should), because they have constructed the analysis that supports them. They are beginning to think in a different, more scientific, way.

I see a sort of symbiosis between the mathematics the students do for these assignments and the issues that the assignments address. On the one hand, the compelling nature of the issues motivates my students to study mathematics; the students are more engaged in the classroom and the mathematics becomes meaningful and engaging within the larger context. On the other hand, the mathematical work for each assignment, the focus on data and the mathematical treatment of that data, offers a grounded way to think about the underlying issues; it offers a perspective on the issues that is different in kind from that obtained by simply talking about or reading about them. As a result, students seem to be able to see beyond their preconceptions and to consider the problem anew.

Just as an analysis of the nuclear waste problem belongs at the core of any discussion of nuclear power, a look at data about the earth (whether it is carbon-dioxide levels, the shrinking of the Arctic ice cap, or any of the numerous other data sets available) should be central to discussions about global warming. And a careful study of world population patterns is essential for any analysis of the issue of population growth. Discussions of the effectiveness of the death penalty as a deterrent to crime, of the reintroduction of wolves into the Yellowstone ecosystem, of the effect of sex education on the rate of teenage pregnancies, and of the exhaustion of the world's petroleum reserves will all benefit from a careful examination of the data and evidence. Yet it is precisely such a careful look at the data that is largely missing from our national discourse on these and other important issues. Until we have a population that is capable of looking at important issues in this way, and that demands that our politicians address issues with analyses built on a solid foundation of data, I fear that our country will make unwise decisions about the important issues of the day.

Mathematics has given me a way to view the world, and I want to share that world view with my students. I want them to understand the importance of examining the data when looking at any question; I want them to know how to analyze the data, and how to draw appropriate conclusions from their analysis. The spreadsheet, combined with a knowledge of high school algebra, is a powerful tool for such an analysis, well within the reach of our students. And this is a liberating message for my students. They are learning that they can draw conclusions for themselves directly from the data. They do not have to rely on the opinions of others. They are emancipated from a political culture that values sound-bites over substance, anger over reason, emotion over thought. I want to use these tools of analysis, along with provocative exercises, to produce citizens who will demand that political decisions be based on data and evidence, who will demand a healthier political culture. I want to literally change the way in which our students think.

Dialogue

A COMMENTARY FROM DAVID GEELAN
School of Education, University of Queensland

It's something that I've ranted about on my blog in the past: people invoking the old "lies, damned lies, and statistics" quote to induce a kind of numerical nihilism—the idea that because statistics have been abused to mislead in the past, no statistics are ever to be trusted again, and all arguments that involve numbers or statistics are lies. Cars kill people, but we don't ban cars, because they are very useful. Rather, we try to mitigate the danger with care and skill and education.

Mike's chapter is the perfect antidote to the idea that mathematical evidence is no longer useful or trustworthy. Rather than abandoning the use of quantitative evidence in making judgments about social issues, the appropriate response is to help citizens develop the knowledge, skill, and critical reasoning ability to judge the quality of numerical arguments. In teaching his students this kind of approach, Mike uses a number of rich, thoughtful contexts and specific mathematical skills to explore issues of global concern. Like Matt Fisher's chapter, Mike's work lifts students' attention from the circumstances of their own lives and helps them to develop a global vision.

I was also struck by the extent to which the discussion spread and broadened, and brought in a variety of social issues and forms of knowledge. Mike, like so many college teachers, is a broadly read person, very interested in the world around him and engaged with a wide variety of issues. As I read the chapter I could see how Mike felt liberated to bring more of himself, his personality and his interests, to the classroom; I have done the same in my courses, to good effect. He loves teaching calculus, but a lot of that love is due to its power as an analytical tool. He also loves to discuss ideas, and this approach allowed the focus of the course itself to lift from specific mathematical knowledge and skills to apply those skills to real world problems, richly defined.

A COMMENTARY FROM RONA TAMIKO HALUALANI
Department of Communication Studies, San Jose State University

In his interesting chapter, Mike Burke highlights the power of data and numerical evidence for his students in a mathematics course. Mike pushes beyond the disciplinary presentation of data "as is" to the underlying issues, questions, and contexts around such data (the origins of the data, conflicting presentations of data, unreliable and invalid uses of data). Math students are thus encouraged to complete calculations but then push beyond that to think about the data in context of an issue—an issue that they had formed opinions and preconceptions about in a "pre-data" stage. Students must therefore go beyond the numbers and piece together what may be unseen and influencing the very data that show up on their tables.

Similar to the notion of culture as fixed (as discussed in my own chapter), our society's overreliance on data and numbers as absolute truths cultivates a passive approach for citizens to interface on real issues. For example, what accounts for a country's financial crisis? Why have there been massive price hikes and then de-escalating prices on gas in the country? What is the rate of global warming and climate change for our world? How much does an unregulated immigration stance cost us in terms of the economy and population overflow? What will our multicultural society look like in 2040? These issues can all be understood and framed in terms of numerical data and calculations. However, the key elements, conditions, and contexts surrounding and informing such data and calculations require more thought, processing, and question-posing on the part of citizens. This is the kind of engaged practice that Mike strives to create among his students. It is the kind of practice that all citizens and societal members should be encouraged to invoke.

Survey data and formulae are rarely questioned or second-guessed in the Western world; only narratives, first-person accounts, and interview data are cast with suspicion. Why is that? Why have we reached a point at which numerical data can be so easily and widely accepted (and unquestioned) and that it becomes novel for us to invite our students to articulate what is behind, beneath, and around the data? We have to explicitly authorize ourselves and our students to re-engage who they are in relation to evidence. Citizenship should always necessitate the recognition of value-laden data and evidence and the importance of engaging one's values, expectations, and perspectives when interfacing with any social issue in the face of any kind of evidence (even seemingly certain, irrefutable data). As a social scientist, I contend that science is never completely value-free; that numbers are never without human intervention or influence; that statistics are never prima facie or "evident." To remind our students of this and how this makes the social world (and their role in it as critical citizens) more compelling stands as an exciting challenge for us in the academy.

A REPLY FROM MICHAEL C. BURKE

Whoa! What am I to make of this? David and Rona offer seemingly contradictory responses to the work I describe in my chapter. David describes, with some evident frustration, a common attitude toward arguments that rely on numbers and statistics. This is the tendency on the part of many to distrust, even to reject out of hand, all such arguments because statistics have in the past been used to mislead. Rona laments, to the contrary, that all too often numbers and statistics enjoy a privileged position in our dialogue, that numbers cited in support of a position are accepted implicitly, never examined, never challenged. How am I to reconcile these two conflicting responses to the use of quantitative information and quantitative methods in an analysis of an important issue?

Actually, I think that, although the two responses described by David and Rona are indeed contradictory, these responses are nevertheless of a piece; David and Rona describe for us two opposing reactions to the same underlying problem. Both impulses (the impulse to reflexively reject the argument and the impulse to implicitly accept the argument) are natural responses for our students (and our citizens) when they are asked to make a judgment that they do not feel competent to make. Specifically, they are asked to evaluate quantitative claims, yet they lack the experience with and the feel for quantitative argument. If we perceive quantitative arguments as too complicated to evaluate, too technical to understand, best left to the experts, then our ignorance leaves us with two possible responses: either the complete rejection or the unquestioned acceptance of the conclusions of these arguments. The term "professional incompetence" that Rebecca and David have used elsewhere in this volume (in the commentaries on David's chapter) fits perfectly here.

David and Rona have identified a central problem, a problem that lies at the core of the work I have been engaged in: the tendency of our students (and our citizens) to fail to consider a scientific perspective when they are thinking about the important issues of the day. I am most interested in the fact that our students do not use mathematics as a tool for the analysis of critical issues, of course, but their failure to adopt any scientific perspective at all is equally distressing. For example, in the public sphere one can listen to an entire debate about global warming, consisting mainly of the familiar talking points used by both sides, without ever hearing someone suggest that perhaps we should take a careful look at the data. I suspect that our students do not see that the mathematics they are taught is relevant to an analysis of such issues because we rarely (never?) explicitly make those connections in our teaching. We expect our students to, somehow, naturally make these connections. And so my approach has been to create assignments that require the use of mathematics to explore important environmental, political, and social issues.

As they progress through the course, my students are gaining experience with quantitative thinking, and through this experience they are developing a feel for quantitative argument. I am convinced that we must encourage our students, science majors or not, to adopt an appropriate scientific perspective when they think about compelling issues of global importance; I hope that by requiring the use of mathematics to explore such issues, I am making some progress toward that goal.

Works Cited

Abraham Lincoln's Cooper Union address. 2005. http://www.c-span.org/Lincoln200years/video/?title=prepresidency (accessed May 25, 2009).

Bethe, H. A. 1976. The necessity of fission power. *Scientific American* 234 (1): 21–31.

Cohen, David, with Theodore B. Lee and David Sklar. 2006. *Precalculus with unit-circle trigonometry*. Belmont, Calif.: Thomson Brooks/Cole.

Corry, John A. 2003. *Lincoln at Cooper Union: The speech that made him president.* Xlibris.

Huber, Mary Taylor, and Pat Hutchings. 2004. *Integrative learning: Mapping the terrain.* Washington, D.C.: Association of American Colleges and Universities.

Lincoln, Abraham. 1860. Lincoln at Cooper Union by Abraham Lincoln. http://www.gutenberg.org/etext/26250 (accessed May 25, 2009).

Steen, Lynn Arthur. 2004. *Achieving quantitative literacy: An urgent challenge for higher education.* The Mathematical Association of America: MAA Notes #62.

Stewart, James. 2000. *Calculus: Concepts and contexts.* Belmont, Calif.: Thomson Brooks/Cole.

8

Science, Technology, and Understanding

Teaching the Teachers of Citizens of the Future

David Geelan

In late 2006, Southeast Queensland, where I live, was in the grip of a drought, with severe water restrictions that were on the verge of becoming more severe. Brisbane had Level Three water restrictions: gardens could only be watered with a bucket and cars couldn't be washed with a hose. Prisoners in the city's jails had the length of their showers reduced. A city 100 km or so further inland, Toowoomba, had Level Four restrictions, with no watering of gardens allowed at all and other restrictions on personal water use.

The citizens of Toowoomba voted in a referendum on whether to recycle treated wastewater back into the reservoir from which the town drew its drinking water. The treatment process yielded water cleaner than that already in the reservoir on every chemical and biological measure, so opposition to the recycling was essentially emotive ("drinking sewage") rather than scientifically informed. And there was no alternative source of water available. Nonetheless the motion to recycle water was defeated at the referendum, leaving the town in a desperate situation.

Science Education and Citizenship

This story is an example of democracy in action, but it's also a cautionary tale that illustrates the importance of scientific understanding for informed engagement in civic life. So many of the issues faced by the middle school and high school students my teacher education students will teach after they graduate have some scientific component—global climate change, nuclear energy, bioengineering and nanotechnology, to name just a few—that helping them to develop the skills of scientific thinking seems crucial to the whole concept of citizenship. This chapter explores some of my commitments and experiences in my fifteen years as a teacher of science teachers, and in particular the ways in which I have tried to integrate a concern for educating scientifically informed and engaged future citizens into my teacher education practice.

Part of my understanding of civil society and my political commitments developed out of a research project I worked on in Perth, Australia, in 2000 and 2001. My colleagues John Wallace and Bill Louden were studying the ways physics education perpetuates advantage in society.[1] Science education, which I had always seen as socially neutral or as a tool for social mobility, was strongly implicated in the broader social processes by which opportunity is held out disproportionately to those who already have the most options and resources. This developing understanding was coupled with dramatic political shifts in Australia and the United States over the past decade, accelerated by the events of September 2001 and the subsequent wars and social changes. The Howard government in Australia had been in power for around six years in 2000, and its privatization-focused agenda—one that very intentionally strip-mined social services and public education—was accelerating the trends we were observing in our research.

The development and growth of the Internet and web discussion forums also played an important role in my evolving view of citizenship and science education. The fact that I have friends in countries all over the world with whom I regularly discuss ideas around education has definitely informed my perspective on a wide variety of issues. Beyond that, the web is a reminder that we are part of a global society and are global citizens, and that my decisions (and those of my students and their students) in Australia affect the lives of my friends in Mexico and Denmark and South Africa.

As these commitments have changed my outlook on the world, I have begun to incorporate them into my teaching practice, attempting always to be aware that my classes are pluralistic and that my students have a wide range of perspectives of their own on these issues. Indoctrination is the danger that attends any attempt to incorporate social issues in science education courses—but eschewing such discussion can itself indoctrinate students into the belief that science is objective, ahistorical, and unrelated to social and ethical concerns.

Global Citizenship

Citizenship, as I'm coming to understand it, is almost antithetical to nationalism and even patriotism. Perhaps that's linked with an awareness of globalization as an inexorable process.

David Smith (1999) has identified three meanings often assigned to the term "globalization" (this is my paraphrase):

Globalization One (G1)—movement for "free trade" and free flow of global capital (with its associated growth in the power and influence of transnational corporations);

Globalization Two (G2)—public reactions to G1, both adaptations and resistance; and

Globalization Three (G3)—global dialogues for a sustainable human future.

We could say that G1 is couched in the language of economics and of rights, and that G2 tends to fall into those same ways of thinking and speaking because it is just a reaction to G1. G3, however, is about our responsibilities to the planet, to one another, and to those less fortunate than we are. Perhaps that is a way of saying that we are citizens of our families, our local communities, and the world, much more than we are citizens of nations or states, and that this (arguably) already existing state of affairs will become more and more obvious in the next couple of decades.

Climate change is a specific headline example of an issue to which citizens are expected to respond. It also stands as an icon for many other current and developing environmental, social and techn(olog)ical issues—including biotechnology, genetically modified organisms and foods, nanotechnology, pollution, space exploration, military spending, medical technology and spending (I shouldn't have started a list because I can't enumerate all of them—and the really dramatic ones we might not even be able to see yet). Climate change is also an example of the kinds of science-related problems that cannot be appropriately addressed exclusively in the nation-state framework, and in that sense is an indicator of the need for a trans- and post-national image of citizenship in order to allow problems to be engaged at the appropriate level.

Educating Citizens

Being a citizen, then, means being able to participate in an *informed* way in the ongoing social conversation around the issues and problems—as well as the opportunities and the broad vision—facing a society. That is, a citizen seeks out information and ideas, and makes decisions/takes positions based on evidence. A citizen is able to argue for those decisions and positions, as well as listen to and

critically evaluate the arguments of others. Numeracy and the ability to critically read graphs and statistics and evaluate evidence are also part of informed
citizenship—and an antidote to the growing trend to discount *all* numerical
evidence as "lies, damned lies, and statistics." Mike Burke's chapter in this volume
about helping students to develop the mathematical skills and a disposition to
engage in this kind of critical discussion of evidence describes an essential facet of
this process. An appreciation of and ability to deal with complexity and ambiguity, rather than flee to simplistic solutions, is crucial—and is, I believe, very much
under threat at the moment in Western societies.

Citizenship can be seen as antithetical to uncritical consumerism but essential
to critical involvement in consumption/production/life. That is, informed citizens make *conscious* choices about what they do and do not buy, use and discard,
and about energy usage and a range of other matters, rather than uncritically fall
into the patterns of consumption set by society and the advertising industry. In
this sense a citizen has an ideal view of how society could be improved (and what
counts as improvement is itself a matter for debate and discussion), while recognizing that ideals are something we work toward in our daily choices but never
fully reach.

Incorporating a concern for citizenship in my own teaching practices has
been a gradual process that has developed alongside the development of my own
skills in and perspectives on teaching itself. When I was a junior high and
high school science teacher I developed a commitment to social constructivist/
constructionist perspectives on knowledge and learning.[2] This led me to consider students' existing knowledge (conceived of as rich, well-elaborated schemes
for making sense of their experiences in the world, not a simple list of "school
science facts" to be learned) and to think about how students develop new
scientific ways of understanding the world through experiment and experience.
That approach to teaching and learning science naturally places science education within the context of students' lives and of topical issues like climate change
or the Toowoomba water referendum.

The challenges of teaching in the light of such commitments, then, have to do
with managing the demands of the syllabus and the state, as well as the expectations and aspirations of students and parents, and with finding teaching practices
that honor all of those things. It involves helping to develop students' understanding of science as a way (not "The Way") of thinking about real human and
environmental situations and the actions and decisions those situations require.

The history of my own teaching over the past eighteen years, first in school
classrooms and then in university teacher education classrooms, has been the
history of my attempts—in a reflective, ongoing process of attempting to link my
personal theories with public theories in education (Griffiths and Tann 1992)—to
resolve some of the "living contradictions" (Whitehead 1989) that I experience.

These include the contradiction between, on the one hand, my aspirations to offer "science education for all/science education for citizenship" and, on the other, my actual practices (within the web of constraints arising in the situation and in myself).

Science, Technology, Society, and Environment

Science, Technology, Society, and Environment (STSE) approaches to science education, coupled with the idea of "curricular emphases," have provided part of the theoretical framework that has supported this ongoing change in my practices.

The Science, Technology, and Society (STS) movement began in the 1970s and has been influential (though more at the edges than the center) in science education since. It is focused on placing science education in social context and on exploring the ways in which science and technology interact in informing and changing our society. More recently the concept of "Environment" has been added to the mix to yield "STSE." The STSE approach involves more than adding content to science education courses; it is a different way of approaching science education that ties it much more strongly to the ways in which students will be expected to use their scientific understanding as they act in the world as citizens, as well as to their own current experiences of the world around them.

There tends to be a key tension in science education: on one hand, science education is about preparing the small proportion (around 10 percent in most Western countries) of our students who will go on to pursue university study in science and careers in science-related fields. On the other, science education is about preparing *all* students to live as citizens in society, a perspective often described as "science for all." The concept of "scientific literacy" is a disputed one, with a variety of definitions, but sufficient understanding of science to function well in society for all citizens is a worthy goal. Sadly, under many definitions we find that only around 10 percent (probably the same group as go into science careers) of citizens can be considered to be scientifically literate. This dual focus in science education, coupled with the fact that it tends to be the "preparation of future scientists" rather than the "science for all" emphasis that predominates, means science education has tended to be much less effective than we would hope in its role of preparing citizens.

The challenge is in finding space within the content-packed curricula of science courses—content which tends to be state-mandated—to teach all students the skills and ways of thinking that constitute "scientific literacy" or "science for citizenship." Matt Fisher's and Mike Burke's chapters address this same tension between packed curricula and teaching for citizenship—and also illustrate the importance of teaching science ideas in the context of specific real-world problems and of students' own life experiences, rather than as a separate, add-on component of the course.

Curricular Emphases

One means toward the goal of science education for citizenship is the idea of "curricular emphases." This approach was developed by Douglas Roberts (1995) in Canada, and developed further by Frank Jenkins at the University of Alberta. I owe Frank an enormous debt of gratitude for the huge influence he has had on my own development as a science educator, and his work on curricular emphases is a key facet of my approach to science education for citizenship.

Teaching science and planning for teaching are already very complex processes, and state-mandated science curricula, particularly in the senior years of high school, are often tightly prescriptive and contain large amounts of "essential" science content to be taught. In such an environment it is difficult for teachers to find the time to attend to all of the dimensions of STSE all the time. The concept of "curricular emphases" is to give each planned unit of teaching an "emphasis" that underlies it. The emphases essentially parallel the dimensions of the STSE approach:

- Units with a "nature of science" emphasis include the history and philosophy of science and some of the epistemological "rules of the game" as a way of complementing and contextualizing the scientific content.
- Units with a "technology" emphasis explore the complex and dynamic relationships between science and technology.
- Units with a "science and society" emphasis look at the social impacts, benefits, and consequences of the associated science, and also address the "environment" element.

In planning a science curriculum, teachers can use the curricular emphases concept as a way to attend to as many of these issues as possible by choosing one of these emphases as a theme for each unit of study. I very explicitly teach my teacher education students about the "curricular emphases" concept and method of unit planning. I see this as a manageable incremental step, an evolutionary rather than revolutionary approach to change. It is too easy to burden young teachers with the aspiration to fundamentally transform science education in ways that accord with their strongly held values and to serve the goal of teaching for global citizenship, but that are outside the scope of their power and influence as beginning teachers in a system with enormous institutional inertia. Such aspirations, and their frustration, may well be part of the reason half of the new teachers we graduate leave the profession within five years. The curricular emphases approach enables us to "get there from here" in steps that a teacher can conduct in his/her own classroom.

This approach also serves the purpose of allowing teachers to honor the goals and aspirations of the students they teach and of the students' parents. Parents understand the processes by which science education acts as a gatekeeper for opportunity, and understandably want their children to successfully pass through the gate. This means that any approach to teaching science for all that fails to also deliver high-quality science education for future scientists and excellent outcomes on high-stakes tests is doomed from its inception. Curricular emphases offer teachers a way to achieve "both-and" outcomes, rather than to be placed on the horns of an "either-or" dilemma.

It is quite possible that once they leave my classroom and come under the pressures of packed curricula, jaded colleagues, and external high-stakes standardized tests, many of the teachers I teach revert to the content-focused approaches to science teaching that they have experienced in their own school and undergraduate science education. I continue to believe, however, that exposure to these approaches to teaching—and to my own attempts to model an approach to science education that exemplifies these features—has a role in preparing science educators who will at least have a predisposition to be committed to science education for all and for citizenship.

Science Teacher Education

The education of science teachers follows a number of different paths in different jurisdictions and for particular students, but typically involves the completion of a science degree followed by (or concurrent with) the completion of some studies in educational theory and practice. My own courses in Canada and Australia over the past seven years have been in the nexus of these two fields—neither science content courses nor "generic" education courses offered to all teacher education students, but specific courses in science education. These correspond to the process of beginning to develop Shulman's (1986) "pedagogical content knowledge."

From 2002 to 2006 I taught an intensive five-week set of three linked courses at the University of Alberta for fourth- and fifth-year science education majors, who immediately after my courses went into classrooms for nine weeks of student teaching. My courses involved helping students integrate the knowledge of science gained from their science courses with their knowledge of educational practices gained from education courses and from their own lives as students.

Since moving back to Australia in 2006 I have been teaching a similar course for physics education students as well as a science teacher preparation course for middle school teachers. The two courses are quite different. The physics education students all have at least a bachelor's degree in physics, but many have honors degrees or even PhDs. They are committed to science and knowledgeable about it, and are typically the kinds of people who enjoyed science and did well in it at school. They will be teaching small, selected groups of students who are similar to themselves in many ways, and who are also good at science and interested in science. Student teachers in the middle years program form a much broader cross section of the community. They are training to be generalists. The usual middle schooling (usually defined as grades 6–9 but sometimes expanded to grades 4–10) approach is one of generalist teachers teaching in all subject areas, sometimes with the support of specialists in areas such as music, science, and languages other than English. The students in my classes have a wide range of experience with and knowledge of science. Some—perhaps 5 to 10 percent— have completed science degrees or have very strong science backgrounds. The majority have at least completed high school science, but another 5–10 percent have virtually no science background, and some students find science very scary and dread having to teach it. My task in this course to help them develop specific skills in teaching science but also to demystify science and help the student teachers feel that they understand it and can teach it.

I'd like to briefly revisit the issue of "science for all" vs. "science for future scientists" in relation to the two levels at which my teacher education students will teach. Teachers in the middle school group will have the full cross section of students in their classes, because they are generalists and because science education is mandated for all students up until grade 10 in Queensland. Their focus, therefore, is more strongly toward the issues of science for all, scientific literacy, and preparing all students with the scientific knowledge, skills, and attitudes that they need to participate as active citizens in society. They also have considerable freedom in terms of the syllabus requirements and the government mandates, the amount of time spent on science learning, the ways in which science is integrated with other subject areas, and the contexts and approaches used to teach science. The syllabi for the other subject areas they teach are also concerned with citizenship and with situating students' learning within their communities, and these teachers typically develop good community ties and skills in connecting learning to students' worlds.

The students who go on to teach chemistry or physics at the senior high school level (grades 11 and 12 in Queensland) are likely to have a stronger focus on teaching science for future scientists, because the students who are in their classes have chosen to study these subjects based on their abilities and interests, and most will go on to study science at university in some form. These students are typically easier to teach, because they are motivated and want to study these subjects. The challenge for these teachers, though, is that they must *also* prepare their students for citizenship. While these students will achieve a high level of scientific knowledge, there is a qualitative difference between the specialized scientific knowledge and skills required by a scientist and the more general knowledge and ability to argue and reason using scientific evidence needed to become an engaged citizen. It is easier for my students in Queensland to achieve these dual mandates in their teaching, both during their teaching practica in our courses and once they begin their careers, than it was for those I taught in Alberta, where the syllabus was much more tightly specified and traditional. The Alberta situation is probably more typical of the experience of high school science education in most Western jurisdictions, and I will draw on some specific examples from my teacher education with those students in the remainder of this chapter.

Evidence and Pedagogy

The evidence for my assertions about the value of complementing the teaching of science content knowledge with curricular emphases on the nature of science, technology, and the relationship of science and society comes from my observations of the students in my teacher education classes. I have had a number of opportunities to observe these students teaching science classes for middle school and high school students during their practice teaching sessions, and to observe the ways they incorporate the kinds of knowledge and critical reasoning that are relevant for preparing their students to be informed, participatory citizens. (Incidentally, two graduates from my courses have also become teachers of my own daughters, giving me another perspective.) But I have not had an opportunity to conduct more formal analyses of the impacts of my students' teaching on the learning of their students, and do not intend to make claims about that learning in this chapter. It seems highly plausible that if teachers are teaching with a strong commitment to science education for all and science education for citizenship, and if they are prepared with skills and approaches that facilitate their efforts to embody this commitment in their practices, students will develop the relevant knowledge and critical thinking skills to a greater extent than they would without such teaching. The evidence presented here, however, relates to the teaching approaches of the students in my teacher education classes.

My own teacher education pedagogy is based, as far as possible, on modeling the kinds of teaching that I am encouraging my students to develop. There is not a direct one-to-one match between my approaches and activities and theirs, because they are teaching high school or middle school students with adolescent concerns and levels of behavior and attitude, while I am teaching university students, and for a number of other contextual reasons. But it is clear that the underlying commitments—to learning in authentic social contexts, to experiment and experience as keys to learning, and to developing scientific ways of knowing and thinking—play out in my teaching. This occurs both as a way of modeling these things for my students—both "practicing what I preach" and "showing as well as telling"—and because teaching in this way embodies my own values and commitments. Teaching out of who I am, and more fully embodying my values in my practices, is what makes teaching the engaging and fulfilling activity that it continues to be through the years.

I use a variety of simple experiments—everything from using red cabbage juice as an acid-base indicator, to using simple pendulums to determine the value of the acceleration due to gravity, to sorting the shoes of class members to illustrate classification of living things—with the middle school teachers. The goal is not to teach the underlying science content—some of the students already have it, but the course is simply too brief to allow the teaching of much science content for the others, so they will need to develop their content knowledge in other ways. Rather, the point is to address teachers' knowledge of the rules of scientific knowledge and empirical experiments, of how knowledge claims are made and tested in science. There is a focus on graphing and analyzing data, and on using evidence to explore social issues.

I use fewer experiments with the high school physics teachers I teach, since their content knowledge is stronger, but I have them set up experiments themselves and teach other teacher education students how to take measurements and about the underlying science concepts. With this group I focus both on modeling a wide variety of specific teaching strategies and approaches and on explicitly addressing the "rules of the knowledge game." I also require them to research and present to their colleagues in the class something about a new physics discovery from the past decade—a kind of antidote to the fact that so much high school physics dates back well over a century.

Examples of Curricular Emphases-based Teaching Plans

Rather than focus on my students' self-reports of changes to their knowledge and commitments resulting from their involvement in my classes, I have chosen to present three specific examples of the ways in which they planned rich science units to be taught to their students, and of the ways in which they taught those units. I have tried to explain them as clearly as possible in order to provide practical examples of the curricular emphases approach to planning in science education and the ways in which these units of work lend themselves to developing in my students' students the kinds of knowledge, skills, and attitudes that prepare them to be scientifically literate, engaged citizens. As always, I'm humbled and amazed by my students' commitment, energy, and creativity.

Cassandra's (all student teacher names used are pseudonyms) unit was for grade 10 science, for a topic introducing the basics of chemistry. It had a Science or Nature of Science curricular emphasis. It might seem redundant to have an emphasis on science in a science unit, but the specific focus of the Nature of Science emphasis is on introducing students to the epistemological foundations of science, the kinds of evidence and arguments that are relevant when making and defending scientific knowledge claims. Frank Jenkins refers to this process as letting students in on "the rules of the knowledge game," and suggests that failing to do so often means that students are more focused on trying to guess the rules of the game we are trying to get them to play—which is often reduced, from their perspective, to attempting to guess what is in the teacher's head—than on knowing the rules and actually playing the "game" of science. In particular, in relation to the issue of science education for citizenship, a good, explicit understanding of the rules of the knowledge game allows students (as citizens) to know when someone is cheating: they are equipped with the skills to evaluate for themselves the knowledge claims made in advertisements, media reports, and web pages. They know what kinds of evidence are appropriate for judging the claims made about a dietary supplement or medicine, or the health effects of living close to power lines.

Cassandra's unit was based on chemical change, but her planning drew on an understanding of the rest of the students' science program for the year, as well as of what they learned last year and earlier in their school career. Her plan included a section explicitly considering who these students were, and what experiences and aspirations they might share, as well as some ways in which they differed. It included about 25 percent lab activities, as well as guest speakers, video snippets, student presentations and even some student-written and -presented dramatization of issues relating to chemicals in the environment. Most chemical concepts were explicitly linked to everyday contexts, and Cassandra knew that one of the "Big Ideas" underlying chemistry teaching is that "everything is made out of chemicals": chemistry isn't just about colorful solutions in sterile glass bottles in the lab, but about explaining the properties of the materials all around the students.

Student discussions formed one important set of activities in the unit, and Cassandra focused on explicitly teaching the students the skills of making scientific claims and supporting them with scientific evidence. These were not "bull sessions" or opinion-sharing discussions, in the main, when they focused on scientific issues, but hard-headed scientific conversations in which students learned real skills in evaluating and synthesizing their knowledge and a respect for evidence and honesty. Other discussions focused on social issues such as pollution, and did focus more on students' opinions, since these issues involve balancing complex social, environmental, and economic interests and students can legitimately arrive at different conclusions about what should be done in a particular situation. It is important that students are informed but never indoctrinated about social issues, but it is also important that teachers realize that there *are* correct answers to *scientific* questions, and that this care about indoctrination does not lead to an "anything goes, whatever you believe is right" approach to science.

Cassandra intentionally planned to use a variety of different teaching strategies and student activities, both to avoid boredom (for herself as well as for the students) and to appeal to the interests and learning styles of as many students as possible. She saw her role as "lighting a fire rather than filling a bucket," and measured her success in teaching in part through her students' attitudes toward further science learning at the end of the unit: if they understood what they had learned in this topic but evinced no desire to learn more, she felt as though she needed to revise her approach.

Michael's unit was for a grade 12 physics class, and focused on subatomic particles and the nature of matter. The curricular emphasis chosen was Science and Society, specifically the history of human understanding of the nature of the atom in relation to other historical events. Direct experience of subatomic particles is simply impossible, even for working scientists; all our evidence for the structure of the atom is indirect evidence, drawn from inferences based on observing the interaction of atoms with one another.

Michael made extensive use of computer-based simulations in the unit: his students still did around 25 percent of their classes "in the lab," but in this instance the relevant laboratory was the computer lab as the students worked with well-designed interactive simulations of the subatomic world, and particularly of the key experiments in the history of scientific understanding of the atom. Students explored J. J. Thomson's experiments with cathode ray tubes in discovering the electron, Rutherford's alpha particle scattering experiment, Millikan's oil drop experiment, and the photoelectric effect.

Students studied the history of Einstein's key papers in 1905 and 1915, and recognized that World War I formed the historical backdrop to the later part of this period. They watched video of the play *Copenhagen*, by Michael Frayn, about the conflict between Bohr and Heisenberg and the ethics of the atomic bomb, and considered whether perhaps Lise Meitner might have shared the Nobel Prize awarded to Otto Hahn if she had been male. They considered the paradox and the fate of Schroedinger's cat, and arguably developed knowledge of quantum phenomena and theory that went beyond what was required by the syllabus. In keeping with the Science and Society emphasis they debated the use of nuclear power and the associated issues of risk and waste (the approach described in Mike Burke's chapter would have fit very neatly into Michael's class), and used both scientific evidence and social and economic information to make cases for and against the use of nuclear power as a partial solution to climate change caused by the use of fossil fuels as the predominant energy source.

Michael is a self-described "geek" and has an enormous fund of anecdotes and applications in his head—for pretty much any scientific innovation or experiment, he can tell a story or link it to a technology. He embraced the idea of "teaching out of who he is," and used this knowledge and ability to make his lessons compelling for his students and to link the scientific concepts learned to technological inventions and social issues in ways that supported both their scientific learning and their ability to apply that learning to their lives.

Wytze's unit was focused on electric forces and fields. It was for a grade 12 physics class and had a Technology curricular emphasis. This meant that Wytze taught the scientific content, but as far as possible linked it with the various technological innovations that apply those concepts. The unit also focused on helping students to understand the complex relationship between science and technology. They discussed, and dismissed, the idea that technology is simply applied science, recognizing that in many cases technologies (such as brewing and steelmaking) led the underlying science by millennia. They came to recognize that sometimes science is halted in its progress until the appropriate technologies are developed to allow the necessary experiments to be carried out, and studied examples as diverse as the use of the atomic clock to study special relativity and the development of high temperature superconductors. They studied the electrostatic issues implicit in the assembly of nanomaterials.

Wytze used a variety of different experiments in the classroom. Some used sophisticated apparatus, but many used the everyday materials found in the classroom such as small pieces of paper, plastic rulers, and students' hair. The use of everyday materials in experiments helps to link scientific understanding with students' everyday lives, and to take science out of the laboratory and into the world. I tend to advocate using everyday materials unless there is no alternative, rather than defaulting to using sophisticated but alien scientific apparatus.

The fact that the unit had a technology focus did not stop Wytze from including social and historical ideas in relation to technological development. Students studied the development of electricity and the lurid history of the conflict between Edison and Tesla over whether alternating or direct current would become the standard for household use. They recognized that the designation of electrons as negatively charged and of electric current as the flow of (nonexistent) positively charged particles was an arbitrary convention, and that in many ways life would be simpler if the opposite convention for charge had been chosen.

There are many other examples I could choose, and if space permitted I could talk more about the pedagogy that each of these beginning teachers brought to implementing these plans. In many ways, though, their attention to STSE in planning to teach set them up in such a way that it was easier and more natural for them to teach out of their own strengths and personalities, develop strong professional relationships with their students, and help their students to develop rich, fluid mental models of the scientific phenomena. Further, it helped the beginning teachers to help their students develop fuller understandings of the links between science and their lived experience: a necessary condition for scientifically engaged citizenship.

Educating all students in our schools in science so as to allow them to participate in our democracy in informed, engaged ways is an essential part of developing citizens for the twenty-first century. Science and technology, and their effects on society and the environment, pose increasing challenges for democratic societies around the world. An educated and engaged citizenry is essential to ensuring that these challenges are handled in ways that increase equity and opportunity for all.

Intriguingly, at the same time as the recycled water referendum was defeated by adult voters in Toowoomba, an informal poll of a large number of school students on the same issue was also conducted, and it was found that, had these students been the voters, the proposal to use recycled water would have been supported. My students and I can't take the credit for that, since as far as I know none of them teach in Toowoomba. This result suggests that science education in Queensland is *already* helping students to bring their science knowledge to bear on important social issues. I would argue, however, that approaches to science teaching and science teacher education that use a curricular emphases model to attend to the Science, Technology, Society, and Environment elements of science education have significant potential to offer a new focus on "science education for all" and "science education for citizenship."

Dialogue

A COMMENTARY FROM REBECCA S. NOWACEK
Department of English, Marquette University

As I read David Geelan's chapter, I found myself reliving some of my best experiences as a student in science classes and reflecting on their importance in new ways. David's point that science classes serve a powerful gate-keeping function reminded me how grateful I am to have had the high school physics teacher I did. My current academic home is an English department, and the humanities have always been a comfortable place for me intellectually. That was true during high school as well. But I signed up for physics and found myself, to put it kindly, in over my head. The exact content of those classes and labs, so many years ago, are lost in a haze. Did my very patient and good-humored physics teacher,

Mr. Bechtel, use a curricular emphases approach? I can't say. But I do know that I left that class feeling like I could learn physics and I could understand the science involved and I could see how it applied in my everyday life. It didn't come easily— it took a lot of work and a lot of persistence—but I left that class knowing I could understand (at least to some degree) some important and complicated scientific principles. Even if I hadn't entirely mastered the "rules of the knowledge game," I now recognized that there *were* such rules for making knowledge—and indeed that scientific knowledge was made, not simply discovered as an eternal unquestionable truth. And *that* knowledge, more than anything else that I might have gained from the class, has been of immeasurable value.

Such knowledge can help students avoid what Cheryl Geisler (1994) calls "professional incompetence"—an attitude that Geisler argues is the result of a general education curriculum structured to teach students just enough about any given subject to convince them that it is a complex matter best left to professionals who possess an expert knowledge simply not available to the rest of us. It is a sense of professional incompetence that leads citizens to look at a complex scientific and/or social problem, shrug our shoulders, and conclude that it can only be understood and solved by the "experts"—and to conclude that we have no way to understand or monitor or challenge the conclusions of those experts.

One benefit of the curricular emphases approach to science education that David describes is, I suspect, students who refuse to accept scientific professional incompetence, students who have some of the basic tools and aptitudes to engage critically with expert knowledge. In some cases, they may empower citizens to negotiate contradictory expert claims. In other cases, they may enable citizens to reconsider the kind of gut instinct that would lead them to refuse recycled water, even at tremendous social cost. In all cases, I think as students and teachers we have much to learn from the idea of making the rules of the knowledge game visible and inviting our students—even our most humanities-oriented students— to see themselves as citizens capable of understanding science.

A COMMENTARY FROM HOWARD TINBERG
Department of English, Bristol Community College

Early in this essay David Geelan notes the tension between teaching science for future scientists and teaching science for all. Don't educators have to choose? As David correctly notes, the question in itself suggests flawed "either/or" thinking. Resolving the pedagogical challenge becomes more than an academic matter if we consider that an engaged citizenry depends on access to good science in order to make good public policy. Access does not necessarily derive, however, from reliance on others to make the hard and informed decision to recycle treated (and perfectly safe) water during a drought. Each of us needs a way of thinking scientifically to resolve dilemmas that inevitably confront us as individual citizens. That said, and David is right to emphasize this point, the responsibility of citizenship must transcend nation and state and even local community, as climate change has just begun to teach us.

The key to promoting global citizenship, ironically, is to ground science in the lived experience of the individual citizen. Unless and until we see ourselves as constructed by science, we stand little chance of seeing the utility of scientific knowledge for the larger, global community. David notes the effective use by science educators of "every day materials . . . such as small pieces of paper, plastic rulers, and students' hair" to conduct experiments in the classroom. Pedagogically, science educators, David suggests, would do well to employ narrative in their science classes. By that he means, teach science as a meaningful set of interconnected phenomena rather than as discrete and fragmented facts.

We all too often view science itself as discretely removed from history and from the comings and goings of nations and individuals. Such a way of thinking, as history has demonstrated, can lead to unethical and tragic behaviors—indeed, to Auschwitz itself. David's own journey, from regarding science as ethically neutral to positioning it within historical and social contexts, inspires us all to undertake similar journeys. Science needs to be seen as an altogether human endeavor, designed to assist us in resolving altogether humanly constructed challenges.

A REPLY FROM DAVID GEELAN

The notion of "professional incompetence" that Rebecca introduces is a very nice way of framing many of the concerns that have driven my attempts to understand and develop my science teacher education practices over the years. Coupled with Howard's emphasis on developing students' global understanding of science and the world through having them engage with their local perspectives, it also encapsulates some of the issues that I've been discussing with my students recently.

I talked about not despairing of the value of evidence and of our ability to make decisions about complex social and scientific issues. There seem to me to be several reasons why citizens in our societies fall into the apathy that makes them feel disempowered to take an active role in such decision-making.

One is professional incompetence—the idea that science is simply too difficult for a lay person to understand. The strong emphasis on the selection and training of future scientists, at the expense of "science education for all," is definitely implicated in the development of these attitudes: we implicitly tell our students and future citizens that 90 percent of them simply aren't smart enough.

A second is an increasing sense that all the important decisions are made by the markets, or by transnational corporations or (many people believe) by shadowy cabals, and that the individual citizen cannot have a meaningful role. This is a challenge to democratic societies that goes far beyond science education, and empowering citizens with knowledge and understanding of the scientific issues is necessary but not sufficient to engage them in being active citizens.

A third influence is a profound cynicism on the part of young people about the motivations and agendas of scientists. An interesting recent study in Brisbane by Clare Christensen (2007) into the ways young adult students address the issue of the brain tumor risk from using cell phones in the face of apparently conflicting scientific evidence shows that scientists are seen as essentially driven entirely by funding rather than by curiosity or the quest for knowledge. Their activities are seen as being about searching for evidence to support their opinions, rather than finding evidence empirically in the physical world. Understanding scientific methods and peer review will help to some extent with these issues, but looking at the attitudes and values of scientists, and perhaps interacting with some actual scientists to come to understand what really drives them, might be important antidotes to this attitude.

I suspect to some extent these attitudes on the part of citizens arise from a phenomenon of "Fox News"-ing issues and debates. This can be described as the idea that all issues have two (and only two) sides, aligned with particular political philosophies, and that as long as both sides are given equal time, the most extreme and ill-founded claims can be made without being tested. This approach claims that everyone, all the time, has a political agenda, and their actions can only be understood in terms of that agenda.

While modern approaches to the history and philosophy of science eschew science's earlier claims to complete impersonal, objective, value-neutral knowledge, perhaps we have moved too far in exploring the human, fallible, and constructed nature of scientific knowledge. Although we don't know what it is yet, there is a right answer about whether consistently using a cell phone close to the brain increases cancer risks. While the ways in which the question is explored may be human constructions, they do not predetermine the answer, if the science is "done right." The issues I'm struggling with in my teaching of science teachers right now are related to how we empower students to understand science more fully, in all its aspects, so that they have realistic expectations about its flaws, but also a greater respect for and understanding of its value to our societies.

Notes

1. In brief, wealthier students tend to pass and excel in physics courses at a much higher rate than less advantaged students, and physics tends to be a "gatekeeper" course for professional programs leading to high paying careers in medicine, engineering and architecture.

2. These emphasize the idea that knowledge is constructed within the learner and within the social groups in the classroom, on the foundations of their existing knowledge, rather than directly transmitted from teacher to students.

Works Cited

Christensen, Clare 2007. *Waiting for certainty: Young people, mobile phones and uncertain science.* PhD diss., Queensland University of Technology, Brisbane.

Geisler, Cheryl. 1994. Literacy and expertise in the academy. *Language and Learning in the Disciplines* 1(1): 35–57.

Griffiths, Morwenna, and Sarah Tann. 1992. Using reflective practice to link personal and public theories. *Journal of Education for Teaching* 18(1): 69–84.

Roberts, Douglas A. 1995. Building companion meanings into school science programs: Keeping the logic straight about curriculum emphases. *Nordisk Pedagogik (Journal of Nordic Educational Research)* 15(2): 108–124.

Shulman, Lee S. 1986. Those who understand: Knowledge growth in teaching. *Educational Researcher* (February 1986): 4–14.

Smith, David G. 1999. *Pedagon: Interdisciplinary essays in the human sciences, pedagogy, and culture.* New York: Peter Lang.

Whitehead, A. J. 1989. Creating a living educational theory from questions of the kind, "How do I improve my practice?" *Cambridge Journal of Education* 19(1): 41–52.

I feel as if I have gained a stronger sense of ownership of the area. To spend four years at a college or university and not gain any knowledge on the institution's environment would truly seem like an incomplete college experience. Before I came to Ithaca, like most freshmen I presume, my historical understanding of the area was virtually nonexistent. As embarrassing as it may be, my knowledge of Ithaca was extremely limited; I knew that Cornell, as an Ivy League school, had to be old and that Ithaca College was established a bit more recently, and that the area was prime for outdoor enthusiasts like myself. [My research into twentieth-century urban planning in Ithaca] has created a new connection with the city. This new relationship will likely foster a greater sense of ownership the next time I stroll through downtown, for I will be fairly cognizant of the efforts behind the sidewalks I tread on or the flowering trees I admire.

—ADAM, RR, S08[1]

The problem of living in a place without understanding or even knowing the first thing about its natural and human history is not unique to college students, though they are usually among the most transient inhabitants of the towns and cities, of the watersheds and bioregions that host them. One can be a good citizen in many ways without comprehending the complex *local* historical and ecological forces that shape everyday life. But without at least contemplating those connections, we are unlikely to develop a culture prepared to adapt to the significant ecological changes that will be a hallmark of the twenty-first century.

Over the past three years I have discovered that local environmental history projects help my students develop connections and commitments to their host community in a way few other learning experiences can, especially in the humanities. As the epigraph that opens this chapter demonstrates, students have not only been able to better understand the community in historical and ecological context, but they have learned to *see* their community differently, to feel affection and respect for it. Each of these transformations is a precondition for a more highly developed capacity for citizenship I and other scholars call ecological citizenship (Dobson 2003; Light 2002).[2] The local environmental history project I have developed as a partnership between the History Center of Tompkins County (New York) and my environmental history course has produced abundant evidence of transformation, evidence that suggests that such projects should be an essential part of teaching citizenship across the curriculum.

Declarations of Interdependence

As the second industrial revolution played out over the course of the twentieth century, it became clear that Aldo Leopold was right when he argued that we are citizens of more than a human-created polity. Leopold's was one of many twentieth-century voices issuing declarations of *inter*dependence, expanding the notion of rights and responsibilities to include what he called "the land" (by which he meant nonhuman nature) (Leopold 1970/1949). As Donald Worster (1994) has observed, their moral emphasis focused not on relations among humans alone but on relations among all things. Leopold hoped that by helping people recognize that our connection to and dependence upon nonhuman nature was inescapable, we would reach a new stage of ethical development that would benefit all life.

Leopold noted that the education system played a vital role in the inculcation of values necessary for a healthy, sustainable society. But, Leopold argued, "the most serious obstacle impeding the evolution of a land ethic is the fact that our education and economic system is headed away from, rather than toward, an intense consciousness of the land," a consciousness he believed was a precondition for what he called "biotic citizenship" (261). The trends he identified in the mid-1940s have only become more pronounced in the decades since, especially the mediated nature of our interaction with the world and the fundamental "placelessness" of the digital landscape:

> Your true modern is separated from the land by many middlemen, and by innumerable physical gadgets. He has no vital relation to it; to him it is the space between cities on which crops grow. Turn him loose for a day on the land, and if the spot does not happen to be a golf links or a "scenic" area, he is bored stiff. If crops could be raised by hydroponics instead of farming, it would suit him very well. Synthetic substitutes for wood, leather, wool, and other natural land products suit him better than the originals. In short, land is something he has "outgrown." (Leopold 1970/1949, 261)

Following the lead of Leopold, Dewey (1938), Boyte (2004), Palmer (1993), and a host of other theorists and moral philosophers who have pondered the meaning of citizenship, I believe that the cultivation of both the attitudes and habits of citizenship is the most important work teachers in higher education can be doing, regardless of their discipline. This is especially true at a time when industrialized and industrializing human civilizations are faced with either adopting something like Leopold's land ethic or facing a much diminished existence.

In this pivotal historical moment when our capacity for adaptation has yet to be calibrated with the inconvenient truth that rapid, anthropogenic global climate change threatens every human achievement of the past several hundred years, ecological citizenship is not a luxury. What habits of mind and behavior would suggest that something we have done in one of our classrooms has set students on the path toward ecological citizenship? Four interrelated sensibilities seem especially important. The first is an evolving sense of oneself as an agent of change—that is, a citizen understands that although institutional and other systemic forces can limit personal action, agency remains. Scale is crucial for developing such agency: as E. F. Schumacher (1974) wrote thirty years ago, "small is beautiful." I believe the kinds of active learning exercises described in this chapter and in the rest of this book are critical for developing this kind of self-awareness.

The second sensibility is an evolving capacity for complexity and ambiguity. Unless citizens are comfortable with complexity, ambiguity, and contingency (and simultaneously avoid empty relativism or, worse, nihilism), they cannot be very sophisticated change agents and often are reduced to a Manichean worldview that does nothing to solve the complex problems of our century. Like Rona Halualani (in chapter 2) and Jeff Bernstein (in chapter 1), I have observed that most students need guidance as they develop this comfort level.

A third sensibility that marks ecological citizenship is an evolving understanding that citizenship entails obligations to the nonhuman parts of our planet

—a vision of citizenship that ultimately strengthens our obligations to other people, for without viable ecosystem services people suffer. Finally, ecological citizenship embodies an evolving sense of connection and commitment to a place. Too often our sense of political commitment is only defined by political boundaries (neighborhood, city, county, state, nation), if it is defined at all. This kind of commitment is important, both in and of itself and as a starting point for a deeper sense of connection. But ecological citizenship entails a sense of place based on groupings like watersheds, foodsheds, and, overarching everything else, the planet writ large. In some ways this is essential, yet the least important: if we develop commitments to local places and empathy for the challenges other people in other communities face, a planetary commitment will evolve too.

Most of these competencies fall into categories of affective learning that range far from the content-oriented learning goals of conventional history and environmental studies courses. It is simpler to assess temporary retention of specific course content through the conventional tools: essay exams, papers, identifications, chronologies, and the like. Yet study after study has shown we focus too exclusively on content—and therefore on outcomes rather than process (Brew 2003; Fink 2003; Healey 2004). Though some content-oriented learning is essential, our presentation of it is often unimaginative. Perhaps above all, our means of assessing learning too often send the message to students that the skills and knowledge we have worked so hard to provide them over the course of a semester need only endure until the final blue book exam is handed in. The resultant diminished student interest and ephemeral learning are unlikely to foster the kinds of intellectual, ethical, and relational commitments necessary for ecological citizenship (or any other kind of citizenship for that matter).

Contexts for Learning

It took me several years to develop both the knowledge of my institutional context and the confidence that allowed me to design new learning experiences for my students. In 2005 I began to refine my United States environmental history course, a course designed to help students develop some historical perspective on the complex relationship between human beings and the North American environment over the past five hundred years. Each semester the course enrolls approximately twenty-five students: environmental studies and outdoor recreation leadership majors generally comprise half the class; the rest tend to be history majors or minors, students from the natural sciences, and others drawn by the course title, History of American Environmental Thought. What almost all of the students have in common is an affinity for that word "environmental"—which made my task of innovation somewhat easier. I just needed to pull them more deeply into material they were already inclined to find interesting.

In the first four years I taught the course, students usually demonstrated adequate foundational knowledge and expressed a general sense of satisfaction with the course. Nevertheless, I finished each semester with the sense that I had pushed few of them consciously and reflexively to integrate, to develop new feelings for Ithaca, New York, their host community, or to apply what they had learned beyond writing a narrative essay that they knew had only me as an audience. My students' learning experiences were, to use the language of Dee Fink (2003), disconnected rather than significant. Through course evaluations and conversations they expressed that the material seemed remote from their lives. The environmental changes that have so dramatically affected the social, political, and economic landscape of this country since Europeans arrived in North America remained abstract. As Leopold (1970/1949, 6) writes, abstractions are dangerous when it comes to developing an ecological consciousness; there is a danger in believing food comes from the grocery store shelf and heat comes from a furnace. If I wanted to cultivate the sense of connectedness out of which ecological citizenship develops, I would need a more ecological pedagogy.

From Problem to Opportunity

In the context of an *environmental* history course, I needed to interrogate the very notion of a good learning environment more carefully. The places where my students were learning—Center for Natural Sciences 119, their rooms and apartments, other study and work spaces—were all in Tompkins County, New York, but could have been almost anywhere. When they did research (for my course or most others) their point of departure was the Google search bar, a portal into a world of information sorted and prioritized by algorithms few of us understand, run by computers far away returning deracinated data. The learning environment I was creating was reinforcing the very tendencies of American life and culture I believe inhibit ecological citizenship. My problem was an old one in the history of education: I was reproducing the very values that I wanted to challenge.

In his influential essay, Randy Bass (1999) examines the way most academics see teaching "problems" as very different from research "problems." The problem-solving venture at the heart of discipline-based scholarly inquiry is celebrated. Problems are the puzzles that send historians to archives for answers, the impetus for our evidence-gathering and analysis, the very foundation of knowledge building. Teaching problems, on the other hand, are an embarrassment, something to be hidden away and scrutinized only in the solitude of our own offices. Rarely—even as the scholarship of teaching and learning has matured in the years since Bass wrote his essay—do teaching problems become the basis for scholarly inquiry the way our research problems do. Even more rarely do we make the results of our inquiry public, the culmination of the scholarly enterprise. Instead of recognizing and embracing teaching problems as an opportunity for conducting scholarly work using the material closest at hand, we just hope no one will notice.

When a student wrote on an evaluation in the spring of 2005, "I personally would enjoy the encouragement and even force of asking us or requiring from us research on many of these topics . . . ," I had the rudiments of a question and a research project. This student's comment expressed a desire not only to learn more, but to take a more active role in the learning process, to develop agency as a learner rather than be a "sponge," the metaphor used by many of the students Carmen Werder describes in chapter 3 of this volume. But how could I couple this desire with an experience that would both render the history of environmental change less abstract and help situate students more consciously in a place (Tompkins County, New York, in particular, but giving them a set of portable tools that would help them connect more deeply with other places they might live)?

My department's budding relationship with the local historical research library and museum, the History Center in Tompkins County, helped answer these questions. The History Center staff was interested in exploring what elements of their collection might be used for a future exhibit on local environmental history. I proposed that my students work in teams of three or four to research a local environmental history case study. They would choose the topic with guidance from the History Center staff, develop research questions and try to answer them, and present their findings to the public at the end of the semester. Perhaps most importantly, they would at several points in the process reflect in writing on what they were learning about history, about the community, about environmental history, and about themselves.

I wove this local environmental history project into the fabric of the rest of the course. In analyzing and writing about the primary sources in a course reader, students would develop the skills necessary for analyzing primary sources they themselves found in the History Center archives. Reading Steinberg's (2002) overview of U.S. environmental history and Price's (2000) investigations into how nature itself has ever-shifting meanings in American culture would provide broader context for the local stories they would tell. Class sessions spent discussing texts, images, and main themes of U.S. environmental history could help them communicate what they learned about local environmental history to the community at the end of the semester.

With this course revision in place, I developed my own research question: How might infusing the course with a student research project on local environmental history lead to more enduring learning? Even more importantly, how might I cultivate and measure a particular kind of enduring learning through this project? Guided by the work of Leopold and Dobson, as well as Orr (1992, 2004),

Wilson (1984), Bowers (1993, 1995, 1997), and Thomashow (1996), I wanted to see whether ecological awareness could nurture and reinforce the core ideals of citizenship—reciprocity (rights *and* responsibilities), connections to place, empathy, a sense for what is just. Ultimately, I wanted to know how (and whether) a service-learning research partnership between teams of undergraduate environmental history students and a local historical society could help students develop this expanded notion of citizenship.

Embarking on the Journey

I knew I could not begin to answer these questions without having some sense of how my students understood themselves as citizens (socially, politically, and ecologically) before they experienced my course and the research project. I needed some benchmark for how their understanding was evolving during the course. And I needed some sense of where my students were at the end of the course.

In order to help me track the evolution of their ideas about history, nature, and citizenship, I developed a survey. I was interested not only in what my students imagined "ecological citizenship" might be but also in what kinds of experiences had shaped their understanding of history, of nature, of ecology, and of the community of Ithaca. This survey tool proved as useful to the students themselves in assessing their progress through the course as it was to me as a researcher.

Since the fall 2005 semester I have had students gather all of their work for the semester—including the material from the local environmental history research project, which was about one-third of the total grade for the course—in a course portfolio (Michelson 2004; Zubizaretta 2004). The final assignment asked them to reflect on their learning in the course, using material from the portfolio as evidence to support their claims. In the spring 2006 semester I replaced the research paper each group had produced in the fall[3] with a series of short individual reflection papers that focused on the experience of doing the research at the History Center (and, in a few cases, other community repositories of local history). These papers proved to be a very rich source of data.

Like many new scholars of teaching and learning, I came to this work a bit intimidated by the vast social science and education literature on student learning and more than a bit alienated by that literature's tendency toward sterile quantitative methodology and jargon-laced analysis. I initially worried my qualitative approach would fail to persuade. But the more I tried to shoehorn my evidence into quantitative boxes or systematize my "data-gathering" in a way few historians are comfortable with, the more inauthentic both my voice and my students' voices seemed. The Carnegie Foundation's efforts over the past several years to root the scholarship of learning in the methods and styles of the disciplines reassured me that I could present my research into ecological citizenship and environmental history using the narrative style and qualitative evidence I am most comfortable with (Huber and Hutchings 2005; Huber and Morreale 2002; Hutchings 2000).

What I have brought together in the rest of this chapter is the story of journeys —of process, not outcomes. I am conscious of the fact that even a carefully designed study of student learning can yield false positives. Bass, Gardiner (1995), and other scholars of learning have noted that distinguishing between "performed understanding (or transformation)" and "deep (or enduring) understanding" is one of the most intriguing challenges we face. In some important respects you never *can* know whether enduring learning has taken place, because the journey continues long after the course has ended. Even if students know their grades will not be influenced by what they conclude about their experience so long as their conclusions and reflections are supported by evidence from their own portfolio, there remains the incentive to show change and deeper understanding (and a new awareness of ecological citizenship) because they know it is what I want to see happen. I have tried to guard against this problem by having students formally and informally document what they are learning/experiencing along the way. When they reflect on the local environmental history project and the course overall at the end of the semester, their conclusions about the journey must be at least partially substantiated by what is in their portfolios.

If I am to persuade readers of this volume that an environmental history course with a local environmental history component propels students along the path to ecological citizenship, it is the student voices rather than my own that will do so. I believe they reveal that many students did develop a stronger connection to a place, an expanding sense of obligation and responsibility, and a higher degree of comfort with complexity and ambiguity leading to a stronger sense of oneself as a change agent.

Many of the students expressed—forcefully in many cases—a much greater awareness of Tompkins County, New York, as a result of their experience in my course. "I have heard before that Ithaca is a product of the unique society that occupies it," wrote Jeremy. "However, over this past semester, I have grown to realize that it is not the people who make the town. Rather, it is the town that makes the people" (RR, F06). Ethan, a Boston native, described how his view of upstate New York changed. "By researching this area where I have been living for three years," he wrote, "it has opened my eyes so much more to the history of the area. . . . By focusing on a smaller area, an area which is closely connected with all students in Ithaca, it offers so much more insight and turned the static, sometimes lifeless disconnect that students often have with history into a more living, breathing past." He went on to describe a moment of intense connection to place:

I found the most exciting aspect of research in this project came with the actual contact with the living history. I remember standing on the foundations of the Old Mill in Caroline [a township in Tompkins County] feeling displaced from my own life, thinking how over two hundred years prior there had been the founding father of Caroline, General Cantine, building this mill, standing where I had stood. As a student so interested in history, I could not explain the feeling I had when introduced to the actual areas where our forefathers had stood before. That is where the project came together for me— the contact with the history we were researching. (RR, F06)

In each of these cases the writer hailed from an urban area in the Northeast, and part of their experience in the course was learning to appreciate a very different landscape than they were accustomed to.

The experience of exploring the history and landscape of this community was even more powerful for a student from the Rocky Mountains. "I began school in Ithaca having never set foot in this region of the country in my whole life," wrote Edith. "I knew almost nothing about the city except for a few things a buddy at Cornell had told me. . . . If not for this project I probably would have gone on with the rest of the semester, college, and life without knowing. . . . The more I learned about the environment in general, and especially humans' impact thereof, I realized that there was a lot more to each landscape, each city I saw or lived in than was perhaps in a history text book" (RR, F06).

But it did not take the experience of being thrust into an entirely new environment for the local environmental history project to lead to deeper connections to this place. David, who had lived his entire life in Ithaca, observed that "because I live here it [the research project] was interesting to me because I have my own history with the place I was researching. I always knew there was a bird sanctuary or something like that down by Stewart Park; from the research I learned more about it. And because of my research I went down and walked around the bird sanctuary to see it myself" (RR, S07). The research project cultivated (or re-cultivated) powers of observation and inquiry often dulled by the passive educational methods employed at every level.

Since I began this project students have written dozens of other reflections about how it has made them think in new ways about this home, whether it is what role a particular industrial site played in the human and ecological history of the place or where their drinking water comes from. The files and boxes at the History Center helped answer questions they could answer in no other way. As a repository of local knowledge the History Center is also firmly situated in a place—in a way that the Internet is not. Many students have also commented on how refreshing it was to do research without recourse to Google. As one student put it, "[The History Center] seems old fashioned compared to the Internet age we're in now, but it's also entirely necessary and more personal than doing Internet research. It's nice to work with real people, and the staff is passionate about history and about getting students excited and curious in their hunt to answer questions and make connections . . ." (Lisa, RR, S07).

Although others were not so explicit about how the Internet depersonalized (and therefore decontextualized) their research and learning experiences, the number of students who noted this dimension of the experience was striking, especially since they received no prompt of any kind from me to reflect on this. "So often in my classes I simply use the internet," wrote James. "This project forced me to get away from the internet crutch" (RR, S06). "It was refreshing to not start a presentation or paper with the Google search engine, and I proved to myself that I can use other ways to gather information," Robert reflected (RR, F05). And in one of the most well-developed reflections on this topic, Sandra wrote:

> I saw for the first time in what feels like forever that people still research in a traditional way instead of opening up my homepage of google.com and typing in a keyword. Instead of scrolling through web pages and quickly skimming tons of material from online sources and databases, I put on a pair of gloves and gently turned the pages of a scrapbook created by someone in 1925. It made the experience so much more real; I was *doing* history instead of just reading about it. This really created a feeling of intimacy with this project; I certainly feel more connected with it and the things I have learned than if I would have done this research the traditional way. (RR, S06)

In addition to suggesting one further way the local environmental history project fulfilled my goal of developing ecological citizenship, these examples (and there are several more in my files) offer the scholar of learning some rich material for trying to understand how students perceive the knowledge creation process (Bain 2006). The student who wrote that "I have become so accustomed to having all the information I can imagine at my fingertips through the internet that I didn't really know what to expect at the beginning of the project"—and went on to describe what he learned as "mindblowing" (Brian, RR, S06)—is expressing a moment of difficulty with its origins in our heavily mediated and placeless reality (Salvatori and Donahue 2004). For these students, the Internet has become the "traditional" way to do research (as Sandra describes it above); there is not a hint of irony in this description.

They are, in the words of Mark Prenksy (2001), "digital natives." Prensky urges college faculty (mostly "digital immigrants" in his view) to go native or become less effective in creating learning environments. Perhaps. But my experience in this project suggests that creating learning experiences that *contrast* with students' habitual ways of knowing can generate learning impossible to duplicate in a digital environment. I suspect (it would take a study on this element of learning specifically to be able to make a bolder claim) that the "intimacy" Sandra describes simply cannot be developed through Internet research. An intimate relationship with a place is critical to both situated learning and the development of ecological citizenship. A sense of intimacy, as other scholars of learning have shown (Feito 2002), can be a key component of learning. Indeed, as Carmen Werder (chapter 3) and Howard Tinberg (chapter 4) show, intimacy can also be a key component for developing the kind of empathy that makes for better citizens.

Several students addressed the issue of ecological citizenship directly, which is not surprising since we began discussing the concept on the first day of class. They were also asked on the pre- and post-course surveys to define the phrase. Nonetheless, students grappled with the concept and made it their own in some interesting ways. Sierra, for example, took her original definition of ecological citizenship—"[it is] almost self-evident that we are taught to value citizenship as a personal responsibility (through one's monetary and social capacity to their country or community)"—and reexamined it in light of her experiences during the semester. "That idea of citizenship presupposes one's individual values as being unique to them, owned by them, yet used toward a common purpose, whether it be environmental or otherwise," she wrote in her final portfolio essay.

> Where once it was easy to see, in myself, the idea that my citizenship was tied directly to the people around me (and perhaps my ability to make them ecologically conscious), the part of myself as citizen that was attached to the land was separate. This part was focused on personal conservation, on formulating my own identity in wilderness, urbanity, metropolis, suburbia, and other environmental spaces, but it was not concerned with how that identity fit into the greater community.

Now, she concludes, she sees citizenship as a process not just of personal evolution but community evolution, "the actions we are responsible for coming not *from* us but *to* us in a chain of historical precedence" (FPE, S07).

Calvin did not invoke the term "citizenship," but in his final portfolio reflection he also described the development of some of the capacities I listed earlier in this chapter, elegantly weaving together his learning in the classroom with the local environmental history project:

> [Historians Jennifer Price and William Cronon] have showed me through historical analysis and modern inquires [sic] that our imaginary disconnect from nature prevents us from appreciating all nature, including human and

nonhuman environments. On November 9th in an in-class assessment on Cronon I wrote, ". . . We look at nature today only as something outside of society, and better for it. We fail to see that a tree in a garden is no less important and meaningful then a tree in the wilderness" (Class Assessment 11/9/05). I also voiced these concerns at the Tompkins County History Center on December 7th in our group's presentation on agriculture in Tompkins County. In my speaking part of the presentation, I tried to convey how this idea of an imaginary separation between nature and man has kept our knowledge of the crops, and what goes into them, a secret that should really not exist. This is one of the most important concepts I have gained from this class and it is allowed to change my conscious perceptions of nature, which will surely come in handy later in life. (FPE, F05)

Like dozens of other students since I began teaching the course with the local environmental history project at its core, these students have made new meaning of abstractions like "community" and false dichotomies like nature/human. As their view of the world has become more complex, it has also become richer and they find themselves with new tools for being in the world. The struggle with complexity, ambiguity, and contingency that is at the heart of ecological citizenship was an important part of many students' reflections on their experience.

Martin wrestled with what seemed like a contradiction in the history of Tompkins County: How could an area now so renowned for its commitment to sustainable living once have embraced a company that contaminated a beautiful gorge for decades? His group's answer was that the concept of civic responsibility (both individual and corporate) had evolved over time, something he had never considered before. Martin's investigation of the company helped him understand not only that historical context is critical for comprehending environmental change ("they were simply a company that existed in a world that didn't even consider the health of the environment"), but also that it was "harder to blame our current environmental woes on the past." Such a shift in his perspective allowed Martin to develop a more complex view of both local and national history than the declension narrative central to the environmental movement (RR, F06).

Alison experienced a similar shift. "I always have and still do consider myself an environmentalist. I worry everyday about the state of the planet and think about what I can do, just a simple individual, to change the course we are on," she wrote. "I used to blame previous generations for our present situation. While past decisions are still resonating today, I see now that our situation is not arbitrary; it is a result of a series of historical happenings caused by changing mindsets that were shaped by situations in a certain place and time. . . . As history unfolded throughout the class I found this theme again and again. I was not so muddled by our environmental situation because I was beginning to see the layers of thought that produced the actions" (FPE, S07).

I will offer one final example of a student who reflected on growth as an integrative, critical thinker who is becoming more comfortable with complexity. "The History of American Environmental Thought, and my project on the Cargill salt mine in particular, became a paradigm shift," wrote Ellen in her final portfolio essay. "I realized that history, in many ways, is science and, likewise, much of biological science is researching, organizing, and recording ancient history. This course was also an immediate eye-opener in that I realized the truly interdisciplinary nature of being an active student and community member, especially in Ithaca. Education and life are essentially inseparable in that you can't really live without learning something, and real learning only happens through experience and stepping outside your comfort zone. Much of this class got me thinking outside of my intellectual comfort zone" (FPE, S07). For us to become ecological citizens we must all engage in this kind of integrative thinking that takes us out of our comfort zones.

Without question, my teaching and my students' experience in my course have benefited from this inquiry. As a teacher I have thought more carefully than ever about aligning course design with learning outcomes. While in the first four years of teaching the course I had hoped my students would make Aldo Leopold's ecological ethics their own, I had provided no concrete way for them to experience what that might mean. The local environmental history research project has clearly done this. Moreover, the students—not all, but most of them—have embarked on a journey toward a sense of ecological citizenship. And they have documented this journey in a way that not only helps scholars of learning but also (and more importantly) helps them come to terms with their learning experience.

In his short story "The Mappist," Barry Lopez (2001) draws the reader into the process of documenting change over time by showing how mapping is both a literal and metaphorical enterprise. After years of searching, Phillip Trevino, the narrator of the story, finally tracks down Corlis Benefideo, the author and draftsman of a series of urban historical maps. Each of these maps is a kind of geographical palimpsest of some of the world's great cities, each distinguished by its exquisite attention to detail and its loving evocation of place—and of what it would mean to understand that place deeply. Trevino finds Benefideo in a modest house far from any town out on the North Dakota prairie. He learns that Benefideo has been working for decades on a series of maps of North Dakota so richly layered that almost every element of human and natural history is represented, from fencelines, past and present, to ephemeral streams, to trails and roads, all compiled through "close personal observation and talking with long-term residents." Trevino, breathless with admiration says, "But nobody has the time for this kind of fieldwork anymore."

"That's unfortunate," Benefideo replies. "Because this information is what we need, you know. This shows history and how people fit the places they occupy. It's about what get erased and what comes to replace it. These maps reveal the foundations beneath the ephemera" (Lopez 2001, 158).

We have increasingly lost our commitment to and deep understanding of particular places on this earth; without this commitment and understanding, the foundation of citizenship, our social and political institutions are endangered. I have my students read this story at the beginning of the semester, at the outset of their own mapmaking journey. When they read it, they do not know that most of them will come to care more about this place they call home for a few years. They do not know that through a process of consistent reflection on *how* they are mapping the terrain not only of Tompkins County, NY, but also of their own ways of knowing the world, they will be transformed. Many will understand what ecological citizenship entails for the first time. And it is my hope that they will in turn transform the world.

Dialogue

A COMMENTARY FROM JEFFREY L. BERNSTEIN
Department of Political Science, Eastern Michigan University

I am struck, in reading this chapter, by the notions of complexity and ambiguity in Michael Smith's study of his attempts to cultivate an ethic of ecological citizenship in his students. Certainly, the substantive issues within the realm of "environmentalism" present their own complexities; if they did not, we'd have successfully solved this environmental "stuff" by now. But as a society, we disagree on how true is this "inconvenient truth" that Al Gore and others present to us— disagreement that encompasses both how bad the situation is and how we got into this mess. And, perhaps most importantly, while in principle we all value environmentalism, we also all value economic growth and the creation and preservation of jobs in our local, state, and national communities. What separates us on these issues is the relative weights we place on each of these ideals.

Sorting through how we got here is a job society typically reserves for historians. The discipline of history offers methodologies for doing this, and for communicating its findings to others. To the historian, context matters—historians are known for traveling to the place where an event happened and immersing themselves in its time period, to aid their understanding of the event. Primary sources matter—historians usually learn more reading a document from that time than they do from reading a retrospective narrative of the event. Historians do their work in a certain way—and yet, too often, history is presented to students as a closed record of the past, documenting what happened without sufficiently exploring why it happened, or why what didn't happen didn't happen.

By pushing his students outside their comfort zones, rejecting Google in favor of studying the context through primary sources, Michael encourages them to learn how to construct a rich narrative, with all its complexity, the way a historian would. Thus, when Martin considers the temporal context in which a company had contaminated a beautiful gorge, he understands that today's environmental sensibilities did not exist at that time. Many students simply want the answers. In this case, Martin had an easy answer readily available—demonize the company, blame the past. That he doesn't rely on it suggests that Michael's students can accept that easy answers often do not exist.

More important than this product, though, is the process students go through to tell this story. For example, when Sandra talks about putting on white gloves and turning through the pages of a 1925 scrapbook as an act of "doing history," and about how that "created a feeling of intimacy with this project," she shows an understanding of what historians do. I would submit that the lessons she learns— about Tompkins County and about the environment—will be more long-lasting as a result of that process.

How do we help our students to view themselves as ecological citizens, as part of a collective larger than their narrow sense of themselves and their own community? We do it by acknowledging ambiguity and complexity, helping students understand that there are no simple answers (and, for that matter, no simple questions). We do it by giving students the disciplinary tools to develop their own understanding of complexity—whether those are the tools of the historian, the chemist, or the poet. And, we do it by grounding them in a setting that they can study, appreciate, and make their own. When our students learn to dig deep into complex issues, they learn to learn, and engage in significant learning experiences. The evidence presented in this chapter makes clear to me that this has certainly occurred in Michael's class.

A COMMENTARY FROM MICHAEL C. BURKE
Department of Mathematics, College of San Mateo

David Geelan (chapter 8) and Michael Smith each propose a more expansive conception of citizenship than most of us are accustomed to. David suggests a citizenship that transcends national boundaries, which he finds artificial and which, he argues, can inhibit the search for solutions to many global problems, problems that do not respect the political divisions we have inscribed upon the world. Michael, echoing Aldo Leopold, advocates an ecological citizenship, a citizenship that transcends human society. Michael argues that the interdependence of mankind and nonhuman nature makes such a conception of citizenship necessary. Although the fact of this interdependence is clear to many of us today, we are still, as a society, struggling to understand its full implications. Most of us are estranged from "the land"; we live in urban environments, we rely on machines for nearly every aspect of our lives, and the information we receive about the world is often delivered to us electronically, via television or the internet. As an antidote to all of this, Michael asks his students to immerse themselves in the history of Ithaca and of Tompkins County; he hopes that the study of this particular place will help foster the connection to "the land" essential for ecological citizenship.

As I began Michael's chapter, I was skeptical of his approach. The students who attend Ithaca College come from all over the United States; they spend only a small portion of their life in Ithaca. Why, I wondered, would they have any interest in the history of Tompkins County? How important would their knowledge of the history of Ithaca, a place they are only visiting, after all, be for them when they returned to their homes? Why cultivate a connection to this particular place, to Ithaca, when they would spend the rest of their lives in other places far from it?

Consequently, I was surprised to read the reactions of Michael's students. First, there is the power of the immediacy and the tangibility of the source material Michael's students work with. When David (who grew up in Ithaca!) writes of visiting the bird sanctuary for the first time, or Sandra describes putting on gloves to carefully turn the pages of an old scrapbook, we see students encountering a reality unmediated by machines, and recognizing the value of such an encounter. Actually, this reaction to Michael's work does not surprise me at all; I've believed for a long time that we must work to attach the material we are teaching to the real world. The habits of textbook learning and, more recently, of digitally mediated learning often induce a kind of a stupor in our students, and the kind of hands-on experience that Michael requires counteracts this. No, the surprise for me was the ways in which the history of Tompkins County seems to contain the seeds of important issues that we face across our country today, issues that transcend the particulars of Tompkins County. Martin, for example, learns that a beautiful gorge in town was contaminated for decades by a local company. And Ellen completes a project on the history of the Cargill Salt Mine. Both students are thinking about the ways attitudes towards local environmental issues have changed over time, and about the implications of those changes for us today, as we try to deal with the environmental problems of our own time. The ideas surfaced by these investigations resonate far beyond Ithaca; I now see that the work Michael's students do in Ithaca will indeed be transferable to their home turf and beyond. Tip O'Neill famously remarked that "all politics is local." I think Michael's work strongly suggests that all history is local, as well.

A REPLY FROM MICHAEL B. SMITH

For me, one of the most important things we can help our students (and children) develop is adaptive capacity. Indeed, suppleness of mind, spirit, and body seem essential for both individuals and civilizations to flourish in the twenty-first century. Too often this capacity—and with it the ability to embrace the world's complexity—is shrunken by the passive, mediated learning experiences so many of our students have, resulting in the stupor Mike has observed. Could a local environmental history project help students become more adaptable, more comfortable with ambiguity and complexity? Could the skills and habits of thinking and being they developed as a result of the project themselves be adapted to new places and circumstances?

Initially I shared some of Mike's skepticism about whether helping my students cultivate a connection to Ithaca would yield a sense of place that would endure. There is something paradoxical about what I am trying to do: generate commitment to a place (and its people, and its human and natural history) that almost all of my students will one soon leave. As much as I want my students to care about this little glacier-carved corner of New York, I am also hoping for a kind of ecological citizenship that is portable—that in whatever place(s) my students pause and eventually end up in their life journeys, they will be able to interrogate in the same way they asked questions about the environmental history of Tompkins County. One student who took the course in a spring semester spent the following summer helping make a documentary film with an environmental theme in Oregon. When he returned to Ithaca in the fall he came by my office to tell me that the first thing he had done upon arriving in the community where the filming took place was to go find the local historical society. He had acquired both the tools and the adaptive capacity to become a little more native to that place.

Which brings me, finally, to Jeff's observations about the role the disciplinary methods of history have played in my students' learning experiences. Though I am now a professional historian who handles archival materials on a regular basis, I still feel that excitement expressed by my students about the tactile experience of "doing" history in this way. The documents, photos, and other artifacts my students examine as part of their research are real, not virtual; their experience with them is mediated by a human archivist, not a search engine. They realize that questions raised during the process of historical inquiry—like the process of living itself—often yield more questions instead of answers. Touching the past, literally, allows students to more readily reach into themselves as agents of their own learning. And it is that sense of agency that opens them to ever wider possibilities for citizenship.

Acknowledgments

Although space constraints prevent me from thanking every person who contributed to this chapter, I would especially like to acknowledge the members of my project group at the Carnegie Foundation, the Chapter House history reading group in Ithaca, New York, the dozens of students who have taken my environmental history course over the years, the staff at the History Center in Tompkins County, and the countless offices, programs, and individuals at Ithaca College who have supported this project.

Notes

1. All of these sources are currently exclusively in my possession, though I hope to make them available electronically eventually. All of the names are pseudonyms. Each acronym designates the source of the quotation: FPE (Final Portfolio Essay), RR (Research Reflection), PCS (Pre-course Survey); and the semester (S = Spring, F = Fall, number = year)

2. Dobson makes a persuasive distinction between environmental citizenship (which he argues fits easily within the traditions of liberal and civic republican citizenship) and ecological citizenship, which obliges us to think of citizenship in terms of nonreciprocal responsibility, of boundaries that range far beyond traditional political boundaries, of private as well as public arenas for civic action, and of "civic virtue" as specific ecological obligations (Dobson 2004).

3. While this experience did demonstrate to students how difficult writing collaborations can be (a valuable lesson in itself), it did not produce great papers. Moreover, the assignment shifted the focus from process to outcome, and I have found that documentation of the process yields richer data about student learning.

Works Cited

Bain, Robert. 2006. Rounding up the usual suspects: Facing authority hidden in the history classroom. *Teachers College Record* 108 (10): 2080–2114.

Bass, Randy. 1999. The scholarship of teaching: What's the problem? *Inventio: Creative Thinking about Learning and Teaching*, Feb., 1(1). http://www.doit.gmu.edu/Archives/feb98/randybass.htm (accessed May 26, 2009).

Bowers, C. A. 1993. *Education, cultural myths, and the ecological crisis: Toward deep changes.* Albany: State University of New York Press.

———. 1995. *Educating for an ecologically sustainable culture: Rethinking moral education, creativity, intelligence, and other modern orthodoxies.* Albany: State University of New York Press.

———. 1997. *The culture of denial: Why the environmental movement needs a strategy reforming universities and public schools.* Albany: State University of New York Press.

Boyte, Harry. 2004. *Everyday politics: Reconnecting citizens and public life.* Philadelphia: University of Pennsylvania Press.

Brew, Angela. 2003. Teaching and research: New relationships and their implications for inquiry-based teaching and learning in higher education. *Higher Education Research and Development* 22(1): 3–18.

Dewey, John. 1938. *Experience and education.* New York: Simon and Schuster.

Dobson, Andrew. 2003. *Citizenship and the environment.* Oxford: Oxford University Press.

———. 2004. "Ecological citizenship." Paper presented at the annual meeting of the Western Political Science Association, Marriott Hotel, Portland, Ore., Mar. 11.

Feito, Jose. 2002. Exploring intellectual community: Group learning processes in traditional "great books" seminars. Carnegie Academy for the Scholarship of Teaching and Learning Final Report. CASTL Electronic Workspace, Menlo Park, Calif.: Carnegie Foundation for the Advancement of Teaching.

Fink, L. Dee. 2003. *Creating significant learning experiences: An integrated approach to designing college courses.* San Francisco: Jossey-Bass.

Gardiner, Howard. 1995. *The unschooled mind: How children think and how schools should teach.* New York: Basic Books.

Healey, Mick. 2004. Linking research and teaching: Exploring disciplinary spaces and the role of inquiry-based learning. In *Reshaping the university: New relationships between research, scholarship and teaching,* ed. Ronald Barnett, 67–79. McGraw Hill/Open University Press.

Huber, Mary T., and Sherwyn P. Morreale, eds. 2002. *Disciplinary styles in the scholarship of teaching and learning: Exploring common ground.* Washington, D.C.: American Association for Higher Education and the Carnegie Foundation for the Advancement of Teaching.

Huber, Mary T., and Pat Hutchings. 2005. *The advancement of learning: Building the teaching commons.* San Francisco: Jossey-Bass.

Hutchings, Pat, ed. 2000. *Opening lines: Approaches to the scholarship of teaching and learning.* Menlo Park, Calif.: Carnegie Foundation for the Advancement of Teaching.

Leopold, Aldo. 1970/1949. *A Sand County almanac with essays on conservation from Round River.* New York: Ballantine.

Light, Andrew. 2002. "Restoring ecological citizenship." In *Democracy and the claims of nature,* ed. Ben A. Minteer and Bob P. Taylor, 153–172. Lanham, Md.: Rowman and Littlefield.

Lopez, Barry H. 2000. The mappist. In *Light action in the Caribbean,* 146–157. New York: Vintage.

Michelson, Elana, ed. 2004. *Portfolio development and assessment of prior learning: Perspectives, models, and practices.* Sterling, Va.: Stylus.

Orr, David. 1992. *Ecological literacy: Education and the transition to a postmodern world.* Albany: State University of New York Press.

———. 2004. *Earth in mind: On education, environment, and the human prospect.* Washington, D.C.: Island Press.

Palmer, Parker. 1993. *The violence of our knowledge: Toward a spirituality of higher educa-*

tion. The Michael Keenan Memorial Lecture, Berea College, Kentucky, The Seventh Lecture, 1993.

Prensky, Mark. 2001. "Digital natives, digital immigrants." *On the Horizon* 9(5).

Price, Jennifer. 2000. *Flight maps: Adventures with nature in modern America.* New York: Basic Books.

Salvatori, Mariolina R., and Patricia Donahue. 2004. *The elements (and pleasures) of difficulty.* New York: Pearson/Longman.

Schumacher, E. F. 1974. *Small is beautiful: Economics as if people mattered.* New York: Harper.

Steinberg, Ted. 2002. *Down to earth: Nature's role in American history.* New York: Oxford University Press.

Thomashow, Mitchell. 1996. *Ecological identity: Becoming a reflective environmentalist.* Cambridge, Mass.: M.I.T. Press.

Wilson, Edward O. 1984. *Biophilia: The human bond with other species.* Cambridge, Mass.: Harvard University Press.

Worster, Donald 1994. *Nature's economy: A history of ecological ideas.* New York: Cambridge University Press.

Zubizaretta, John. 2004. *The learning portfolio: Reflective practice for improving student learning.* Bolton, Mass.: Anker.

The Double Crisis

The Fourteenth Amendment of the U.S. Constitution famously declares "all persons born or naturalized in the United States" to be citizens whose "privileges and immunities" cannot be abridged. For those of us who share the robust view of civic engagement that runs through *Citizenship Across the Curriculum,* however, the Constitution may be wrong. To be sure, it is fundamental to democratic societies that women and men are born into the privileges and immunities of citizenship. Yet, along with these rights and birthrights, citizenship entails the collective work of cocreating and participating in public life; of engaging, overseeing, and challenging government; of naming and solving shared problems, in collaboration with others to whom we are tied by a common fate but not necessarily a common experience. In that larger sense, no one is born a citizen. Citizens have to be made. We become not merely rights-bearing humans but public selves through a complex socialization that endows us with the knowledge, capacities, values, and habits that we need for the reflective practice of democratic life. "[W]e must *learn* to be free," argues the political theorist Benjamin Barber:

> The literacy required to live in civil society, the competence to participate in democratic communities, the ability to think critically and act deliberately in a pluralistic world, the empathy that permits us to hear and accommodate others, all involve skills that must be acquired. (1992, 4)

Here is the animating assumption of this book: there is no citizenship without education for citizenship.

And yet this is not news. For centuries, philosophers and public intellectuals as disparate as Rousseau and Dewey, Benjamin Barber and William Bennett—not to mention politicians, activists, and ordinary citizens of all stripes—have debated what educational practices should underwrite the making of a public of citizens. The very terms of debate are themselves part of the debate, constitutively up for grabs. Is the goal of civic education to inculcate civic virtue—and what do we mean by virtue anyway? Should civic educators aim primarily to induct apprentice citizens, such as immigrants or the young, into a shared canon of heroic memories and creedal values, or to prepare them for navigating the differences of a multicultural society? *Citizenship Across the Curriculum* thus enters a well-worn discussion. Yet it intervenes at a time in which the old problem of how to educate for citizenship is being revisited in new ways. The book makes an important contribution to that reframing, proposing answers to emergent questions and (like all good interventions) provoking further questions that the book cannot fully answer itself. Let me sketch the historical and intellectual context within which, it seems to me, the authors are working; offer my own map of their contributions to that moment; and finally specify some of the issues that the book opens up for further reflection and action.

Notwithstanding its measured tone of collective reflection and dialogue, *Citizenship Across the Curriculum* is a project catalyzed by urgent and timely concerns; or, more precisely, by the intersection of two sets of concerns. It is first of all a response to what Harry Boyte and Nan Kari have called "America's civic crisis" (1996, 4). Jeff Bernstein's essay speaks to this larger context when he laments the "decrease in social capital," "decline in trust of the political system," and "low levels of knowledge" that hobble his students' engagement. Other authors frame the civic crisis in different ways, variously stressing students' difficulty in bridging differences of ideological commitment or cultural identity, their felt sense of distance between their classroom studies and the larger world, and their disbelief in their own efficacy as political actors. Taken as a whole, their vignettes of disengagement echo concerns that are widespread in American society. Civic culture in the United States seems to have devolved into a privatized, fractured landscape of poll-driven policy-making, ideological polarization, gated communities, passive consumption of government services and media specta-cles, cynicism toward politics, and low rates of participation.

At the same time, the book is part of a robust surge of efforts to renew public life. The yearning for active citizenship and political community, of course, fueled the historic candidacy and election of Barack Obama. Yet the 2008 cam-paign was itself the culmination of a "civic turn" that had germinated during the previous fifteen years across many sectors of American society. We have seen calls for "civic professionalism" in the media and philanthropy (Sullivan 1995; Dzur 2008; Boyte 2004a; Rosen 2001; www.pewcenters.org),[1] experiments in "citizen-centered" policy-making and public agenda setting (Sirianni and Friedland 2001; Gibson 2006; www.novemberfifth.org), the proliferation of programs for youth engagement and leadership development (Levine 2007; Kiesa et al. 2008)[2]—and, more to the point here, a rising movement for academic civic engagement to which *Citizenship Across the Curriculum* belongs and contributes (Stanton et al., 1999; Scobey 2005; Benson, Puckett, and Harkavy 2007; Boyte 2004b). As the editors of *Citizenship* write in their introduction, "there is an emerging con-sensus that cultivating an enduring ethos of civic engagement is one of the most important things higher education should do."

Indeed the volume underscores one striking aspect of the current civic turn: how deeply *higher education* has been implicated in the health of American citizenship. Unlike their Progressive or New Deal counterparts, contemporary theorists and activists such as Barber (1992), Boyte (2004a, 2004b), Peter Levine (2007), Kiesa et al. (2008), and Martha Nussbaum (1997) assume academic in-stitutions and undergraduate education to be important settings of civic disen-gagement *and* civic renewal. This assumption seems to me quite new. To be sure, U.S. colleges have long promoted education for the public good as a core value of their mission statements, and they have fitfully included civics courses as core components of their curricula. Yet, until the student activism of the late 1960s, the campus was mainly a sidebar in the larger story of American democratic movements: either an antithetical space of elite social privilege or (in the case of land-grant universities) a support space of expert training for public service.[3] It was not scholars and students, but other social actors—the citizen-worker, the citizen-farmer, and the citizen-immigrant—who embodied the possibilities (for some) and risks (for others) of an expansively democratic public life (Boyte and Kari 1996). Yet, as the courses, community projects, issue briefs, and reflection journals that populate *Citizenship Across the Curriculum* underscore, all this has changed. The campus and the curriculum have come to be regarded as conse-quential arenas for the making of citizens (Colby et al. 2007).

In one sense, this is not remarkable. The half-century since World War II saw a genuine, if uneven, democratization of U.S. higher education. This had many

causes: the demand for new skills, technologies, and professions in a moderniz-
ing economy; the expansion of state university and community college systems;
increases in working-class upward mobility; and governmental commitments to
tuition aid and affirmative action advancing the novel policy that higher education was itself a public good. As a result, more than half of young Americans now
enter institutions of higher learning. It would be surprising if such institutions
did *not* serve as crucibles of civic socialization, much as grange halls, union halls,
and military barracks did in earlier eras. Yet the movement for academic engagement involves more than just a response to expanded access and expanding
diversity. It was catalyzed by concerns and conflicts that were unintended consequences of the expansion of higher education, especially in the past fifteen years
or so. With almost startling precision, the civic crisis has coincided with a crisis
in higher education, a growing worry that the relationship between the American
academy and American society is broken. Here is the other key context for
Citizenship Across the Curriculum.

Public and academic anxiety over the health of higher education gets expressed at several levels. The first is of course economic. Colleges and universities
have faced a perfect storm of fiscal pressures in recent years—rising health and
energy costs, declining public investment, more complex programs and missions
—that sharply increased institutional costs and public disgruntlement. Budget
shortfalls and tuition sticker shock in turn clothe a deeper problem: a legitimation crisis that threatens to undermine the social compact on which our enormous claims to resources and autonomy depends. A decade ago, this was played
out in culture wars and critiques of "tenured radicals" (Kimball 1998; Bloom
1988); today we see it in calls for accountability and assessment, often associated
with former Secretary of Education Margaret Spellings's Commission On the
Future of Higher Education, that call on (and call out) the academy to justify its
effectiveness and value (U.S. Department of Education 2006; Scobey 2006). The
editors of *Citizenship Across the Curriculum* situate their project as a response to
such concerns, rightly citing "public frustration about the cost-to-value relationship of a college education" and the need to "evaluat[e] just what a college or
university graduate has gained from . . . our classrooms" as challenges that the
movement for academic civic engagement needs to take seriously. The book
speaks even more eloquently to the educational crisis in its pedagogical stories.
The essays offer a montage of evidence that undergraduates do not find (or
worse, expect) their educational experience to be meaningful, integrative, and
transformative. Carmen Werder's analysis of her students' metaphor of the "self-
as-sponge" is the most vivid testimony to this pattern of alienation and passivity.
Yet the lived experience of what I am calling the legitimation crisis of higher
education—and students' sometimes inchoate longing to change that experience
—runs powerfully throughout the book. It is also there, just beneath the surface,

in the authors' own vignettes of escape from conventional disciplinary teaching into more integrative, experiential, ethically mindful, and socially engaged pedagogy: "breaking the silence," in Matt Fisher's poignant phrase.

Citizenship Across the Curriculum, in short, seems to me prompted by two intersecting urgencies: mounting disquiet over the devolution of civic life and mounting disquiet over the failures of higher education. The book is animated (like the larger movement for academic engagement) by the notion that we will meet these challenges most effectively by joining them together; each crisis has spurred the development of ideas and strategies for engaging the other. New pedagogies enable the campus to serve as a crucible for the making of citizens. The movement for civic renewal offers an important catalyst for making our educational practices deeper and more consequential—and in the process, reweaving the frayed social compact between the academy and the larger society. These essays translate that rather grandiose double project into rich and grounded stories of teaching and learning.

Teaching Citizenship in the Plural

How, then, does the book contribute to these aims? In thinking about its achievement, I want to start with a fact that may be so obvious as to escape notice: *Citizenship Across the Curriculum* is an anthology. It comprises an exploratory and wide-ranging collection of studies that documents the community of inquiry forged by an exploratory and diverse set of scholars. The book's genre represents more than just the inertial result of a scholarly convening or academic publishing habits. Its "anthology-ness" is organic to its goals and context: to the complexity of the problem of educating for citizenship, to the breadth of practice wisdom the collaborators bring to bear, to their collective process, to the unfinished quality of the historical moment to which they are speaking. Of course, we have (and need) books that assert focused, even polemical claims about civic engagement in a singular voice: Boyte and Kari's framing of citizenship as public work in *Building America* (1996) or Nussbaum's argument for the centrality of the narrative imagination in *Cultivating Humanity* (1997) come to mind as indispensable examples. Yet *Citizenship Across the Curriculum* is right, it seems to me, in *not* privileging some particular model of engaged pedagogy or civic competence. Its achievement is precisely to map a domain of work that is irreducibly heterogeneous and to offer a network of pathways—intersecting but not unidirectional—across that domain.

The range of settings and approaches through which the book explores the teaching of citizenship is not simply broad, but multidimensional: a plurality of pluralities. The authors' home institutions are diverse in sector, location, size, and mission, from Rebecca Nowacek's urban Jesuit university to Mike Burke's community college to Rona Halualani's comprehensive public university to David Geelan's research university (the sole non-U.S. institution in the mix). The essays bring together an expansive mix of fields—some disciplinary, others interdisciplinary—and an array of topics from the literary history of the Shoah to U.S. environmental history to mathematical modeling. Even more striking is the panoply of pedagogical approaches described in the essays: not only the issue briefs, community projects, and reflection journals that one might have expected in a book on civic learning, but also simulations, interview projects, dialogue exercises, kinetic games, and visual productions. The collaborators model a commitment to ongoing, reflective experimentation in their teaching that is inspiring.

Perhaps the most important dimension of the book's plural imagination is its treatment of civic education itself. Some authors—Jeff Bernstein and Mike Burke, for instance—place informed citizenship at the heart of the project; they focus on the nurturing of students' capacity to assimilate data, produce publicly useful knowledge, and engage conflicting viewpoints with attentive civility. Other essays theorize what might be called the characterology of citizenship, using developmental and ethical categories—"self-authoring" for Carmen Werder, "vocation" for Rebecca Nowacek—to sketch models of public personhood that civic educators ask our students to inhabit. Still other chapters foreground the urgency of key "meta-issues"—ecological citizenship for Michael Smith, intercultural engagement for Rona Halualani—that no contemporary agenda for civic renewal can ignore. The authors make clear that these are importantly different but not conflicting emphases; indeed, the essays do a wonderful job of putting their diverse approaches in dialogue, and I will have more to say about the through-lines that seem to me to connect them. My point here is that the "anthology-ness" of *Citizenship Across the Curriculum* is an important part of its argument. The book maps citizenship as a complex practice that integrates various forms of knowledge, core values and competencies, and capacities for reflection, collaboration, and action. It maps higher education as a complex field of institutions and disciplines, in which different settings are apt for different aspects of civic socialization. As the title underscores, this sort of citizenship cannot be distilled or inculcated from some singular, Archimedean point. It must be taught "across" the whole educational landscape.[4]

This stress on the heterogeneity of the problem may seem commonsensical to us. Yet it reflects quite recent changes in practice and attitude among American academics, changes that eroded older strategies of civic education and catalyzed new ones. The most important change was the decline of civics itself. Until the 1960s, calls for civic education meant, with few exceptions, proposals for civics courses. There were important disagreements, both educational and political, about what that entailed: perhaps a primer on government, or an introduction to core problems of American life, or a survey of civilizational history or canonical texts that were taken to teach civic virtue. Yet advocates and critics shared the assumption that teaching "civics" meant investing particular faculty at a particular curricular address with title to the issues, materials, and methods required to lead young Americans into citizenship. All this changed with the transformation of higher education after World War II. The expansion of public systems and student access, the proliferation of specialized fields, and the professionalization of scholarly communities to oversee them worked together to undermine confidence in a unitary model of civic preparation and the willingness of the professoriate to teach it. By the 1960s, civics had become a disreputable curricular category, redolent of patriotic boosterism or stale models of character-building.

Yet, as I have discussed, these changes generated a sense of crisis about the divide between higher education and the larger society—concerns that led academics and academic institutions back to the issue of citizenship. Beginning some twenty-five years ago (we might take the founding of the Campus Outreach Opportunity League in 1983 and Campus Compact two years later as benchmarks), a new movement for campus-based community engagement revitalized interest in the public purposes of higher education. The first wave of the movement saw a proliferation of campus volunteerism and service-learning pedagogy that was impressive in its energy but often neglectful of larger issues of social change and democratic politics (Stanton et al. 1999). Over the past decade, spurred by critique within the movement itself, many academic institutions have launched ambitious centers and community-learning initiatives, committed to more sustained, intellectually rigorous, and socially transformative work. This second wave of engagement has tended to reframe the discourse of community service into one of collaboration and citizenship, to reconnect community work with systemic issues of policy, power, and justice, and to work for change not only in individual courses, but at the level of the curriculum and the campus as a whole (Scobey 2005). To be sure, such efforts still struggle for legitimacy among mainstream academics, disciplinary associations, and campus administrators, but their stature has risen steadily. If "civics" once connoted the musty practices of dead wood, "civic engagement" now evokes an insurgent claim to the future of undergraduate education—the kind of claim that leads national foundations to convene faculty innovators in projects like this.

Moreover, the civic turn has coincided with and drawn on other initiatives that have made the past twenty years an extraordinary, if unheralded, era of institutional creativity in undergraduate education. The editors rightly cite "writing across the curriculum" as a success story from which they borrow not only a title but a strategic model. I would add the efforts to institutionalize learning communities, experiential education, interdisciplinary programs, and diversity requirements in U.S. colleges and universities. These initiatives (all roughly contemporaneous) are characterized by a similar, transcurricular model of change and a deep ambivalence toward disciplinary authority. They all work strategically within the disciplines, even as they propose learning goals and teaching methods that problematize field-bound definitions of knowledge, methods, and skills. *Citizenship Across the Curriculum* evokes the same creative tension with disciplinarity. The essays take shifting, multiple stances toward the professional communities of inquiry within which the authors work and teach. The result is to situate civic education at once in, across, and against the disciplines.

The book, in short, belongs to a larger moment of civic energy and programmatic creativity in U.S. higher education. It is within that moment that its commitment to heterogeneity, its synthesis of large themes, grounded stories, topical diversity, and exploratory practice, makes sense. I do not mean to imply that the collection is "merely" eclectic, a grab-bag of good local stories. Quite the contrary: the essays are interwoven in a rigorously collaborative practice. Not only in the formal inclusion of coauthors' commentaries but also in the skein of internal conversations that criss-cross the essays, *Citizenship Across the Curriculum* enacts the ideal of dialogical citizenship proposed by Carmen Werder. The result, we might say, is a kind of "federal writers' project," where diverse, interconnected approaches to a complex problem coalesce around a relatively integrated conceptual frame. *E pluribus unum.*

Or rather, *e pluribus duo.* For to my mind, there are two persistent throughlines, two key "meta-claims" about education for citizenship, that align the essays together. The first is that the crux of civic education lies in the pedagogical encounter between teacher and student. It is striking that, although these essays teem with illuminating glimpses into the architecture of particular syllabi and assignments, they are not fundamentally focused on the craft of designing courses or assembling curricula. We do not find generalized discussions about, say, how to embed community partnerships in departmental courses of study or develop capstone projects using participatory or policy research. This is not a matter of neglect; the authors have other issues on their minds. They are thinking across the curriculum, but not so much about it.

What they are thinking *about*, it seems to me, is the power of pedagogy, the relational dramaturgy of teaching and learning, in the making of citizens. Nearly every essay includes—in fact, turns on—some powerful, moving, and complex scene in which the transaction between teacher and students serves to model, theorize, or problematize some aspect of citizenship. Rona Halualani's kinetic game, in which students array themselves according to the perceived norms of their ethnic cultures, playfully surfaces their sometimes inert assumptions about cultural identity and intercultural judgments. Howard Tinberg's iterative use of journaling, audio-memoir, and oral history, through which his students (and he himself) respond to, resist, and reflect on the literature of the Shoah, enacts a space of "intimate citizenship," a kind of ground-zero for nurturing compassion toward strangers. Mike Burke and Jeff Bernstein rework (seemingly traditional) analytical assignments into little dramas of disruption through which students experience the difficulty of producing accessible policy knowledge and engaging divergent viewpoints with critical, but fair-minded scrutiny. Each of these teachable moments, of course, carries important "content lessons" for civic learning. Yet running through all of them is a belief in what might be called (borrowing from Freud) the transferential power of engaged pedagogy. Civic learning takes place through scenes and moments in which teachers and students relationally enact, make visible, and reflect on the power, pleasures, and problems of being a public self.

This attention to the development of what I have called the public self, to civic education as the achievement of a kind of personhood, seems to me the second overarching theme of the book. Students do much important public work in these essays: they test and demystify policy debates, apply scientific analysis to social problems, research and interpret local environmental history, work in a variety of community organizations. Yet the book is fundamentally focused less on the change they make than on the change they undergo. I do not mean to imply that the authors dismiss the significance of the engaged research, policy analysis, and community partnerships in which they immerse their students. What I mean is that the essays tend to present such public action less as the *telos* of civic education, sufficient unto itself for a goal, than as catalysts for the student's development as a public person. This emphasis is clearest in Werder's rich appropriation of the psychology literature on "self-authoring," or Nowacek's equally rich appropriation of the Jesuit category of "vocation," as ways of theorizing civic learning. Yet, even with the more issue-oriented studies of the scientists and social scientists, the narrative center of gravity remains the blossoming of students into public selves—committed, compassionate, collaborative, critical, self-critical. Taken together, the essays offer a portrait of the student as a young citizen.

Or perhaps, a cubist collage. For like the book as a whole, that portrait is marked by the tension between heterogeneity and integration. The student-citizen who emerges in these pages will have learned to bring together capacities, values, and habits that are sometimes in tension with one another, and she will have learned to bring them to bear across a public sphere that is itself plural, complex, and conflicted. From Howard Tinberg (and others) she will have learned the civic necessity of moral empathy; from Mike Burke (and others) the demystifying power of critical analysis. Jeff Bernstein will have emphasized the need to bring civility, epistemological modesty, and a tolerance for ambiguity to political dialogue; Carmen Werder will have stressed the claiming of voice as both a precondition and an outcome of such dialogue. From all of these teachers, she will have learned that the public sphere is a complex, fractured domain, full of significant others with divergent experiences, interests, and values. David Geelan, Matt Fisher, Mike Burke, and Rona Halualani will have underscored the range of literacies (scientific, quantitative, intercultural) needed to talk with those others, to argue with them, to work with them. Conversely, Rebecca Nowacek will have taught her to listen for the personal call to responsibility and compassion in the midst of the cacophony. Finally Howard Tinberg, Rona Halualani, David Geelan, and Michael Smith will have enlarged her sense of the distances and scales at which civic peers must engage one another, challenging her to cross not only ethnic and national boundaries, but also ecological and existential divides. She will have had, in short, an extraordinarily complex, dialectical education for citizenship—bracing, at times daunting, but exhilarating too.

New Questions

Even the best answers—especially the best answers—beg new questions. Precisely because *Citizenship Across the Curriculum* offers such a wide-ranging response to the double context of civic and educational crisis, it opens up issues that the book cannot fully engage. Let me end by pointing to three issues that invite further thought.

The first has to do with what seems to me the one real lacuna in the book's disciplinary range: attention to the role of the arts and humanities in civic life and civic education. The humanities are of course richly represented here in Howard Tinberg's discussion of reading as empathetic practice, Carmen Werder's analysis of the poetics of students' self-descriptions, Rebecca Nowacek's analysis of citizenship as vocation. Yet, along with such modes of ethical pedagogy, I would argue that the interpretive and creative disciplines offer an essential arena for modeling and theorizing the centrality of story-telling and meaning-making in civic life (Scobey 2007). We cannot become a democratic community, a "we the people" (whether that "we" is local, national, or planetary), except through the cocreation of stories about our commonalties, our divisions, and our problems. Culture, then—the practice of collective meaning-making—is an indispensable medium of citizenship; and the cultural disciplines are equally essential to civic education. Our students become public selves in part by learning to practice a kind of story-telling in which listening, interpretive discernment, and collaboration are deeply integrated.

A second issue concerns the role of non-academic peers. As I have noted, *Citizenship Across the Curriculum* explores with depth and passion the transferential power of the student-teacher relationship in civic education. That relationship unfolds largely on campuses that constitute spaces of separation and sometimes privilege within a diverse democracy; indeed such set-apartness is part of what makes possible the playfulness and risk of the pedagogical encounter. At the same time, however, preparing students to engage significant others who have quite different experiences, values, and interests means breaching that separation *within* the educational process. A pedagogy that remains too exclusively focused on the dramaturgy of the teacher-student encounter, or the community of students in a classroom, may inadvertently send the message that students will remain the center of their own civic experience. Community partners have a crucial role to play in this de-centering process, not simply as fellow citizens, and certainly not as objects of academic expertise or philanthropy, but as interlocutors and coeducators. The authors clearly know this: the essays include powerful stories of community projects, oral history interviews, and other extramural public work. Yet the importance of such practices—the inclusion of the community partner as a "third party" in the pedagogical encounter—raises a host of new questions. How does the partner change the dynamics of teaching and learning? What kinds of pedagogical roles can he or she appropriately play? How can faculty and community partner best work together? How do they negotiate the connections between their project partnership—with its own goals, responsibilities, and frictions—and their division of labor as teachers and mentors? The partnership practices spawned by the community-engagement movement, in short, offer both opportunities and complexities for civic pedagogy that deserve fuller attention.

Finally *Citizenship Across the Curriculum* touches suggestively on the complex issue of the *geographies* of citizenship, and this too, it seems to me, cries out for further thinking. The book's stress on the heterogeneity of civic life and civic education speaks in particular to one of the most vexed questions in current citizenship theory and practice: the relationship between citizenship and nationality. To many theorists and activists, the dominant association of civic life with national membership seems blinkered and ethically problematic in a globalized and multicultural world. For some, the very category of citizenship is exclusionary, a legal means for nation-states to marginalize internal minorities and demonize immigrants. For others, national borders prevent effective responses to global-scale problems like climate change and North–South inequality. Still others defend the resilience and value of civic nationalism, arguing that democratic politics flourishes best in a public sphere that is neither particularist nor abstractly universal, but grounded in a shared but expansive way of life (Hollinger 2006; Scobey 2001).

The authors of *Citizenship Across the Curriculum* speak to these debates with varying degrees of explicitness. David Geelan strongly objects to equating the civic with the national, arguing that the ideal of citizenship is "almost antithetical to nationalism," while the editors offer a gentler transnationalism: "[M]any of the issues and problems we must deal with in the twenty-first century... require that we be citizens of the world rather than a nation-state," they exhort in the introduction. "While we may be citizens of towns, cities, states, and nations, we are also citizens of the planet." The book as a whole models this notion that civic educators prepare students for multiple geographies of affiliation—even as the authors tacitly accept the primacy of U.S. institutions and policy agendas for their students' lives. More generally, however, I would argue that the book's focus on the diversity of engaged pedagogy and its ambivalent relationship to disciplinary authority proposes a potentially important contribution to the debates over citizenship and national authority. Just as civic education needs to work at once in, across, and against the disciplines, so civic agency in our (globalized, multicultural, nationally organized) world must work simultaneously in, across, and against the nation-state (and at the same in, across, and against the racial, religious, and regional subcommunities that divide and compose nation-states). By exploring the teaching of citizenship across the curriculum, in short, the book offers a suggestive map of the workings of citizenship across all the geographies and attachments that claim our attention as democratic actors.

These observations constitute an agenda of issues for a sequel to take up, however. As it stands, *Citizenship Across the Curriculum* makes an important intervention in the double crisis with which I started this chapter. The authors are exemplary in the creativity of their pedagogy, their compassion for their students, the three-dimensionality of their vision of the civic, and the intentionality of their commitment to collaborative reflection. I am hungry for more.

Notes

1. Philanthropy for Active Civic Engagement (PACE) has been a leading voice for the development of civic professionalism among foundations and grant-makers.

2. For an introduction to the extraordinary array of youth leadership initiatives that have emerged over the past fifteen years, see the social-enterprise coalition America Forward (www.americaforward.org).

3. Scott Peters's historical scholarship (2007) helpfully complicates this overall understanding of the land-grant system, pointing to populist traditions of community-based scholarship that ran counter to the model of expert "outreach" to the public. This remained, I would argue, a counter-tendency within the larger, technocratic land-grant tradition.

4. It is worth noting the resonances between the authors of *Citizenship Across the Curriculum,* brought together under the aegis of the Carnegie Foundation for the Advancement of Teaching, and the Carnegie Foundation's Political Engagement Project. Both initiatives reflect Carnegie's interest in using the scholarship of teaching and learning to investigate the role of civic and political engagement in undergraduate education; both include a diverse array of projects and practices in their inquiry. For an account and analysis of the Political Engagement Project, see Colby et al. (2007).

Works Cited

Barber, Benjamin. 1992. *An aristocracy of everyone: The politics of education and the future of America.* New York: Oxford University Press.

Benson, Lee, John L. Puckett, and Ira Harkavy. 2007. *Dewey's dream: Universities and democracies in an age of education reform.* Philadelphia: Temple University Press.

Bloom, Allan. 1988. *The closing of the American mind.* New York: Simon and Shuster.

Boyte, Harry. 2004a. *Everyday politics: Reconnecting citizens and public life.* Philadelphia: University of Pennsylvania Press.

———. 2004b. *Going public: Academics and public life.* Dayton, Ohio: Kettering Foundation.

Boyte, Harry, and Nan Kari. 1996. *Building America: The democratic promise of public work.* Philadelphia: Temple University Press.

Colby, Anne, Elizabeth Beaumont, Thomas Ehrlich, and Josh Corngold. 2007. *Educating for democracy: Preparing undergraduates for responsible political engagement.* San Francisco: Jossey-Bass.

Dzur, Albert W. 2008. *Democratic professionalism: Citizen participation and the reconstruction of professional ethics, identity, and practice.* University Park: Pennsylvania State University Press.

Gibson, Cynthia. 2006. *Citizens at the center.* Washington, D.C.: Case Foundation.

Hollinger, David. 2006. *Postethnic America: Beyond multiculturalism.* New York: Basic Books.

Kiesa, Abby, Alexander P. Orlowski, Peter Levine, Deborah Both, Emily Hoban Kirby, Mark Hugo Lopez, and Karlo Barrios Marcelo. 2008. *Millennials talk politics: A study of college student political engagement.* Medford, Mass.: Center for Information and Research on Civic Learning and Engagement, Tufts University.

Kimball, Bruce. 1998. *Tenured radicals: How politics has corrupted our higher education.* New York: Ivan R. Dee.

Levine, Peter. 2007. *The future of democracy: Developing the next generation of American citizens.* Medford, Mass.: Tufts University Press.

Nussbaum, Martha C. 1997. *Cultivating humanity: A classical defense of reform in liberal education.* Cambridge, Mass.: Harvard University Press.

Peters, Scott J. 2007. *Changing the story about higher education's public purposes and work: Land-grants, liberty, and the Little Country Theater.* Ann Arbor, Mich.: Imagining America (Foreseeable Futures Position Paper #6, published by Imagining America: Artists and Scholars in Public Life. www.imaginingamerica.org [accessed June 6, 2009]).

Rosen, Jay. 2001. *What are journalists for?* New Haven, Conn.: Yale University Press.

Scobey, David. 2001. "The specter of citizenship." *Citizenship Studies* 5: 11–26.

———. 2005. "The second wave of engagement: Learning from West Coconut Grove." In Samina Quraeshi, ed., *Re-Imagining West Coconut Grove.* Washington, D.C.: Spacemaker Press.

———. 2006. "Legitimation crisis: The Spellings Commission and the civic engagement movement." Plenary, Imagining America: Artists and Scholars in Public Life national conference (Columbus, Ohio).

———. 2007. "The arts of citizenship in a diverse democracy: The public work of the arts and humanities." Lecture, Wesleyan University, Middletown, Conn.

Sirianni, Carmen, and Lewis Friedland. 2001. *Civic innovation in America: Community empowerment, public policy, and the movement for civic renewal.* Berkeley: University of California Press.

Stanton, Timothy K., Nadinne I. Cruz, and Dwight Giles. 1999. *Service-Learning: A movement's pioneers reflect on its origins, practice, and future.* San Francisco: Jossey-Bass.

Sullivan, William. 1995. *Work and integrity: The crisis and promise of professionalism in America.* San Francisco: John Wiley & Sons.

U.S. Department of Education. 2006. *A test of leadership: Charting the future of U.S. higher education.* A Report of the Secretary of Education's Commission on the Future of Higher Education. Washington, D.C.: U.S. Department of Education.

There are at least two perspectives from which one can view the preceding collection of essays. As the volume's title suggests, the contributing chapters all deal with some form of "citizenship" and the ways in which citizenship can be incorporated into the academic curriculum as a legitimate teaching–learning objective. But they are all at least as intensively focused on the teaching–learning process itself. It is no easy task to put together a collection of essays all of which have something important to say. To put together a collection that simultaneously contributes to two important academic conversations is even more of a challenge. *Citizenship Across the Curriculum* meets that challenge.

In the spirit of this volume, it seems only appropriate to begin with a brief personal statement. Interestingly enough, the statement my work calls for parallels in many ways that made by Michael Smith in his chapter "Local Environmental History and the Journey to Ecological Citizenship." As in Michael's case, and indeed as is true for many of the book's other contributors as well, my commitment to new forms of teaching and learning as well as to education for citizenship grew out of a sense that traditional discipline-defined teaching strategies were not enough. Like Michael, I could say that I had been creating good learning environments that students found generally satisfying. My students learned to read critically and make meaning from books and other sources, and they often engaged in lively discussion and wrote fine analytical papers. But also like Michael, I felt something important was missing. Teaching and learning *about,* located exclusively in the context of the classroom, was inadvertently "reproducing the very values I wanted to challenge" (see Smith's chapter in this volume for these thoughts). What both my teaching and my students' learning lacked was quite literally a *palpable* sense of reality. As a teacher of literature, I was not moving my students beyond a learning experience that was, in Parker Palmer's words, "objective, analytic, experimental," a way of knowing that "itself breeds intellectual habits, indeed spiritual instincts, that destroy community" (Palmer 1997, 22).

My solution to this challenge was the same as Michael's: I learned to draw upon the power of primary experience coupled with structured reflection. Eventually I would learn that others had already discovered the power of such a combination and had named it "service-learning." But back in 1989 my discovery of a fledgling national movement took place only *after* I had personally experienced the upsurge in student interest and motivation that real-world connections can bring about. This experience was exhilarating, and it led me as a teacher to appreciate the profound difference between something academically correct and, to appropriate a phrase from Keats, something "swelling into reality" (1970/1817, 42). It seems to me that all the contributors to this volume testify—each in his/her own distinctive way—to some such discovery of the power and pleasures of teaching and learning as transformational experiences.

The Scholarship of Teaching and Learning

As the introduction to this volume makes clear, an intensive concern with the scholarship of teaching and learning was indeed the culture out of which the present volume grew. A concern with some kind of citizenship may well have been encoded somewhere in that culture, but it was heightened *academic* engagement that paid the bills. This is evident everywhere throughout the chapters both in the quantity of time, space, and energy devoted to pedagogical issues—quite irrespective of any civic dimension or civic implications—and in the sophistication with which these pedagogical issues are addressed. In other words, even if one were not at all personally concerned with "citizenship" and preparation for citizenship as items that should be on the academic agenda, one could still learn so much from these chapters that one might recommend them simply because of what they have to say about good teaching and deep learning.

What, then, does this collection tell us about good teaching and deep learning? First and foremost, it tells us it is impossible to underestimate the importance of *active learning*. In every instance, from the real-world problem-solving modeled by those working in scientific-mathematical fields to the agency-intensive focus of the humanists and social scientists, all the courses described place a premium on students as knowledge producers (see Nowacek's chapter in this volume). Such an emphasis demands that students acquire not only effective intellectual tools and analytical skills but also habits of critical inquiry and the kind of self-knowledge that anchors their skills in a dynamic sense of self. Perhaps no chapter makes this clearer than Carmen Werder's "Fostering Self-Authorship for Citizenship: Telling Metaphors in Dialogue" (original emphasis). Here the work at hand is first and foremost to help students recognize just how poorly they are served when they choose for themselves as learners the metaphor of "*Self-as-Sponge*." Unless they can begin to move beyond such an inherently limited self-image, even their acquiring sophisticated analytical skills may not save them from shallowness.

But truly active learning, whether it be of a more technical or existential kind, cannot draw exclusively on cognitive development. Equally important is the affective domain, a domain as likely to be ignored in contemporary courses on literature as in courses on water purification. As Michael Smith remarks of the competencies he seeks to develop: "Most of [them] fall into categories of affective learning that range far from the content-oriented learning goals" of the disciplines that inform his own teaching; namely history and environmental studies. Cultivating such competencies can take many forms. In Howard Tinberg's seminar on the Shoah, it assumes the personally intimate form registered in the title of his chapter: "We Are All Citizens of Auschwitz: Intimate Engagement and the Teaching of the Shoah." In David Geelan's course for teachers of science—described in "Science, Technology and Understanding: Teaching the Teachers of Citizens of the Future"—it reveals itself in an "approach to teaching and learning science [that] naturally places science education within the context of students' lives." In other words, what matters most is one's ability to tap and develop a genuine sense of personal connection.

All the contributors to this volume pay careful attention to the connection between the "content" of their course(s) and their students' "lived experience," whether this entails choosing illustrative materials with which the students are already familiar (Fisher and Geelan); working with the students' personal (Tinberg and Werder), ethnic (Halualani), or geographical (Smith) identities; or some other kind of connection. Especially interesting in this regard is Rebecca Nowacek's chapter, "Understanding Citizenship as Vocation in a Multidisciplinary Senior Capstone," for while several contributors work with the professional/

disciplinary identity students bring to the course(s) in question, Rebecca makes this professional/disciplinary identity the very center of her capstone seminar. In this way she is able to help them "identify the worldviews and ways of knowing they [have] cultivated during their university studies." Here the word "vocation" is meant to have full resonance. As one of her respondents, Mike Burke, notes: "I must admit to an initial sense of discomfort when I first saw Rebecca's chapter. . . . The use of a term ["vocation"] so laden with religious history and meaning seemed problematic to me." But it is very much in the spirit of these essays that Rebecca does not back away from the weight of this term. For her, as for each of her colleagues in his/her own way, the connection between academic study and something larger than academic study, between course work and an individual's sense of himself/herself as someone capable of addressing what Rebecca calls "the world's 'great hunger'" lies at the very heart of the teaching–learning experience.

Finally, Rebecca's phrase "the world's 'great hunger'" serves to introduce one other critical dimension of the teaching–learning complex we have been delineating—a dimension Matt Fisher identifies when he notes that an important similarity between his work as a teacher of chemistry and Mike Burke's work as a teacher of mathematics is the priority they make of "contextualizing data and ideas." As important as it is to link the course to the learner, to anchor it in a student's potential for agency and ability to contribute, so it is of equal importance that student potential be focused on issues worthy of deep learning. If we imagine the course, and the discipline(s) it embodies, as a bridge that allows holistically engaged students to go somewhere, to move beyond the familiar, to develop new skills and expand their sense of self, the place they use that bridge to get to must be worthy of their effort. Hence, we can understand the care all the contributors take to connect their course not just to their students and their students' evolving identities but also to the great questions and issues that challenge our country and our planet.

It would be easy to underestimate the importance of this move. There is probably no faculty member anywhere who does not believe that what he/she teaches is important not only for the students in his/her class but also for society in general. Moreover, there are probably few faculty members who do not see their teaching as relevant to some contemporary issue. Matt Fisher speaks to this point when he notes that undergraduate science education "assume[s] that majors who have a basic understanding of the scientific concepts will automatically make connections between those concepts and global challenges. . . ." Unfortunately, experience shows that this is not the case, and so one word from Matt's chapter that especially stands out is "explicit," as in "explicit recognition of the important connection between science and social issues." But even in chapters without this verbal emphasis, it is clear Matt's cocontributors are very much on the same page when it comes to contextualizing their teaching within a set of urgent contemporary issues. I will return to this topic when I discuss the volume's approach to citizenship, but for now I simply want to underscore the importance of embedding learning in such issues. As Mike Burke remarks at one point, ". . . I have never before taught courses in which the level of student interest was so high. . . . I was never asked the question, 'Why do we have to learn this?' " How many faculty who simply assume students see a connection between course content and the "the world's 'great hunger' " can make this claim?

In the end, what all these observations suggest is the primacy of design, and design, in turn, implies intentionality, scaffolding/structure, assessment, and experimentation. Many of the chapters include a detailed design history in which we see authors struggling to "get right" the various elements and activities that constitute their courses. Active experimentation assisted by diagnostic assessment creates a pattern of constant improvement. We are here at a far remove from teaching and learning as simply a teacher's delivery of technical expertise combined with students' commitment to "apply themselves." To return to Michael Smith's experience cited above, we are no longer satisfied with merely "conventional" success. Jeff Bernstein knows, for example, he can deliver "course content" as well as the next person but questions whether "educating [his] students as future political scientists" is all he should aspire to. Is there not, in his words, some "better legacy," "something more lasting"?

It is ironic, but also not surprising, that in rejecting conventional disciplinary strategies and a narrow academic understanding of success, each of the volume's contributors succeeds not only in helping his/her students achieve "something more lasting," but also in more effectively mastering, if not disciplinary "content" in the traditional sense, then something even more important: essential disciplinary skills. Demonstrating their courses' ability to deliver the latter is a key function of the outcome assessments most chapters include. Matt Fisher, David Geelan, and Mike Burke have no interest in sacrificing scientific or mathematical competence to some fuzzy notion of "relevance." The courses they describe and document allow students to develop and strengthen essential technical competencies while at the same time developing a sense of agency in addressing real-world problems. Indeed, as David explicitly notes in his response to Matt's chapter: ". . . there's a very strong argument to be made that engaging with the science content in the context of an authentic social or public-health issue leads to a deeper and richer level of engagement with and understanding of the science." In some of the less technical courses, the potential for tension between discipline-based expertise and contemporary relevance may be less apparent, but here too it is clear that contributors see relevance as way of strengthening, not undermining or diluting, discipline-based competencies. Indeed, Rona Halualani, a professor of communication, suggests in her response to Carmen Werder's chapter: "Perhaps we have it backwards." Perhaps our students' sense of themselves as "part and parcel of a society that needs them" could turn out to be the single most important factor driving their mastery of "key skill sets." It is time we turned directly to questions of citizenship.

Citizenship

As much of the research Jeff Bernstein cites in his chapter shows, youth participation in the political process—as well as youth appreciation of the importance of staying informed about current events—traced a steady and fairly steep decline from the late 1960s through the middle of the 1990s. More recently, a marked increase in youth participation in the 2006 and 2008 elections suggests this trend may have bottomed out and has led some researchers to express guarded optimism. This includes Robert Putnam, whose *Bowling Alone: The Collapse and Revival of American Community* (2000) raised enough concern about declining "social capital" to put the book on the *New York Times* bestseller list. In March 2008, Putnam wrote in a *Boston Globe* op-ed piece:

> Last month the UCLA researchers reported that "For today's freshmen, discussing politics is more prevalent now than at any point in the past 41 years." This and other evidence led us and other observers to speak hopefully of a 9/11 generation, perhaps even a "new Greatest Generation."

Whether or not we really are experiencing some kind of renaissance in political engagement, other studies clearly establish that with regard to *non-political* forms of civic engagement, today's young people are not, in fact, any less engaged than their elders. (See, for example, Cliff Zukin et al.'s *A New Engagement? Political Participation, Civic Life, and the Changing American Citizen* [2006] for a comprehensive review of the data that support this finding.) Furthermore, young people themselves have vigorously rejected the blanket implication that they are *civically* disengaged. As a group of thirty-three student leaders who met at the Wingspread Conference Center in Racine, Wisconsin, in 2001 write in *The New Student Politics* (2001):

> For the most part, we are frustrated with conventional politics, viewing it as inaccessible. We discovered at Wingspread, however, a common sense that while we are disillusioned with conventional politics (and therefore most forms of political activity), we are deeply involved in civic issues through non-traditional forms of engagement. We are neither apathetic nor disengaged. (1)

One of the present volume's editors, Rebecca Nowacek, implicitly corroborates this claim when she notes that most of the students at her university, Marquette, "actively embrace the Jesuit goal of becoming 'men and women for others,' volunteering their time to social justice work in impressive numbers. And yet . . . many of them remain wary of the obligations of democratic citizenship."

Thus, the question of how best to promote "citizenship" demands that we disabuse ourselves of both unexamined assumptions regarding young people's civic indifference and a reductive understanding of "citizenship" as simply—or even primarily—participation in electoral politics. Richard Battistoni, the author of *Civic Engagement Across the Curriculum: A Resource Book for Service-Learning Faculty in All Disciplines* (2002), has developed an exercise that asks each participant to look at a list of fifteen possible responses to the question, "How do you define citizenship?" and then to rank them in the order that "most closely models" the participant's "own idea of good citizenship." The items include: voting, working for a candidate in a local election, tutoring a migrant worker, walking a frail person across a busy street, leaving one's car at home and biking/walking to work/school, talking with a friend about a social issue of importance, and joining the armed forces. Such an exercise helps us appreciate the many legitimate ways in which one can understand civic participation.

This is especially important in the present context because one can easily imagine each of the volume's contributors making a different first choice—or adding still another item not on the list. Thus, the exercise suggests the wisdom of an expansive approach to "citizenship," one in which the term can mean or imply, among other things: developing traditional political skills or "tools" (Bernstein), building "a soulful relationship with others" (Tinberg), the ability "to participate in an *informed* way in the ongoing social conversation around the issues and problems" (Geelan), being "actively involved and immersed in one's surrounding community and civic society" (Halualani), a vocation, "something we are called to do" (Nowacek), and "the manner (skills, disposition) in which an individual responds to membership in a community and the mutual relationships that come with such membership" (Fisher).

It is important to note that such variety is not to be equated with conceptual incoherence. Many of the definitions stated or implied in the volume's chapters overlap, and even when they do not, they are more likely to be complementary than contradictory. Thus, while contributors like Jeff Bernstein and Mike Burke stress skills sets as key to citizen participation in American democracy, David Geelan, the only non-American in the group, suggests "we are citizens of our families, our local communities, and the world, *much more than we are citizens of nations or states*" (emphasis added). Taken together, the volume's stated and implied definitions model an understanding of citizenship that necessarily works on many different levels. This interrelated diversity represents one of the collection's primary strengths. While helping students acquire the skills that will make them more likely to contribute to what the Wingspread participants (2001, 1) call "conventional politics," we must not ignore the very real openings other, "nontraditional forms of engagement" provide. Rather than merely insisting on the importance of conventional politics, we must be prepared to help students foster a commitment to civic awareness and public action in all relevant spheres. And we must do so, not only because such a strategy allows us to tap into acknowledged interests and inclinations, but because we have good reason to believe forms of civic engagement do not operate in sealed environments. While researchers disagree as to the extent to which nonpolitical forms of engagement naturally lead to more political forms (Zukin et al. 2006, 193–194), it seems safe to conclude that "widening the many narrow pathways" to public engagement that already exist "can help more young people find their way to active citizenship and public life" (153).

Hence, the wisdom of the editors' explicitly evoking the ideals, insights, and strategies of the writing across the curriculum (WAC) movement as a model for their own work. Like the development of writing skills, the development of citizenship skills *must* be a cross-curricular undertaking, and that, in turn, necessitates respect for a wide diversity of disciplinary interests and priorities: citizenship in a chemistry course will not, cannot look like citizenship in a communication studies course. The challenge is not to seek uniformity but to nurture distinctive possibilities. Citizenship across the curriculum cannot succeed if it is merely "sequestered" in a single discipline like political science, but it can also not succeed if it is not *naturalized* in every discipline in a convincing way. As the editors write, it must work in a way that furthers legitimate disciplinary goals "while also helping students become more aware of citizenship."

I believe all the chapters in this volume succeed beautifully in "naturalizing" citizenship—however the term be defined—in allowing it to emerge holistically from legitimate discipline-specific activities and concerns. I also believe that, just as WAC encourages "writing to learn" as well as "writing in the disciplines," all the chapters convincingly demonstrate not only that preparation for citizenship can take a wide variety of discipline-appropriate forms, but that incorporating a discipline-appropriate commitment to citizenship can itself contribute mightily to the social value and the educational resonance of the disciplines. This is a point I have already alluded to in the preceding section of this chapter.

Another Civic/Civil Dimension

There is, moreover, one special way in which this volume makes a distinctive and important contribution to education for citizenship. I refer here to its exploration of the importance of civil dialogue and informed disagreement. Both Jeff

Bernstein and Rebecca Nowacek contextualize their courses and their educational goals with reference to "the crippling effects of living in a society dominated by the shrill talk radio of Limbaugh and Franken" (Nowacek). Mike Burke is at pains to stress the need to ground "our national discourse" in "analyses built on a solid foundation of data." Again and again the contributors return to the importance of helping students learn "to engage in extended dialogue across difference" (Nowacek), to move beyond the "dominance of consecutive monologues." Surely Michael Smith is correct when he notes in his response to Rebecca's chapter:

> We *all* "need practice and coaching in the art of principled and civil disagreement." Without this capacity differences fester and the cost of conflict rises. In a world in which we are all increasingly pulled toward people and media whose worldviews primarily resonate with our own, civil disagreement becomes one of the more important mechanisms for civic engagement. (Original emphasis)

Furthermore, in the very way in which the volume is structured the contributors try to model what it means to go beyond the "dominance of consecutive monologues." While they take pains to be respectful and supportive of each other's work, they also work hard to learn from each other, to appropriate concepts, concerns, and distinctions that can enrich their own thinking. As many of us can recall from our graduate student days, the academy need not take a back seat to any legislative body when it comes to aggressiveness, hypersensitivity, and barely disguised disdain. By placing such a premium on civility with substance, the book does more than simply explore another dimension of citizenship; it recognizes civility as a *foundational value*. As the expression goes, this by itself would be worth the price of admittance.

Opportunities

When it comes to teaching and learning strategies, none of the contributors to *Citizenship Across the Curriculum* needs any advice from me. Still, I would like to offer a few observations that follow primarily from their students' observations— or from their own observations on what their students have told them.

Several years ago I was fortunate to be able to spend a year working with John Gardner on active and civic learning in the first-year classroom (Zlotkowski 2002 and in press). One of my assignments was to visit approximately two dozen campuses to talk to students as well as faculty and staff about their first-year experiences. No word or term came up more frequently in my meetings with students than "hands-on." By this students meant not just issues and assignments with real world significance but work that took them out into the real world. On just about every campus, this was the way a majority of students characterized their preferred learning style. I see a similar inclination running through many of the course narratives. Michael Smith's work, of course, deliberately focuses on the power of such hands-on learning, but it also appears explicitly when Carmen notes in her response to Matt's chapter: "Students often try to remind us of this need for genuine opportunities for practice" and implicitly when Rebecca describes how "Seeing that cavernous pipe [that dumps raw sewage into the Milwaukee River] while paddling down the river brought home to me and (I know from conversations) to others the reality of the Deep Tunnel problem."

Rebecca's experience in the context of a course at a Jesuit university brings to mind a point made in 2000 by Peter-Hans Kolvenbach, S.J., former Superior General of the order. Emphasizing the need to "raise our Jesuit educational standard to 'educate the whole person of solidarity for the real world,'" he referred to a recent statement by the pope in which the latter observed that such solidarity "is learned through 'contact' rather than through 'concepts'" (Kolvenbach 2000). Whether or not one agrees with this judgment, I think there can be no doubt that "contact" can serve as a powerful complement to "concepts." It seems to me Carmen has it exactly right when she proposes that "across higher education, we continue to emphasize the cognitive domain exclusively" (in Fisher's chapter) or Mike Burke when he suggests that "[t]he habits of textbook learning and, more recently, of digitally-mediated learning often induce a kind of stupor in our students, and the kind of hands-on experience that Michael [Smith] requires counteracts this." The fact that Howard has designed the research assignment in his course on the Shoah around each student's interviewing a Shoah survivor and that Rona sees her intercultural communication course as leading to "concrete action," big or small, ranging in "different degrees and levels" indicates to me such a recognition of the power of the sensuous and the concrete. I am by no means suggesting that every course should include a field-based component, only that a failure to make greater use of field-based experiences must rank among instructors' most important "missed opportunities."

A second important opportunity, perhaps of equal importance, comes into focus in Jeff's description of the mechanism that makes possible his experiential version of an American government course. I refer here to his use of undergraduate honors students to facilitate the course simulations. They are, in Jeff's own words, the "linchpins in making this arrangement work," but they do more than "just" make possible the course's experiential dimension. They also alert us to the untapped potential of seeing at least some of our students as genuine colleagues. Indeed, so impressive have been the leadership roles students have assumed in service-learning programs around the country that several years ago my colleagues Nicholas Longo, then the director of Campus Compact's Raise Your Voice initiative, and James Williams, then a junior at Princeton, set out to capture some of what was happening. The result was *Students as Colleagues: Expanding the Circle of Service-Learning Leadership* (Zlotkowski, Longo, and Williams 2006), a collection of essays and vignettes that document the many ways students themselves are facilitating their fellow students' learning through community involvement. If our goal is to graduate more students who possess a strong sense of civic agency, we could hardly go wrong in making more students our partners both in designing and in implementing opportunities for citizenship across the curriculum.

By now it must be clear how much I have enjoyed working with my "virtual colleagues" on this important collection of essays. I must say, I envy them their personal–professional connections, not to mention their Carnegie residencies in "the golden foothills of the California Coastal Range." Although we come to the "problem" of the academy's failure to take seriously education for citizenship from somewhat different perspectives, I have no doubt we share the same core vision of an academy that does justice to our students' need for genuine engagement—academic and civic. I also have no doubt we see these two forms of engagement as intimately intertwined. The academy and its disciplines need something beyond themselves both to inspire and to ground their activities. As the historian Thomas Bender (1993) writes in *Intellect and Public Life: Essays on the Social History of Academic Intellectuals in the United States:*

> The integrity of the academic intellect is not endangered by competing discourses of social inquiry. The risk now is precisely the opposite. Academe is threatened by the twin dangers of fossilization and scholasticism . . . The agenda for the next decade, at least as I see it, ought to be the opening up of the disciplines, the ventilating of professional communities that have come to share too much and that have become too self-referential. (143)

At the same time, as the chapters in this collection repeatedly demonstrate, citizenship—on any level and in any context—cannot flourish without the skills, values, and habits of heart and mind that the academy is uniquely positioned to develop.

John Dewey, America's most important philosopher of education, spent the better part of his life trying to convince his fellow citizens that the problem of the schools and the problems of democracy are ultimately one and the same. We cannot address the weaknesses of our society unless we also address the weaknesses of our education system. We cannot demand an engaged, informed populace while allowing, or even encouraging, our young people to develop lifelong habits of intellectual passivity and moral disengagement. I believe there are many reasons Dewey would have been pleased with this book.

Works Cited

Battistoni, Richard M. 2002. *Civic engagement across the curriculum: A resource book for service learning faculty in all disciplines.* Providence, R.I.: Campus Compact.

Bender, Thomas. 1993. *Intellect and public life: Essays on the social history of academic intellectuals in the United States.* Baltimore, Md.: Johns Hopkins Press.

Keats, John. 1970. *Letters of John Keats,* ed. R. Gittings. Oxford: Oxford University Press.

Kolvenbach, Peter-Hans, S.J. 2000. The service of faith and the promotion of justice in American Jesuit higher education. http://www.scu.edu/ignatiancenter/events/conferences/archives/justice/upload/f07_kolvenbach_keynote.pdf (accessed June 6, 2009).

The new student politics. 2001. Providence, R.I.: Campus Compact.

Palmer, Parker J. 1997. Community, conflict, and ways of knowing: Ways to deepen our educational agenda. *Change* 29(5): 20–25.

Putnam, Robert D. 2000. *Bowling alone: The collapse and revival of American community.* New York: Simon & Schuster.

———. 2008. The rebirth of American civic life. *Boston Globe,* March 2. http://www.boston.com/bostonglobe/editorial_opinion/oped/articles/2008/03/02/the_rebirth_of_american_civic_life/ (accessed June 5, 2009).

Zlotkowski, Edward. 2002. Service-learning and the introductory course: Lessons from across the disciplines. In *Service-learning and the first-year experience: Preparing students for personal success and civic responsibility,* ed. E. Zlotkowski. Columbia, S.C.: National Resource Center for the First-Year Experience and Students in Transition: 27–36.

———. In press. Taking service seriously. In J. Saltmarsh and E. Zlotkowski. *Higher education and democracy: Essays on service-learning and civic engagement.* Philadelphia: Temple University Press.

Zlotkowski, Edward, Nicholas V. Longo, and James R. Williams, eds. 2006. *Students as colleagues: Expanding the circle of service-learning leadership.* Providence, R.I.: Campus Compact.

Zukin, Cliff, Scott Keeter, Molly Andolina, Krista Jenkins, and Michael X. Delli Carpini. 2006. *A new engagement? Political participation, civic life, and the changing American citizen.* London: Oxford University Press.

CONTRIBUTORS

Jeffrey L. Bernstein is Professor of Political Science and Faculty Development Fellow at Eastern Michigan University. His work has appeared in the *Journal of Political Science Education, Politics and Gender,* the *Journal of Public Affairs Education,* and numerous edited volumes. He is currently secretary of the International Society for the Scholarship of Teaching and Learning.

Michael C. Burke is Professor of Mathematics at the College of San Mateo, where he has served as a co-coordinator of the Integrative Learning Program. His recent published work has appeared in *Peer Review,* a publication of the Association of American Colleges and Universities.

Matthew A. Fisher is Associate Professor and Chair of Chemistry at Saint Vincent College. He was director of Saint Vincent College's Teaching Enhancement and Mentoring Program for seven years and is a senior fellow with the National Center for Science and Civic Engagement. He also is a member of the Program Committee for the American Chemical Society's Division of Chemical Education and the ACS Committee on Environmental Improvement, where he coordinates education activities.

David Geelan is Senior Lecturer in science education and Director of Middle Years Education at the University of Queensland. He is the author of two books on educational research, *Weaving Narrative Nets* and *Undead Theories,* as well as co-author of six middle school science textbooks.

Rona Tamiko Halualani is Professor of Language, Culture and Intercultural Communication in the Communication Studies Department at San Jose State

University. She is the author of *In the Name of Hawaiians* and two forthcoming books, *Critical Intercultural Communication Studies: An Introduction* and the *Blackwell Handbook of Critical Intercultural Communication.* Her work has appeared in the *International Journal of Intercultural Relations, Journal of International and Intercultural Communication, Communication Theory,* and the *International and Intercultural Communication Annual.*

Mary Taylor Huber is Senior Scholar at the Carnegie Foundation for the Advancement of Teaching. She has worked with Carnegie's scholarship of teaching and learning projects, including the Carnegie Academy for the Scholarship of Teaching and Learning. A cultural anthropologist, Huber's books include *Disciplinary Styles in the Scholarship of Teaching and Learning: Exploring Common Ground* (co-edited with Sherwyn Morreale); *Balancing Acts: The Scholarship of Teaching and Learning in Academic Careers;* and, with Pat Hutchings, *The Advancement of Learning: Building the Teaching Commons.*

Pat Hutchings is Vice President of the Carnegie Foundation for the Advancement of Teaching. She has worked closely with a wide range of programs and research initiatives, including the Carnegie Academy for the Scholarship of Teaching and Learning. Her publications include *Opening Lines: Approaches to the Scholarship of Teaching and Learning; Ethics of Inquiry: Issues in the Scholarship of Teaching and Learning;* and, with Mary Taylor Huber, *The Advancement of Learning: Building the Teaching Commons.*

Rebecca S. Nowacek is Assistant Professor of Rhetoric and Composition at Marquette University. Her work has appeared in *College Composition and Communication, College English, JGE: The Journal of General Education,* and *Research in the Teaching of English.*

David Scobey is Donald W. and Ann M. Harward Professor of Community Partnerships and Director of the Harward Center for Community Partnerships, Bates College. He is the author of *Empire City: The Making and Meaning of the New York City Landscape* and other studies of nineteenth-century U.S. cultural and urban history. He serves on the National Advisory Committee of Project Pericles and was chair of the National Advisory Board of Imagining America: Artists and Scholars in Public Life.

Michael B. Smith is Assistant Professor of History and Environmental Studies and coordinator of the School of Humanities and Sciences Community Service Program at Ithaca College. His work as an environmental historian has appeared in *The Historian, Feminist Studies,* and *Environmental History.*

Howard Tinberg is Professor of English and Founding Director of the Writing Lab at Bristol Community College. He is the author of *Border Talk: Writing and*

Knowing at the Two-Year College and *Writing with Consequence: What Writing Does in the Discipline* and co-editor, with Patrick Sullivan, of *What is College-Level Writing?* Tinberg was the 2004 recipient of the Carnegie/CASE Community College Professor of the Year award.

Carmen Werder is Director of the Teaching-Learning Academy, Director of Writing Instruction Support, and Affiliated Faculty in the Department of Communication at Western Washington University. She is co-editor, with Megan M. Otis, of *Engaging Student Voices in the Study of Teaching and Learning.* Her essays have appeared in *Campus Progress: Supporting the Scholarship of Teaching and Learning* and *Inventio: Creative Thinking about Teaching and Learning.*

Edward Zlotkowski is Professor of English at Bentley College. He is editor of *Successful Service-Learning Programs* and *Service-Learning and the First-Year Experience,* and co-editor of *Students as Colleagues: Expanding the Circle of Service-Learning Leadership.* Dr. Zlotkowski is a senior associate at the New England Resource Center for Higher Education.

INDEX

Page numbers in italics indicate pages on which the individual is an author.